May God Bless You All

© 2016 Joseph J. Soukenik IV Author. All rights reserved.
ISBN 978-0-692-68335-4

May God Bless You All

Joseph J. Soukenik IV

Preface

An unforgiving blast of Artic air cut through the pass with a vengeance clawing its way through tents, gnawing at every anchor rope that kept the tiny shelters in place and finding its way through any exposed layers of a man's blankets and clothing until it once again irritated his already raw, pink flesh. Winter had arrived in the Ardennes and it felt like weeks since Frank had gotten any sleep. The 793rd Field Artillery Battalion had fired a record number of rounds protecting the 9th Army in answer to Germany's last major offensive.

Frank had finished his shift and didn't feel very much like eating. He crawled into his tent and curled up in his four blankets, three U.S. army issued and one German blanket found during their most recent advance. As he prepared himself for three hours of restless sleep, he looked down at his boots, soaked clean through with a thin layer of ice and snow that had built up almost like a protective shell encompassing the entire foot. Frank knew they had to come off and his socks had to be changed even though his spares were almost as wet as the ones he was wearing. His feet had developed a type of fungus from having been perpetually wet for the past six weeks, but to stop caring for them all together due to exhaustion would spell disaster. He understood why the British were such sticklers for the diligent care of a soldier's feet. You sure couldn't get very far without them, he chuckled to himself.

With his socks changed, Frank thought maybe he would try to write a couple of quick letters to help him try to relax while letting his family back home know that he was doing alright... *Dearest family,...*

These are the stories of common men living by God, prayer and family and their experiences captured in almost three hundred letters, v-mails and postcards written by two sets of brothers during their service in World War II. The letters share laughter, hardship and perseverance. It is a story that touches on issues of citizenship, farming and service. It is a story about all of us.

Every person living in the United States of America shouldered additional responsibilities during the Second World War. Viola, whether she realized it or not, assumed the role of writing letters to her two brothers, two brother-in-laws and approximately a half dozen other servicemen from the small rural area of Greene, Ohio. Her tireless correspondence provided hope and morale for these men as well as for her young family and neighbors.

Viola (Valeria) was the eldest child of Polish immigrants Charles and Blanche Lulek. Her siblings included Cashmere (Claude), Helen (Drabek), John and Veronica (Sulek). She married a man of Czech heritage named Joseph Soukenik. Joe was the second eldest child of Joseph and Josephine Soukenik. His siblings in order included Mary (Jackson), Lillian (died early on), John, Cecelia (Ceil Romanchik) and Frank. Anne became Joseph's stepmother following the death of his mother, Josephine.

John Soukenik was the first sibling to be enlisted into the service followed by his brother Frank. Frank's close friend, Viola's brother, John Lulek was next to be enlisted and finally, brother Claude entered the service. There was a brief mention of Charlie Jackson entering the service and being stationed in the South Pacific. Charlie was the son of Mary Jackson, Joe's sister.

Amongst the four men, two served in the Pacific theater and two served in the European theater. Frank served during the D-Day invasion, both Frank and John served in the Battle of the Bulge, the Roer River crossing, the Elbe and later would meet up with the Russians during the surrender of Berlin. The two serving in the South Pacific described their encounters dealing with the Japanese army and their experiences along the way with the locals. John Soukenik fought in the Munda Campaign on New Georgia, Bougainville, and the Luzon Campaign. Claude fought in Guam and the Battle of Leyte.

Throughout the letters, all four men came to grips with each card dealt them keeping God, prayer and family in the forefront of their correspondence and actions. Although they each had their trials, they persisted in remaining selfless discussing the well-being of their family members and each other ahead of themselves.

Viola and the boys best tell the majority of this story in their letters, and the letters are best read in an italicized font that exemplifies the character of each writer. In addition, there are passages from the Bible found throughout the story that reveal our family's life and faith in God and though we are all sinners and harden our hearts until life is at its most difficult and we feel most vulnerable, these passages remind me, personally of God's infinite mercy and love for us.

My hopes are two-fold. First, that as you read these letters you feel as though you are actually sitting around your kitchen table with your family sharing some news following a Sunday meal, or that at times you feel as though you are in a leaky tent exhausted and trying to read or write by candlelight. It should remind us how precious life is, that we are only visiting here for a short time and that every soldier that served in the armed forces or family member left waiting at home had feelings, hopes and dreams of their own that were interrupted and sometimes ended by war. Second, that you feel a continued or renewed relationship with God, the power of prayer and the importance of family.

My grandmother, Viola and grandfather, Joe spent their lives quietly conveying the lessons of God, prayer and family to their children, grandchildren and great grandchildren. It is only fitting that they would have kept a collection of letters from presumably one of the most tested times of their lives to continue teaching future generations. It is with honor and great pleasure that I present to you my Grandmother Viola's collection of letters from the war. May God bless you and your family.
Joseph J. Soukenik IV

Family Tree - Lulek	Family Tree - Soukenik
Charles and Blanche Lulek	Joseph and Josephine / Anne (stepmother)
Viola	Mary
Claude	Joseph
Helen	Lillian
John	John
Veronica	Cecelia
	Frank

May God Bless You All.

Chapter One

February 3, 1941 Hattiesburg, Mississippi

"I arrived at Camp Shelby Saturday morning 7:30. The army is a fine place." "May God bless you, all. With love, John."

John Soukenik tucked away the letter and grabbed his standard issue duffle bag with all of his belongings. The B&O had stopped and for the first time, John could hear the sound of a winter rain deflecting off the top of the steel cars of the passenger train like a young child incessantly beating on the bottom of a tin coffee can with that perfect stick.

John stepped off the train with bag slung over his unusually broad shoulders for he was a man of average stature for the times, 5'9" tall and maybe 175 pounds soaking wet. His hair was dark like a raven's wing and well groomed with thick, seemingly endless waves. The only feature broader than his shoulders was John's smile! It began with those eyes, deep dark honest smiling eyes that could light up a room and welcome any stranger into an eventual friendship, radiating toward his slightly oversized ears, over his full cheeks and finishing at his sculpted chin. John's smile was comforting and reassuring that everything was going to be alright while commanding the respect of a leader, a rare combination found in this fourth child of six. His parents were immigrant farmers from Czechoslovakia now living in the small rural town of Bloomfield, Ohio.

John was content with his lot in life loving God, family and his fishing! Being drafted into the armed forces was like watching a summer storm approach the farm. At first, he could see it a long way off slowly rolling and billowing gradually replacing the afternoon sun with purplish white ominous clouds all the while wondering how many more casts he could make into his favorite fishing hole before the storm was upon him and left him running for cover.

Just two days prior, he was sitting at his Aunt Chepek's kitchen table enjoying a coffee with his younger sister, Cecelia or Ceil as she was known. Ceil lived with their father's sister in Cleveland since the age of five when their mother had died. It was customary for the girls to be shipped off to women family members to be raised and for the boys to stay on and work the farm while their father found another suitable wife and remarried. Once remarried, their new stepmother Anne wanted only to keep the boys for work because she was not fond of raising children and found the girls to only increase her own burden. Their father Joe would not hear of it and asked for the girls to return to the farm, as well.

Auntie Chepek, a woman seemingly too small of frame for the size of her kind heart, always wanted a little girl to raise as her own and was fond of Ceil and so asked her brother if she could stay in Cleveland. Twenty two years later, Ceil was taking her older brother to the war terminal in downtown Cleveland where she stood on the platform waving and crying as John waved back also crying until the train pulled out of sight.

Now he was in the army, even with his left leg almost a full inch shorter than his right. John pulled his collar tight around his neck to keep the rain from dripping down his back as he trotted toward the train station to deliver his letter and then board the bus headed for Camp Shelby.

Camp Shelby Mississippi was used during World War I for basic training but deactivated shortly after the war. In 1940, it was once again established as a U.S. military installation for the training of troops in anticipation of the United States inevitably joining the conflict in Europe. John was assigned to the 145th Infantry Regiment, 37th "Buckeye" Division which had transferred training operations from Columbus, Ohio to Camp Shelby in October 1940.

    John along with the majority of the men stationed at Camp Shelby would be housed in tents during their basic training. The tents were a crude but efficient method of housing a large number of troops and somewhat easy to construct and tear down if either need arose. Each tent measured roughly sixteen feet in width by twenty feet in length housing sometimes as many as eight soldiers per tent.

    The floor was a series of two by fours strapped over a two by ten inch frame. The walls were constructed of seven stacked two by fours on top of the flooring followed by an additional three feet of lightly framed screening. This design was the same for all four walls of the tent with the exception of the front of the tent which contained the only screen door. Above the framed in screening sat another two by four which made up the frame for the roof. The roof had a forty five degree angled frame that rose an additional three feet in height to a squared top or ceiling giving the tent a total height from the ground to the ceiling of approximately nine feet. A thick khaki green tarpaulin covered not only the roof frame but also extended down each quarter panel of the side walls the length of the screening. The portion of tarp covering the screen could either be rolled up to expose the screening allowing air and light to enter the tent from any or all four walls or the tarp could be secured to the frame using bungee straps in order to protect the men and their supplies from the elements. There were various hooks on the inside frame of the tent which provided a place for the men to hang personal supply bags thus affording them additional much needed floor space. At one time, there were 14,000 tents housing over 100,000 troops making the camp both the largest training center as well as the largest tent city in the world![1]

---

[1] www.Custermen.com/AtTheFront/CampShelby.htm October 25, 2008

Past lessons from war on the frontier to the Civil War to the Great World War led the U. S. to this conclusion as this next conflict looked more eminent; mass and mobility would be the foundation on which this young inexperienced army would be built.

February 3, 1941 Tokyo, Japan

The Emperor concluded his cabinet meeting and dismissed his generals. He removed his wire-rimmed spectacles, his eyes looking forever sleepy and wiped the lenses methodically as he stared past them with a slight smirk. Emperor Hirohito was most pleased with his decision to form an alliance with Germany and Italy.

His recent campaigns in both Manchuria and the Philippines had been met with unexpected resistance as the Emperor had resorted to the use of chemical warfare and the mass killings of both prisoner and civilian populations in regions presently occupied by The Imperial Japanese Army. This newly formed alliance would most definitely assist Hirohito in his quest to expand the Japanese Empire into China and throughout the Pacific![2]

Be still before the Lord and wait patiently for him; do not fret when men succeed in their ways, when they carry out their wicked schemes. Refrain from anger and turn from wrath; do not fret- it leads only to evil. For evil men will be cut off, but those who hope in the Lord will inherit the land.
    –Psalm 37:7-9

---

[2] www.Wikipedia.org

March-April 1941 Hattiesburg, Mississippi

"Dear Viola,
I received your most welcome letter quite a while ago, but as usual to busy doing training and shoting. We sure have been having raining weather and plenty of it. I have been marching every day. I just came back from a march today. I was all wet. Ha! Ha! Well, maybe I'm alway <u>all wet</u>. I sure am tired by the end of the day after walking so many miles. Well, how is everything up in Lockwood & Ohio? Hope your family and your folks are all ok. I suppose you are working hard every day and Joe too. Well, I'm still in the army and making $21 a month and all the water I can drink. Up every day A.M. 5:30. Drill all day & then spend half of the night cleaning your stuff up for the next day. But it make me throw my chest out and shoulders back. Well, maybe you will see me someday all dressed up but it take money to come home. It take about $11 one way. It take me 38 hours to come down here on the train so I will need a week's furlough to come home.

Thank everyone for the letters. It sure makes me feel good to know you are still thinking of me. I received the letter from Violet. I will write to her soon. I hope she'll wait. Ha. Ha. Did you go to the dance at the church and have a good time? I wish I was there. Oh boy would I dance.

By the way, thank you for the sweet package candy, and Honey it was so good and so thoughtful of you and it sure made me happy since it came from you Dearest. I also want to thank Little Joe for getting part of his Easter Bunny. The rabbit ears came in good tip-top shape and boy was it good. Ahmmmmmmm...

Well, I must be signing off. I'll see you soon if my furlough go through alright. I may come home about May 20 or so. I'll let you know. I hope Big Joe gets some fishing in. Take good care of yourself and the family Honey and May God bless you all.

With love, John"

"Here are some kisses for the kids
xxxxxxxxxxxxxxxxxxxxxxxxxxxxxxxxxx"

Young men clothe yourselves in humility toward one another. –Peter 5:5

John sealed the letter and blew out his candle. The evening temperature still offered him a good night's sleep as a gentle breeze billowed through the flaps of his tent. John had already been informed all too many times about the fast approaching stifling heat and humidity of summer in the South. What John did not know was that by August, he and the 37th "Buckeye" Division would be participating in the Louisiana Maneuvers, the largest military exercise performed on U.S. soil to date. The maneuvers would keep him and approximately 400,000 troops away from their respective camps until well into early fall.[3]

The seemingly routine events of the following morning roll call were altered by the introduction of a fellow Buckeye and former employee of the same Republic Steel plant that had employed John and some of his buddies. His name was Sergeant James A. Cononico, a seasoned veteran assigned to John's division to instruct the men on rifle shooting and the distribution of the M-1 Garand rifle.

John had spent his initial month in rifle training learning how to shoot and care for the 1903 Springfield. He had acquired a fluid motion regarding the rifle's bolt-action and confident with the five-round clip of .30-03 or 30-06 cartridges. John knew this was the primary rifle used by the U.S. army and marines during the Great World War, and the Springfield remained a reliable weapon and useful as a sniper rifle because of its' dense wood stock and it's weight of almost nine pounds. Any uncertainty about adjusting

---

[3] www.Wikipedia.org

to another weapon quickly subsided as he stepped up to receive his new rifle. He immediately noticed the difference in weight as he hefted the rifle into his two strong hands. The gas-powered M-1 Garand came in at a mere five and a half pounds! This would make a significant difference regarding fatigue in the field especially following one of those thirty-mile hikes! The M1 was also a semi-automatic rifle that held eight .30 caliber cartridges. John suddenly felt grateful to receive this new rifle since production and distribution to the troops was a slow and arduous task. He became proficient in the tear down and reassembly of the M1 by the end of maneuvers.[4]

Tokyo, August 1941 Japan

Hirohito solidified Japan's alliance with Germany and Italy. The three nations discussed supply and distribution of oil and other natural resources as well as each other's agenda for expansion and occupation. The Emperor, from this point forward would prepare his commanding officers for any and all troop deployment or combat action with virtually no warning. His goal was to maintain diplomatic talks with The United States and Great Britain while having long since decided that war with the U.S. was a necessity if Japan was to expand it's empire to include all of the Pacific. By fall, Hirohito's obsession would be with a first strike on U.S. soil; Pearl Harbor.[5]

For such men are false apostles, deceitful workmen, masquerading as apostles of Christ. And no wonder for Satan himself masquerades as an angel of light. It is not surprising then,

---

[4] www.Wikipedia.org
[5] www.Wikipedia.org

if his servants masquerade as servants of righteousness. Their end will be what their actions deserve. -2 Corinthians 11:13-15

Sunday, December 7, 1941 Pearl Harbor Oahu, Hawaii

1:20p.m. : Japan attacks American soil; 3,351 military and civilian casualties.

December 8, 1941 Hattiesburg, Mississippi

It was 4:30a.m. and John lay awake in his tent. Sleep for he and most of the men would become a luxury over the next couple of months. News of events from the prior day trickled in from Washington and around camp as the rumors of possible troop deployment ground in the pit of each man's stomach. John's first thought was to get up for the day and write a few letters to family. He so wanted to know how they were and to reassure his family that he was alright. Unfortunately, the camp was placed on a make ready or red alert status restricting all inbound and outbound communications. John along with the rest of the men in camp would encounter their first taste of battle; anxiety. For the first time, the distant possibility of the United States going to war became a sudden reality and the invincible feelings of youth wrestled with feelings of mortality and those of the unforeseeable future. The glamour of war began its evolution toward duty, resolve and the possibility of never returning home. John wiped his eyes and finished lacing his boots.

The 37th "Buckeye" Division remained ready for possible deployment to the Philippines until late January 1942. At that time the U.S. determined that it was not prepared to neither defend nor retake the islands and so it was decided that they would opt to intensify training of these troops in anticipation of a future campaign in the Philippines.[6]

Humble yourselves, therefore, under God's mighty hand, that he may lift you up in due time. Cast all your anxiety on him because he cares for you. Be self-controlled and alert.   -1Peter 5: 6-8.

February 1942 Indiantown Gap Military Reservation Indiantown Gap, Pennsylvania

"Dear Mother,
Just a few lines to let you know where I am. I arrived in our new camp here in Penn, Sunday morning. I also got your package today it came in pretty good shape, for it went all the way to Camp Shelby first. You see I can't tell you when we move.
Tell Frank and Viola thank you all for the package it was really good, also the drink Ha! Ha! Its came alright too.
Well Mother I began a Corporal today. I hope I make good too. I was going to call you some time this week, but I suppose it would be better to call you Sunday around noon so you can talk to me. I hope Frank will be home yet. If I can I'll come home on a weekend pass. I'll close for this time and May God Bless You All.

Your Son, John

Don't forget to be home Sunday <u>around noon</u> some time.

---

[6] www.Wikipedia.org www.history.army.mil

p.s. Say hello to Dad and Frank- Charles and the Jacksons. Also, thanks to Viola and family. Tell her the new cookies were really good too. I'll write more to you sometime this week."

March 5, 1942 Indiantown Gap, Pa.

"Dearest Viola,

I received your most welcome letter today and was very glad to hear from you. I'm also sorry for not writing you and thanking for those cookies and things. They were really good and no kidding either.

Well Honey we had a very good trip from the South to our present location. We come up on the Railroad with pull man service and everything. The camp is really nice we have most everything and it's all new. We sleep in barracks, which surely seem like living again. After being in a tent for a year, it sure seems good to have a real roof over your head once more and real windows to look out of. Course the pattern of living is somewhat changed now that we are not in tents. Now there is more of us together than it used to be. The barracks have to be scrubbed out every day & a few other things that we will get used to as the time goes on. Of course the privates do the work. Ha. Ha.

It sure is nice being stationed so near home. Now all we are waiting for is for the big shots to shell out some weekend passes. There is some talk of getting 3 day leaves. If it comes true, it will be just swell. Hey kid! It take about 8 hrs. to get home, some of the boys made it in 6 1/2 hrs. if I could make it that way it would be swell Hey!

I was really glad to hear Frank doesn't have to go to the Army right away they really need him there. I also hope Johnny Lulek doesn't have to go too. This Army life is no place for kids like Johnny and Frank. Viola, I was really glad to hear you all that Sunday, when I call up it seem like you were in the next room, it make me so happy to hear Barbara and Little Joe too. I miss them very much, tell them I also say prayers for them too and that if they pray for me all the time it will help me along, so I can come back. You know Honey. I also shed a few tears too. I was so happy to hear you all. Right now I feel like shed a few tears, just writing to you.

I'm glad to hear you had a good time at Tom Smida's wedding. I wish I could had been there too to dance with you. Well Darling. I guess I'll close for this time sending love to all and as always yours. May God Bless you All. With Love, John"

Only be careful, and watch yourselves closely so that you do not forget the things your eyes have seen or let them slip from your heart as long as you live. Teach them to your children and to their children after them. –Deuteronomy 4:9

March 30, 1942 Indiantown Gap, PA.

"Dearest Viola,
I have just received your most welcome letter and was really glad to hear from you as you know I always am. I'm sorry about not calling up Monday nite, but I was so tired and sleepy. You see its took us 9 hrs. to come back to Camp that Sunday nite. I just made it in time, or I would have been A.W.O.L. if you know what I mean Ha. Ha. But things turn out alright so here I am still a good soldier but a little lonesome for home. You see Honey when I go home and see you all have share a good time and every thing I can't help it. I just run out of ink so I'm writing with someone else ink.

Gee it was tough seeing Frank leave for the Army. But Honey we'll all be in it sooner or later. So, all we can hope for is that we all come back home again. And like you said, We'll be one big happy family again! By the way, I received a letter from Frank saying he was O.K. and will let me know when he arrives at his new camp. I hope they place him near home so he can come home and see the Folks. I suppose he is a little lonesome at first, but he'll get used to it in time as I have.

By the way Darling, I was sorry to hear that Frank wrote to Johnny first. But you see that Johnny and Frank had so many things to do together and I suppose that why he wrote to him first. Any way, you Folks read all the letters and cards together, so when we write we write to all of you. But I promise from now on I'll write to you first and then to the others. How is that?

The weather has been pretty good and makes me feel like going fishing. I suppose Joe will be going fishing again soon. I wish I could go with him and show him how. Ha. Ha. When I come home on my furlough I hope I get time to do a little fishing with him.

Well Viola, I'll have to close for this time, because I have to get up early in the morning before taps and take the morning report. So, May God Bless You All. With love, John."

p.s. tell Joe to keep the fishing biting till I come home. Give my love to the little ones."

These commandments that I give you today are to be upon your hearts. Impress them on your children. Talk about them when you sit at home and when you walk along the road, when you lie down and when you get up. Tie them as symbols on your hands and bind them on your foreheads. Write them on the doorframes of your houses and your gates. –Deuteronomy 6: 7-9

Chapter Two

March 1942 Camp Claiborne, Louisiana

He could already feel the heat from the mid-morning sun stinging the back of his neck as he made his way to the front porch of the Post Exchange located on the grounds of Camp Claiborne. No matter. Frank's pace remained a casual friendly stride as was usually the case for the youngest of the Soukenik's and the tallest of the siblings. Frank stood around six feet two inches tall and a slender 169 pounds. Frankie had a knack for making friends of both genders with an easy almost musical tone to his voice, a long elegant glide to his step that quickly reduced the initial awkward space between two people about to engage in conversation, soft twinkling blue eyes with a subtle periwinkle hue and that mischievous smile that reassured you that he was a good guy and that it was okay to enjoy living on that line that teetered between fun and trouble!

The Post Exchange looked like three low roof, single level homes butting up against each other to form a "T". The building was entirely wood-framed and perpetually looked like it was in desperate need of scraping and repainting. Each of the entrances had a door flanked by a window on each side and a series of peaks and covered porches to welcome a man in from the current Southern elements. To the servicemen, it was like a little piece of home that included a post office, stationary and convenient supplies, a soda fountain and a staff of local girls that always seemed available for some light conversation.[7]

---

[7] Postcard of Camp Claiborne Post Exchange

April 8, 1942 Battery 320th 82nd Division Camp Claiborne, La.

"Dearest Viola and Family,
I received your cards and not a letter don't forget to write a letter not like John L. Since you said I didn't write I'll write this letter and hope it makes up for it Honey.

Well here I am in Camp Claiborne La. I sure do miss you all. The army isn't so bad after all. I'm taking all kinds of shots that's why I didn't write to you. Well I'll be a man when its over with not that I'm not one now.

Well I'm meeting a lot of buddies! Well I'll have to be closing now and don't expect me to write too many letters but I want you to write me often. How are Joey and Barbara? I hope they're feeling good. Are Joe and Barbara praying for me? Hope <u>sure.</u> I wishing you has a good Easter.

The weather here is hot its like July in Ohio. I guess I'm going to have my hands full for a few weeks I have K.P. to-day. How is mother feeling? I hope she is feeling good same to your family. Until next time God bless you All.

All my love, Frank"

Frank stepped into the Exchange, smile widening with every step as he approached the counter. Surely, he had a couple of minutes to flirt.

If some of the branches have been broken off, and you, though a wild olive shoot, have been grafted in among the others and now share in the nourishing sap from the olive root, do not boast over those branches. If you do consider this: You do not support the root but the root supports you. –Romans 11: 17-18

Friday, April 24, 1942 Lockwood, Ohio

    Friday could not have come soon enough. Like Joey and Barbara, even their mother, Vi was overwhelmed with the feelings of hope and promise and renewal that were some of the symptoms attributed to spring fever following a long cold winter in the snow belt. She ran to the mailbox as she did each afternoon following the sound of the mail truck. On this day, Viola scarcely noticed the welcoming spring blooms of the azaleas, begonias and apple blossoms surrounding the house. The shades of brown from late winter and early spring finally surrendered to the recent explosion of color in the yard. Viola was so excited to see if John or Frank had sent letters that she practically tore the gray steel door off the hinges of the newly installed box!
    There was an envelope on top of the stack of bills and newspaper. It was from John but looked far different from any of his previous letters. The envelope had a rectangular stamp in the lower left hand corner marked "Passed by Army Examiner" with the hand written initials "LJB". Viola found a second circular stamp in the lower right hand corner much like the other. Along the right-hand edge, the envelope had been torn open and resealed with a bold print seal marked "OPENED Army U.S. Examiner". As Viola hastily split the seal on the envelope, her face went pale and her hands trembled as she violently tried to shake free any content. She stood there on State Route 87 for what seemed like an eternity as she stared inside the empty envelope. She looked from front to back of the envelope for some additional clue when she finally noticed a change in the return address. The letter had been sent c/o San Francisco, California. This was to be the first of many censored letters sent to Viola and her young family. John and the 37th "Buckeye" Division were preparing to ship

overseas! He and the rest of the family would learn quickly as to what was U.S. approved content for a letter.

April 25, 1942 Camp Claiborne, Louisiana (9:30 Sat. night)

"Dearest Viola,

I hope all are feeling fine. I am alright and a Corp. I was made a corporal the 21st of April. They sure are giving me the work but I can take it you no! Thanks for the cookies and candy it was good sure love it. I am a Switch Board Operator and like tonight I had a weekend pass but I couldn't use it because I will have to work on the switch board. So I'll think of you all. I don't know how long we will be here but I do not think we will be here more than three months that was understood we might pull out any time. I hope to see you before I go.

How are Joe and Bab. Tell I love them. About two week from now we are going on a camping trip. I wish you were here to keep me warm. Ha. Ha. I got a letter from John L. and he said he sold my car to Frank P. and got 650 for it. Not so bad. How is Joe working on the farm? Tell him not to go to the mill to work on the farm. Tell John L. that I like cigars and R.G. Dunn. Ha. Ha. Tell him to write me a postcard and if he can a letter. How is the Lulek family? Tell said hello and tell my mother not worry because I am o.k. and like the Army. I have to close my letter here to work on the switch board. God Bless you all.

Love Frank

p.s. did you like my picture I sent you I hope so. Say hello to Joey and Bab. Tell them I miss them."

May 13, 1942 San Francisco, California

"Dearest Viola,
It's been a longtime since I wrote to you but you see I'm now in San Francisco, California. I received your candy the day we left our old camp and could not write until I got here, so forgive me. The candy was really good. I wish I had some now. Ha. Ha.
How is everyone feeling? I hope they are all well. I'm feeling fine and hope that you all are too. When I have more time I'll write you a letter but right now I'm pretty busy. Say hello to Joe, Joey, Barbara and to my folks. Tell them not to worry about me, because I'm all right. May God Bless You All. Yours, with love, John

p.s. Thanks for the candy it was so good!"

Who of you by worrying can add a single hour to his life. - Matthew 6:27

May 26, 1942 Camp Claiborne, Louisiana

"Dearest Folks,
You know you should give me some real hell for not writing to you in such a long time, but really we have been so busy out here that I just don't have the time. How are the kids? I hope that they are feeling fine! I got a letter from mother yesterday. Wish John L. would write me. What, hell with John he don't write to me.
I do not think we will be here more than 1 mo. That was what I understood. I hope to see you before I go across darling.
Tonight we have a dance and it sure is going to be good. 200 girls are coming!
Is Joe working everyday? I hope so. How much is he getting paid, $.50 an hour?
Ha ha. The weather sure is hot. It's 100 degrees. I see in

the Warren paper that it rained for 3 days strait in Ohio. I'll close for this time. God bless you all. Love, Frank"

May 31, 1942 Camp Claiborne, Louisiana

"Dearest Family,

I was glad to hear from you but did not have time to answer your letter soon so I am today. This is 10 letters I am writing tonight. Sure is a hot job to do. I wrote to mother, John, some gal...haha. Boy sure am having a good time with the southern gals every weekend!

What damn brother, my hell, don't he write to me? I wish he'd send me a letter. I like getting him worked up. Ha.Ha.

I hope John don't go to the army.

Boy weather today was 104 degrees sure is hot as hell...I know haha.

Maybe get to be a Staff Sergeant Technician Third Grade sure am working for it. I am Corporal of Telephone and Telegraph repairman installers. I have 3 trucks, 3 cars and 15 men boy all good buddies like them all. Boy doesn't my B.S. work haha. It works just like it works on the girls some~~~~B.S.

Today, C/O going some place around 1200. May be going some place...don't know...maybe I'll be going don't say to mother...hope we are going some place close to Ohio. I have to close at this time. Hugs to Joey and Babs tell them still love them. Tell them to pray for me.

God bless you all.
With love your brother Frank

Write soon maybe we'll be going soon. I hope so. I hope you can read my write and spelling. So long, Honey."

> Sovereign Lord, you are God! Your covenant is trustworthy, and you have promised these good things to your servant. -2 Samuel 7:28

John took in the mild, quickly warming breeze of morning in the South Pacific. The collar of his shirt was just beginning to stick to the beads of sweat on the back of his neck. It was quite a change from the damp chilled air of mid-spring in San Francisco where John and his men had left on the 26th of May. Now, better than two weeks later, the four ships transporting troops had safely reached their destination, the Fiji Islands. The rail of the ship on which he leaned was already warm and would soon be hot to the touch.[8]

June [censored], 1942 Overseas

"Dearest Viola,

How are you and family? I suppose you are all feeling fine. I'm quite well and hope you and family are too. Well Honey, I really been seeing the world lately. I suppose you wonder where I am. Well I can not tell you that, but I got here safely to our present locations and, don't worry about me, because I'm doing alright and feel like a king.

I received your most welcome letter the day I left San Francisco and Honey, I really enjoyed it course it made me a little home sick, but write more like it again. Also tell Joe Jr. and Barbara I love their letters too. You see Viola, we can't make any kisses on the end of our letters, so when I write to Joe and Barbara, I'll spell or write it down, and you can tell them. I know Joe can read it but Barbara can't.

---

[8] www.Wikipedia.org

Well Honey, how is everything going around there? I suppose you're not doing any fishing now? Or are you and Joe still going? I bet Joe really catching some big ones too! Ha. Ha. I guess you are all through with your papering and painting by now. I can't wait till I come home and see the place again.

Well Viola, I'll close for this time and until I hear from you, May God Bless You All. Please write when you have time. I really enjoy your letters. Say hello to Johnny and all the Folks for me. I'll write more when I have time again. Yours with Love John."

"Dear Little Joe and Barbara,

I received your most welcome letter and love to hear from you two. When you wrote to me you asket me if I kill any Japs. Well. So far I have not, but when I see one, I'll get him for you. How is that? Alright?

And Joe and Barbara, when night come I always pray for you and Barbara. I know you pray for me and I love you for it. Tell Mother, Daddy, ⟨censored⟩ and Johnny I also pray for them. Well Joe, now that school is over, I suppose you and Barbara go fishing with Daddy and Mother, hey! I'll close for this time with ocean of Love and Kisses. Your loving Uncle John"

Hear my prayer oh Lord, listen to my cry for mercy. In the day of my trouble I will call to you, for you will answer me. –Psalm 86: 6-7

John sealed the envelope and went to preparing his gear for tomorrow's training exercise. The 37th "Buckeye" Division had been in Fiji for almost two weeks and the anticipation of possible combat was just now giving way to daily routine. Washington assigned new arrivals to the islands with two objectives. First, they were to set up defenses in order to fend off any potential Japanese invasion. Next, they were to continue their extensive training in preparation for combat support and/or a future offensive by the U.S.[9]

    John was about to learn of the great news from Midway that occurred earlier that month. The Battle for Midway was a crushing blow to Japan as it lost all four of its' carriers and many of the country's top pilots forcing the Imperial Navy on the defensive and stepping up the readiness of U.S. troops now stationed throughout the Pacific.[10]

July 6, 1942 Camp Claiborne, Louisiana

"Dear Viola & Joe & All,
    How are you all dear family? I hope you are fine. I sure am feeling fine. I was sure glad to receive your letter but I didn't have time to write. I haven't had much time to write to you dear. We are busy.
    How's the car? I be coming home soon maybe. Tell Joe get some gas. Ha. Ha. Were you over home lately? How is mother & dad?
    Did you have a good time on the fourth of July? I had a good time with some gal ha ha sure was Honey! Did Joe go to the ball game? Boy I would like to see one.
    I have to close for this time we are having thunderstorms this evening it's raining every day sure is hell. We are going on a trip for 360 miles sure going to be hard.
    God Bless You All.
    Your brother in law Frank."

---

[9] www.Wikipedia.org
[10] www.Wikipedia.org

July 20, 1942 Monday Nite Overseas

"Dear Viola,

How are you and family? Fine? I feeling fine and doing alright. I received your two letters together and was very glad to hear from you. So keep on writing when you have the time even if you do not hear from me & don't worry about me 'cause I'm alright.

Viola, I was really surprised to hear about my pal Carl Bayles getting accidentally killed, it's really too bad & him with a family, I really feel bad about it. We used to have such good time together. I feel terrible about it.

Well for pleasant news. I been getting all kinds of mails but no time to answer them. Well, little by little I'll get there. Ha. Ha.

I suppose the Parish had a great day on the 4th of July? Remember last year when I was home on my furlough? Boy we really had fun and this year I was so far away from you all but I was thinking of you anyway, dancing etc. I hope Frank made it. I mean on his furlough.

Say I got a letter from Veronica and Johnny and was I surprised to hear from them. It seems like years since Johnny wrote. I was beginning to think he was in the army. Ha. Ha.

How's the weather there now? I imagine it's wonderful now. The weather here's been swell, a little rain now and then but not bad.

Viola, I am really sorry about not taking my picture in a studio for you and Mother but you know how I am about taken pictures, but as long as you have a snap shot of me it's alright, hey!

Since I been away I pray for the day when we will all be together again and enjoy life like we used to. Well Honey I'll close for this time and will write more when I have time. Say hello to all for me and May God Bless You All. Yours always, with love and kisses John.

To Barbara and Joey,
How are you? I hope you are having a good time this summer! When you go to Grandma tell her I pray for her and Grandpa. Be a good little girl and boy to your mother and Dad. With love and kisses, John."

August 11, 1942 Camp Claiborne, Louisiana

"Dearest Soukenik family,
I received your letter today sure was glad to get it I sure miss you all sure miss mother and home she writes every day that's O.K. with me. I write to night because I have time this week because we have test men from Washington so I got to make good. Not that I cant. Ha. Ha. Tell John to write me soon. Tell him I am going to training for 17 weeks on Airborne Dive. I am going to join the parachute troop when we go across we will go in planes sure going to be O.K. with me.
How is my honey Barbara and Joey? Tell them to pray for me. so it rained in Ohio that sure is hell when it flooded. How are your potatoes? I hope that you made some money on the pickles. Tell mother not to work on the muck because she don't have to hell with the muck this year.
I have to close for this time. God bless you all with all my love Your brother in law Frank

Tell Joe not to work to hard. Ha. Ha. So long "

The 320th had been combined with the 82nd Airborne and renamed the 320th Glider as support for the 82nd.[11]

---

[11] www.ww2-airborne.us

Praise the Lord, O my soul, all my inmost being praise his holy name…who forgives all your sins and heals all your diseases, who redeems your life from the pit and crowns you with love and compassion, who satisfies your desires with good things so that youth is renewed like the eagle's. –Psalm 103: 1; 3-5.

August 14, 1942 Wed Nite

Dearest Sister in law,
Just finished a letter to Mother and of course it made me think of you and family, so thot I would jot down a few lines while I am not too busy. Honey, I received you letter yesterday & you'll never know how happy I was to hear from you, it make me feel so good to know that I have such a sweet Sister in law back home. I love you for it, so keep writing whether you hear from or not, for there are times that I can't write as often as I would like to.
Viola, in your letter you said that I shouldn't marry some of these girls over here. Well Honey, you know me, if I haven't marry any girl back home I'll sure as h~~~ not marry any here. Ha. Ha.
Censored
I can't tell you where I am because our letters are sensored and we can't say anything about the place, but don't worry Honey cause I'm alright. The place isn't bad. All the civilians are friendly, most of them are Native, a few white and some half casts. The money is also changed, we have shilling, lbs. & so on. For a times I had trouble with it, but now I'm used to it. I go to church every Sunday, here in the Village, it remined me so much of the little church in Orwell & that's bad, because it bring back the swell times we had there. I sure remember last 4th of July when I was home on my furlough. Kid I'll never forget it as long as I live, them were the days hey! By the way Viola, I met Johnny Babinchek the other day and he really doing swell, he said to say

hello when I write.

  Well Honey, how's my two little dears coming along? I suppose they're still the same, always wanting to see GrandMa & GrandPa on Sunday. Tell them, I love them & pray for them every nite. I know they do the same thing for me & I miss them very much, & can't wait to hold them in my arms. Tell Joey, I said that I hope he has a hundred more birthdays. I'll send him a Defense Savings Bond for this, & May God always keep him at home, not like his God Father.

  So Joe doing a little fishing now. I suppose he catches the small ones & leave the big ones. Well, when I come home I'll show him how. Ha. Ha. Does he take you along? Remember when we all went together that Sunday. Some fun hey? How's Johnny and this girl friend getting along? I suppose fine? I'm really glad to hear that he and Claude are still home course we can use them to help lick the Axis. That brother of yours must be out of ink or something or maybe he too busy with this honey. I would love to hear from him being such <u>Pals.</u> When I meet him again I'll punch him in the nose. Ha. If I'm big enough~~

  Well Viola dear, Ill close for this time, it's getting late and I have to go to sleep, and my candle is getting short. Say hello to My Folks and Your Folks, also Your Sisters and Brothers. And kiss Barbara & Joey for me. Tell Joe to take care of everything until we come home. Good Luck to you and all, May God Bless You All & unite soon again.

  Yours with love and kisses Corp. John

  Have you heard from Frank lately? I received a letter from him to-day. He doing swell. Keep writing to him too, I know he love you all and misses you.

  September 7, 1942 Camp Claiborne, La.

Dearest Soukenik family,

How are you all? I hope you are feeling I have much time so I am write you this card. I sure miss you and kids how are the kids? Is Joe going to school I hope he like it tell him his Uncle used to like it. Ha. Ha.

Did John go to the Army I hope he likes it its o.k. I think he will like it.

Your brotherlaw Frank

Chapter Three

September 7, 1942 Camp Davis, North Carolina

John walked among the still newly white washed barracks in camp looking for something to eat. He was still getting familiar with the camp grounds having spent the majority of his time in the basic training area and antiaircraft range along the adjacent beach front. He had been the official property of the United States Army for over a week and part of the Battery "B" 411th C.A. Battalion A. A.

John Lulek was a thick man standing maybe 5' 10" and two hundred pounds. The second youngest of five children and Viola's youngest brother, John had a large heart-shaped head that at a glance appeared as if it sat directly on his broad shoulders. His upper body was cut like a keystone with forearms as thick and strong as seasoned hickory posts. He wore his shirt sleeves rolled up just above the elbow and his favorite pair of dungarees when he was working on the farm. John's thighs looked like those of a champion steed rippled and bulging against the baggiest pair of jeans his mother, Blanche could find. He could lift a man to his shoulder as easily as slinging a bale of hay, quick to make a friend and even quicker to stick his neck out for a good cause! The only thing John enjoyed more than a big meal or a good tussle was a fine cigar.

-So Jacob was left alone, and a man wrestled with him until daybreak. When the man saw that he could not overpower him, he touched the socket of Jacob's hip so that his hip was wrenched as he wrestled with the man. Then the man said let me go for it is daybreak. But Jacob replied, "I will not let you go unless you bless me." The man asked him, "What is your name?" "Jacob," he answered. Then the man said, "Your name will no longer be Jacob, but Israel, because you have struggled with God and with men and have overcome." –Genesis 32: 24-28.

Dearest Soukenik's,

We are now in the land of "big mosquitoes" and hot sun. It sure is stuffy around here but I guess I'll get used to it.

You ought to see me in my "zute suit" the boys say I look like a sergeant in my uniform. It isn't such a bad life the only thing you don't know what you're going to do next until you're doing it.

Gee Vi! I sure could go for a meal of dumplings and chicken. They aren't feeding us to good at present. They better improve or I'll starve!

I certainly miss you folks and the family. Please help mother and dad all you can so they won't have to work so hard.

I really miss the kids. Tell Joey to write to me and pray for me. How is my little honey Barbara? I must be leaving you now. Write to me soon Good bye and God bless you. Love John.

September 12, 1942 Camp Claiborne, La.

Dearest Soukenik Family,
How are you all? Hope all feeling good. We are sure busy as hell but I like it. Where is John L.?
Tell me his address of his camp so I can write to him.
I have to close for this time sure miss you all. May God bless you all with all my love,
Frank

September 23, 1942 Camp Davis, North Carolina

Dearest Viola,
How is everything at home, fine I hope? I received the clothes hangers to-day but not the ring I suppose that will come tomorrow. I hear you are doing very well on the market. Did you have a frost yet? The wether down here is hoter then hell and stuffy to. I can't sleep at night it's so hot I wish I could be at home so I could get one good nights sleep. I can't get used to these army beds they're as hard as a board.
Did you get your soybeans put up yet or is it still raining? Is dad cutting our soybeans yet? It rained twice since we've been here. The mosquitoes are terrible around here, my legs are just one raw mess from the bites. If we ever get rid of them maybe we can get some rest I hope.
We got a new battery commander now. Captain Matlock is tough. His bottom lip hangs way down if he don't watch it he's liable to step on it one of these days. No one likes him and he don't like anyone of the guys either sometimes I wonder if he likes himself.
I just got through writing to Ceil. They really keep me busy around here. I think I'll get me a secretary. Ceil gives me hell for not writing then you give me hell for not writing home. I don't even get a chance to go to show I'm busy writing every night to someone. I wish you folks would write more often. I know you're busy but can drop a few lines that means a lot just to hear from you.
How's Barbara and Joey? I really miss the kids. I can just see them praying for me every night. Tell them to keep it up. Sometimes when I lie down at night and think of the kids I could almost cry. It's hard to be separated and so far away from

them. How does Joey like school this year with all the new teachers? I must be closing now cause it's getting late. Give my love to mom and dad and the rest of the family. Don't worry about me I'm doing fine. Good bye for now and God bless you all.
Love your brother John

p.s. Is Joe doing any fishing? I'll bet he goes every time he gets a chance. Tell him to take good care of my dog cause I might be home on furlough around hunting season I hope. So long

October 5, 1942 Camp Davis, N.C.

Dear Joe,
My buddy and I took a little ride out to the ocean to-day. Two blondes wanted to take us out for a boat ride but we already had a date so we had to refuse them. I wish you could be here boy there is some swell places to fish. Give my best regards to all the family.
Love John

October 10, 1942 Fort Bragg, N.C.

It was an uneventful move to Fort Bragg. That should have been Frank's first clue as to the rigors of training that awaited "America's First Airborne". Frank had to hone his skills for both field infantry and as a paratrooper. It seemed like the scenarios drilled into he and his men were endless and with only one common thread; uncertainty! He was taught to be innovative, think on his feet and regroup quickly because once his feet left the plane change became the only constant. Frank was officially a soldier in the "All American Division."

> *Dearest folks,*
> *How are you all in Ohio? I hope you are fine. The weather is O.K. with me. I hope to see your brother some time soon he is about 100 mi. from me. I will write to you a letter when I get time we are so busy.*
> *May God bless you all. Love, Frank*

October 10, 1942 Company B 2nd Battalion Camp Wheeler, Georgia

It was Saturday night and Claude was settling in for the evening to write letters home. The mission and routine of Camp Wheeler became crystal clear to Cashmere Lulek, Viola's next eldest sibling. In his first month of arrival to the infantry replacement camp just east of Macon, Georgia, Claude, as he was known by family and friends, was dealt the worst card of both families; training for front line infantry duty.

He was a good guy with the sculpted facial features of his Polish heritage. Claude's square forehead drew to his distinguished wide eyes that sat atop his carved cheekbones. His cheeks were so chiseled that they seemed as if they pressed his nose to a narrower hawk shape that drew you to his firm lips and pointed chin. He stood 5'8" tall and weighed about 165 pounds with broad shoulders that cut quickly to his waist. Claude was a hard worker on the farm and forever loyal to his family, but he seemed to fight that "glass half empty" syndrome when it came to his own affairs. That was except for Catherine.

> *Dear Viola & Joe,*
> *Just a few lines to let you know how that I feel fine and am*

doing well. And "Boy" was I glad to get that berthday card. You know that was the first mail I received since I have been here. I don't know what is the matter but I seem to be writing some where every day but never get no answer. Maybe every body has forgotten about me.

Well how is Joe is he still working at the Orwell Gardens. If he is why don't he go to the city and make some good money. How are the kids? I hope they are well. "Gosh", but I miss them a lot. How is Joey doing in school? Is he getting good grades? Say hello to them for me will you?

Did mother and Veronica go to see John yet. I haven't had a chance to write to him yet but I will this week. John Ankowski said he was going to write to him too. John and I went to the thearter last night and this morning we went to church, we washed some clothes and then went to another show so we are perty well occupied in our spare time. Well I can't think of any more to say so I will be closing until some other day. Please write because it means a lot to me. Goodby.

Your Loveing Brother Pvt. Claude Lulek

I am sending 2 pictures home one is for you.

Be merciful to those who doubt. –Jude 22.

October 10, 1942 Camp Davis, N.C.

Dearest Viola,
How is everyone at home fine I hope? When is little Joey going to write to me? I've been waiting for his letter for a long time maybe he doesn't want to write to me. I certainly would like to hear from him. How is my beautiful little blonde Barbara? Does she think of her uncle once in a while? I really miss her, tell her that I pray for her every Sunday in church and am thinking of

her all the time. How does Joey like school? I'll bet he's as tough as ever trying to kick hell out of the other kids.

I want to thank you for the cookies the boys certainly enjoyed them you ought to see them dive in the box they were gone in five minutes. We have a pretty nice bunch of boys in our barracks, when anyone of them gets a package they pass it around, one happy family ha! ha! Of course there is always a few greedy ones but we just kind a ignore them. Tell mother and the girls not to bring any more then they need. They will have plenty of clothes to carry. I don't know how long they plan to stay. Just tell ma to bring enough money along because things and rooms are expensive around here. It would be foolish for them to bring anything for me they can send that by mail instead of lugging it along. I told Ceil about the weather here so they can get together on their clothes they are to wear and bring with them.

I see you are doing plenty of canning. Fill your cellar good and full because when I get a furlough I'll take care of it ha! ha! Are you having trouble getting sugar? I hear it's hard to get coffee also.

I'm sending you a picture of myself. This will give you some idea of how hard I have to work even on Sunday. I took a few in uniforms to-day. I'll send them as soon as I get them developed. I wish you would get together some Sunday with Ceil and take pictures of the farm. Corn fields, cows, barn, hay stack and other pictures. I would like to see what it is like at home. Down here you see nothing but pine trees and swamp. I forgot what a cow looks like already and corn fields also. I'm lonesome for that good old farm. Give my best to mom and dad and the rest.

May God bless you always. Love your brother John

p.s. I suppose Joe is working hard. Tell him to get all he can. I really miss Joe and the hunting this year maybe I'll get a chance later in the year I hope.

Love the Lord your God with all your heart and with all your soul and with all your strength. –Deuteronomy 6:5

Thursday, October 15, 1942 Somewhere in the Southwest Pacific

Dearest Viola,
  I hope this letter finds you all feeling fine as I know it will. I'm doing fine and I feel like a King, and I hope I keep on feeling that way. It has been some time till I received a letter from you and begain to wonder whether you have been getting my letters or not, you see honey, I write as often as I can, but right now we are very busy & can't find time to write as often as we'll like to. So, please excuse me if I don't write as often as you would like to have me write, I suppose you are pretty busy now too, and as far as writing go, I know you have plenty to do, with a brother and two brother in law in the Arm Force already. Gee! Vi, I'm sorry I wasn't home to see your brother Johnny off to the Army. After the way he has always show us a good time when we were home from the Army. I bet you miss him awful, after the way he used to be at your place all the time. It's tough to see him go. How's his girlfriend taking it? I hope they station him near home so he can come home often & see you all. I know he'll look swell in a uniform.
  I got a letter from home the other day & they told me Joe went fishing to Canada, I was glad to hear that, because he always wanted to go fishing up there all his life. Fishing is his next thing to eating. Charles wrote that you may have a fish fry some night when he come home, I bet he'll have some big fish storys to tell when he gets back. Ha. Ha. I only hope I could have been home to go with him and enjoy it too. I suppose by this time you know that I'm on a island somewhere in the Southwest pacific. I can't tell you the name of it or what I'm doing 'cause are letters are sensored. But when I can I'll have plenty to write about. Right now it's pretty hard to find any thing to write about.

How's Joey and Barbara? I suppose Joey is going to school now and little Barbara is home with her mother. May God bless them so they never see War.

Well Honey. I'll have to close for this time and write again soon. And in the meantime you write me as often as you can. You see I love to hear about you folks back home & how you are doing. Say hello to your folks & mine and Good Luck to All, we'll keep 'em flying over here & you do the same over there.

Yours with Love & Kisses. John

He will fully bless you, if only you fully obey the Lord your God and are careful to follow all these commands I am giving you today. –Deuteronomy 15: 4-5.

Wednesday, October 23, 1942 Somewhere in the Southwest Pacific

Dearest Viola,

I received your letter mail September 8 yesterday and words can't express how happy I was to hear from you again& to know that you were feeling fine. It seems queer to get letters a couple of months after they are written, because so much happens in the mean time.

First of all, I'll like to know Johnny's address. I been waiting to write to him for some time, I wrote to him before he went to the Army. But I guess he was too busy to write & now that he's in, I guess he doesn't know my address. You know how I feel about Johnny! He was my best pal & friend, I suppose you all miss him very much after the way he always hang around your place and whooping it up. I guess he'll do pritty good in the Army & when he come home on furlough you'll be proud of him.

I suppose by the time you receive this letter Joe will be doing a lot of hunting instead of fishing. Well if he does as well in hunting as he does in fishing he'll be alright, hey?

Well Vi, how are the dances going at St. Mary's now? I suppose now that hunting season is in you'll be a hunting widow at the dances instead of a fishing widow. Ha. Ha. Are you still having dances for the boys in the Army? I suppose I'll get my present sometime next year the way mail gets here. You must have done pretty good at the dance the way you and Joe sold tickets. You always do your part.

I guess the pickle season is over now, Charles wrote that you had your first frost September 26. I got a letter from him today and it was mailed September 28. So you see how it go course he send that one air mail.

How the kids? Barbara & Joey, say hello to them for me, I really miss them and also your little letters. I bet they're getting big. If you have any pictures of them that you have taken lately, please send them to me and I'll send them back in my next letter.

I suppose by this time you know that I'm somewhere on a island in the Pacific, I do fine and hope to keep on, I can't tell you whether I'm fighting or not 'cause our letters are sensored. But keep your chin up like you always have and I'll do the same. I'm eating bananas & coconuts till I feel like a monkey. Ha. Ha. Honey you should see the island, it's really beautiful, with this palm trees, fish and etc. a fisherman dream.

I must be closing Vi 'cause my candle is getting low, I'll write more in my next letter. May God Bless You All. Say hello to your folks and mine. Good Luck.

Yours with Love. John

p.s. Have you heard from Frank lately? I got a letter from him the other day and some pictures, boy, he sure looks swell. Tell Veronica to write, if she's out of ink I'll send her some, or is she too busy going out wither boyfriends. Ha. Ha.

The Lord gives strength to his people; the Lord blesses his people with peace. -Psalm 29:11

Sunday, October 25, 1942 Camp Davis N.C.

Dear Vi,

    I suppose you think I forgot all about you folks but I didn't I'm just busy as hell. You probably heard I'm going to telephone communication school. It keeps me pretty busy school all day then cleaning up at night. Veronica probably told you how I got out of cleaning guns the night they were here. As soon as I got home from school I would take a shower get my pass and beat it for the guest house. I didn't even wait for chow that's something! We had chicken for dinner to-day I'll bet I ate a whole chicken myself. Most of the guys were out of camp, that leaves more for me. I weigh about 202 lbs now I think I'll have to go on a diet. Don't mistake me and think we get that much all the time. That only happens on Saturday and Sunday. During the week I finish eating at the P.X. or cookies that the guys have.

    Those cookies you made were swell. The guys were always around, "Lulek you got any more of those good homemade cookies?" they didn't last very long in our barracks. Thanks a lot Viola I really appreciate it.

    How is everyone at home? Tell Joey I really appreciate his letter it touched the spot to hear from him. I'll write to him as soon as I get the chance. Is Joe still working on the muck? Tell him not to worry I was just kidding about those blondes. They wanted to take us for a ride but we didn't go. I just can't go for these southern women. Not that I didn't have a chance or anything like that. I think too much of Ceil to monkey around with those bags.

    I'll send some pictures of myself this week or next as soon as they are developed. Give my love to the kids and rest of the family. God bless you all. Love your brother. John

October 26, 1942 Fort Bragg, N.C.

Dear Family,
How are you get along with everything? Sure was glad to get that card you send me. I haven't heard from you in a long time. The weather get cool this week.
It sure was good to see mother. I hope she liked it. It was hell went she went back I sure miss her. I sure miss her. She good to me.
Thanks for the cookies you send me the boys sure liked them. I'll write you a letter some time I hope if I don't I'll call you or a card every week will that be o.k. with you?
Yours, Frank

p.s. How is my Barbara & Joey? Say hello for me tell them to pray for me.

Frank walked out onto the airfield and realized that he couldn't stop smiling! It was one thing to practice jumps out of the C-47's but today he was going to have the opportunity to jump out of the Waco-CG4A Hadrian glider. The glider was towed behind the C-47 by a towline that contained a wire fed through the center so that the pilot and co-pilot in the glider could communicate with the C-47. The glider could carry the two pilots, up to thirteen paratroopers and a maximum of 7,500 pounds of payload. The glider was considered expendable once it landed but under certain conditions, it could be snatched by a C-47 during a fly-by if the glider was still operational.

The wood and metal frame of the glider was covered in fabric. This left the occupants more vulnerable to gunfire and shrapnel from anti-aircraft.[12] However, Frank found a certain comfort to the gliders construction. The design reminded him of a giant cocoon for he and his men, and that made him feel secure especially once the glider was freed from the C-47 and the reverberating sounds coming from the engines of the towing plane were replaced by the sounds of wind rushing over the wings of the glider. It was the ideal calm before the storm.

Praise be to the Lord my Rock, who trains my hands for War, my fingers for battle. He is my loving God and my fortress, my stronghold and my deliverer, my shield, in whom I take refuge, who subdues peoples under me. –Psalm 144: 1-2.

---

[12] National Museum of the U.S. Air Force www.nationalmuseum.af.mil

Chapter Four

The 37th Buckeye Division moved from Fiji to several different islands securing locations and training along the way. Their first real encounter with the Japanese was still nine months away, and they were becoming one of the most skillfully trained divisions in the Pacific.

Two weeks on this new island and defensive positions had been established. The work was hard and the days seemed to blend one into the next, but John found it no different than working on the farm and no hotter than those blast furnaces back home at the mill. The humidity, however, was a different story all together. It could drain the will and morale right out of a man if he wasn't careful. Each island was like a beautiful gem that gave a man promise and hope at a glance, only to drag him down with it's seemingly impenetrable jungles, stinging mosquitoes and insects and the stench of decaying foliage and mud beneath each new canopy. John and his men were averaging either side of four hours of continually interrupted sleep each night so, better to work to the point of exhaustion then to try and find comfort in a pool of one's own sweat on his bunk!

John's eyes perpetually stung from the beads of sweat that seemed to race from under the rim of his cap, and he made certain to always have a jar of suave nearby to help minimize the irritable rubbing and chaffing that otherwise occurred along the neck from his shirt collar. Many of the commanding officers had long since abandoned the mandatory orders of dress code while on work detail, but John knew that it was far less work to look after a raw and irritated neck than a blistering back and stomach. The only reprieve was the constant water breaks that seemed to string one into the next in an effort to keep the soldiers hydrated along with some occasional local fare from the gracious natives.

Saturday, October 31, 1942 Some where in the South West Pacific

Dearest Viola,
Hello Honey, I received your letter today and you'll never know how happy I was to hear from you again. And also to know that everything is O.K. back home. Course I know how you feel about Johnny being away from home and Claude going soon. But just keep your chin up and every thing will be all right. I heard Frank may be moved to N. Carolina soon. I hope he's send to the same camp Johnny is in, that would be swell, hey? I haven't heard from Johnny yet, but I suppose he has written to me by now.
Honey, I was so glad to hear that Mother& Dad were well & also your folks, I'm always worried about them. I'm always thinking & wondering how they are. So keep writing whenever you have time. You see there are times when I can't write as often as I would like to so if you don't hear from me, you know I am busy and can't write. I'm still on the Island I wrote to you about. I can't say very much about it at the present time, but when I can I'll write you a long letter. I'm well as can be expected, still keeping my chin up and hopeing for the best. I know you are doing the same and May God Bless You All for it. I go to church whenever I can, course there are times when I can't go, but I try. I pray where ever I am.
I suppose by this time the weather in Ohio is pretty cold. Here it's hot as hell, and no kidding either. Is Joe doing any fishing for pike at the lake this fall? Gosh, I miss those nites when Joe and I uset to go. Well, maybe some day we can go again, I hope. Are you still busy on the farm? I suppose Joe is doing all kinds of hunting now? Has he got Johnny's dog? How are my

two little Honeys? How's Joey like school this year? I hope he love it. Has he got a little sweet heart too? I bet he has. And Barbara is she still as sweet as she use to be. I heard she getting sweeter every day. Beth wrote that the boys will really go after her when she gets big. If you have a little picture of them, please send it to me.

In your last letter you wrote about sending me some candles or some thing I need. I wouldn't send any thing like that because it breaks up before it got here. I could stand some of your homemade candy if you know what I mean. Ha. Ha. Well Honey, I'll close for this time and will write more soon again when I have time. Good bye for now, May God Bless You All and take care of you. Say hello to all my friends, Mother, Dad and your folks and please write again soon.

Yours with love. John

I'll write again in a few days.

Pray continually, give thanks in all circumstances, for this is God's will for you in Christ Jesus. -1 Thessalonians 5:17-18.

Saturday, October 31, 1942 Fort Bragg, N.C.

Dearest family,
How are you all? Hope you are all feeling fine!
Just came back from a trip about 300 mi. in a plane. Could see your brother's camp from the air. Wish I would see him but I will see him soon I hope. I got a letter from him yesterday.

The weather here is cool now is it in Ohio? Sure like to be there but maybe soon I hope. I don't know when we will be going across but I hope soon and get it over so I can come home see you all.

We are training hard for the last 3 or 4 weeks. It's the

Airborne troop, we are the parachute & Glider. Sure is good to be out in a plane.

Tell Joey and Barbara to pray for me. The Army is the same all the time. It's O.K.

I didn't get a letter from John for the last two weeks, but don't worry me cause he'll be O.K. I'll have to close for this time. May God Bless You All. With all my love. Frank

Sunday (11:15A.M.), November 1, 1942

Dearest Sister,

I received your letter today and was very happy to hear from you. I haven't been doing much writing, but you will have to excuse me for that. I feel fine except when I get shot in the arm or have to go to the dentist. We get plenty to eat, but some of the time it isn't so good. Boy could I go for one of your meals. I weighed myself last nite and I weigh 157 lbs. I would like to see Johnny now. I bet he really looks good. I don't think I will gain to much weight be cause my work is to hard.

Johnny wrote to me last week and told me about getting together some time. I think it is a good idea. If it can be fixed up. Boy would we raise cane.

Yes, I am in the Infantry but I am not to proud of it. 13wks. of it will be enough for me. There isn't much of a chance of us to get into anything else, because the Infantry is to important.

I am sorry to hear that Junior is sick. I hope he gets well very soon so he don't miss to much school. Gee but I sure do miss Joey and Barbara a lot. I would give anything to see them rite now. Tell Junior to get all the scrap he can because that will help win this war.

Gosh but the days are going slow. The weather out hear is perfect. The days are warm and bright & the nights are very beautiful. We only had about two days of bad weather since I *have been here.*

I am very glad to hear that mother and dad got that clover up. Did they start husking corn yet?

Well it is 12:30 and we just had our dinner and boy was it a crapy dinner the only thing I liked was the ice cream.

Well I must be closing for now because I have two more letters to write and that will take a long time for me.

Good by and God Bless You All. Love and kisses Pvt. Claude

p.s. excuse the poor writing.

Have I not commanded you? Be strong and courageous. Do not be terrified; do not be discouraged for the Lord your God will be with you wherever you go. –Joshua 1:9

Sunday, November 1, 1942 Camp Davis, N.C.

Dearest Joey,

I received your letter the other day and was very happy and surprised to hear from you. I thought maybe you forgot all about your uncle. Well Joey how is the farm coming along? I heard your cow had a nice little calf. Are you going to raise it? I'll bet your goat is big by this time. You ought to keep him and hitch him to your sled in the winter time.

Your mother told me your report card was perfect. I'm glad to hear that, keep up the good work Joey boy. I'm sorry to hear you had a bad cold and were out of school for four days. I guess you can make that up in no time.

How is Barbara? I pray for you kids every Sunday and I'm

glad to hear you pray for me too. I miss you kids very much. I hope to see you soon maybe for Christmas.

Well Joey I must be closing now. Give my love to Barbara and your mother and daddy. God bless you kids always. Say hello to Grandma and Grandpa for me will you?

Your Loving Uncle John

P.S. I'm sending you a picture of myself. You can show it to the kids tell them that's your tough uncle. ha. ha. Well be a good boy Joey and take care of yourself. So long write soon.

John sat staring at the letter for a moment, thinking about the kids… and home… and how he would just now be pushing away from the Sunday dinner table with the family. He would step outside to light his cigar and take in the crisp fall afternoon admiring the bright and deceptively warm sunshine as thick billowing clouds painted white to a deep purplish hue with flattened bottoms rolled across the sky from Lake Erie. He would make room for supper with an afternoon hunt with his brother-in-law, Joe.

He sealed the letter and thought that the sooner we fight then, the sooner we all get back home to our families and back to how life used to be.

Lift up your heads, you gates; be lifted up, you ancient doors, that the King of glory may come in. Who is the King of glory The Lord strong and mighty, the Lord mighty in battle.   — Psalm 24:7-8

Monday Night, November 9, 1942 Camp Wheeler, Ga.

Dear Viola,
I received your card the other day and it made me very

happy. Any kind of a letter or card from home makes a soldier feel good.

How is Junior feeling? Is he going to school yet? I hope so because I would hate to see him miss too much school. And Barbara how is she behaven? Gee every time I think about them it makes me feel bad. I wish I could go home tomorrow so I could see them.

Is Joe still working at the Orwell Gardens? Or did he get a job in the mill already? Is he doing any fishing now or can't he get tires to drive his car. Did ma by any pigs at the sale the other day. I'll bet she paid a big price for them if she did.

We are very busy around here. I can't even find time to write. I have to do all my writing after dark. I don't like that very much. They give us so darn much to do on our own time. We have to clean our rifles every day. Every Sat. we have rifle inspection an boy we sure have to have them clean inside and out. We had our rifles out on the range and we had to clean them in soap and water 3 days after. Boy that sure was a job. This week we probably will shoot the revolver and the machine gun. I sure am looking forward to it.

Have you been getting any letters from Johnny lately. I got a letter from him about a week or so. And I haven't heard from him since. Well I suppose he is like me, don't like to write very well. I heard he is going to get a furlough for Christmas, "I hope so." I hope I can get one to so we can have a reunion. I hope John Ankowski and I can get a 3 day pass so we can get out and see... Boy would we have a good time.

Tell Junior I am still waiting for the letter he is writing to me.

Well there isn't much more I can think of right now so I better be closing for now. Say hello to everybody.

Your loving brother Pvt. Claude

excuse the poor writing

Wednesday, November 11, 1942 Somewhere in the South West Pacific
(sent 'V-mail")

Dearest Viola,
Received you VMail letter and also the other and words can't express how happy I was to hear from you again. Gee it's swell to hear from you and family. I think of you all often and wonder how you are doing. I received a letter from Johnny the other day. The first since he's been in the Army. I was really glad to hear from him. Also heard from Frank & Veronica. I'm very sorry for not writing sooner, but I've been busy lately so please forgive me. I know you will. How are the children? Tell Barbara I wish her a Happy Birthday. Wish I could sing to her. Her 5th Birthday, Gee she'll be a big girl by the time I come home. And Junior, how's he doing in school must be doing pretty good in the third grade already. How is this girl friend? Ha. Ha. And Joe, I suppose he's been doing all kinds of hunting now. Has he gotten any birds yet? And you Honey, I suppose you're busy getting Junior ready to school also driving your Mother & Dad around. Well Honey, I'll close for this time and will write again soon. I'll send you a picture of my self. May I wish you all a Merry Christmas and a Happy New Year. May God Bless You All.
Lots of Love, John

Wednesday Night, November 11, 1942, Camp Wheeler, GA.

Dear Viola,
Just a few lines to let you know that I am feeling fine. I am

sorry to hear that Junior is sick with the flu. I hope he gets well very soon. How is Barbara feeling, she isn't sick is she.

When Johnny said the dentists in the army are like horse doctors he was right. They do anything they want to with you. Wheather it hurts you or not. They pull any teeth or fill any that they want. You have nothing to say in the army.

When I said I would be here only 9 wks., that was only what I heard I don't know for sure. So don't worry about it. I will get enought training.

When they were catching the heifers did they have a hard time with the bull. You know he was very mean. Has Pa been going to any sales lately. Has he bought any more cows.

I got those pictures you sent me of Ma& Pa and the tool shed. The one with Ma & Pa was alright but the other you can't make out who is on the picture. I guess it is pretty small.

What did John Soukenik have to say in his letter. I think if I have time I will write him myself. I am (ancuss?) to know how he is getting along. I know he can very well take care of him self. Because he always has. Does he know I am in the army yet? I suppose he has seen some fighting by now.

Well I must be closing because tomorrow we go on the range and I must get some sleep. So I will be saying goodby and May God Bless You All.

Love, Pvt. Claude

Friday, November 13, 1942 Fort Bragg, N.C.

Dearest family,
How are you all getting along. I hope you are fine. I hope the children are feeling good by this time with their colds.

I haven't seen John yet but I'm hoping to see him soon because we are going some place soon. I don't know where. We are working hard all the time in the night.

I am so tired when it come to writing I don't feel like writing you. Know I miss you all.

My girl went home yesterday. I didn't see her much, but we had a good time when we went out with her money. Haha, You know me don't you.

I got a letter from John. He is O.K. did you get one from him? I sure wish I would be with him. We will be there before long.

I'll have to get to bed soon. May God Bless You All.
The weather here is cold. Well good night all.
Love Frank

p.s. did you like the gift I got for mother. I hope she likes it.

Tuesday evening, November 17, 1942, Some where in the South West Pacific and doing fine.

Dearest Vi,
Just a few lines to let you know that I'm doing fine and hope this letter finds you the same. How's everything with you? I hope it's all swell, I hope you all are having a good Christmas by now. How's the weather in Ohio? I suppose it's really cold. We are having our hot season and honey it's really hot. Have you heard from Johnny, Frank, and Claude lately? I bet they's keep you pretty busy writing. I haven't heard from Claude yet. Maybe he hasn't got my address if and when you write to him send it to him. How's Barbara and Joey? Swell? I hope so. Is Joe still working on the Ohio muck? How was his hunting this year?

Well Vi, the way things are going now it won't be long, we hope. Then we can all be together again and enjoy life like we use to. I have a funny light and it's hell writing. I'll do my best and maybe you can read it.

By the way I'm sending in my letter a picture of my self

which isn't so good, but I hope you will like it anyway and honey, I know you will, because you're really swell, I can't wait until I come home to see you all, it seems like years still I was home. You know Vi, it been a year ago since I was home from Shelby. I think of the time when I went hunting and all, Boy I really miss it all, but you know how it is, we have a job to do, and when it's over we can all come home right?

Well Honey there really isn't much more I can say. I just want you to know that I'm thinking of you all and wishing you all the luck in the world. May God Bless You All and a Merry Christmas and a happy new year to all. Say hello to my folks and yours. I'll write again soon, and you do the same. Keep your chin up and I'll do the same. Tell Joe to take care of all till we come home.

Lots of Love John.

p.s. Kisses to Joey and Barbara

Are not five sparrows sold for two pennies yet not one of them is forgotten by God. Indeed, the very hairs of your head are all numbered. Don't be afraid; you are worth more than many sparrows. –Luke 12:6-7

Tuesday at noon, Nov.17, 1942 Camp Wheeler, Ga.

Dear Viola,
I received your cards yesterday and was very glad to hear from you. But what I can't figure out is why they both came at the same time. One was dated the 12th and the other the 14th.
I am getting along pretty good except for one thing that is. Too much work for the amount of pay we get.
We went on another hike yesterday. This time it was with a full field pack, about 45 lbs. altogether. But we had a lot of fun

sitting up our tents and then tearing them down again. This time it was about 8 miles long but that wasn't bad at all.

I didn't get a chance to (Wed. noon) writing yesterday because I didn't have time. We went out on alert. That means we sleep in tents. Boy and what a night. We sleep on the ground and boy was it cold. The days are very warm and the nites are cold.

I am getting enough mail but I can't keep up answering them. You know how long it takes me to write a letter.

We haven't had any rain here for three wks. and then it didn't rain very much. It is alful dry and dusty. I suppose when it starts to rain it will rain for 3 wks. but that won't stop us.

(wed. nite) Well this is the therd time I am writing this letter. This time maybe I will finish it. I received your letter and the fruit cake tonight. I wasn't there for mail call but John Ank. got it for me. as soon as I got it we opened it up and had some. I gave John a piece of it and he said it was the best fruit cake he had ever eaten. I thought it was swell too. Although I always did. I found out one thing and it is you can't eat much of it at one time. I don't see how I can ever go hungry with you and every body else sending me cakes & cookies etc. I want to thank you very much for everything. And I appreciate everything you send me. But you are spoiling me. now I will be expecting something every day. I am sorry you had such a hard time to fined string and tin cans. It was too bad about Joe's fishing line. Now he won't be able to do any more fishing. Has he been fishing lately?

I also received Junior's letter. He sure is a good writer. He has me beaten already. It was too bad you had to kill the goat. It was so nice. I can just see Junior playing around with it. How is my goat? Is it still giving milk?

Calves must be pretty high since they got $25.00 for it. Did they get their coal yet?

I didn't know Mother's and Dad's anniversary was so near. I would have gotten them something. well I haven't anymore to say right now. So I will be saying Good by. And may God bless

you all.
Your loving brother Pvt. Claude
I am very glad my nephew is getting better. Excuse the poor writing.

Friday November 20, 1942; Headquarters Battery 320th Glider F. A. Bn. 82nd A/B Division Fort Bragg, N.C.

Dearest family,
I received your card &cake sure was good that all the boys said "I sure like it." Boy I wish I could come home for Christmas but we are going on 15th of Dec. or some and we will be back some time Jan. or Feb. Boy I miss Barb & Joey & you all. But its War so you know. I haven't much to say. I didn't see John but I hope soon. The weather is hot here this week. Did you see mother this week how is dad and all the folks in home.
I have to close for this time see you some time in next 2 mo. I hope. May God Bless you all. Send me a picture of the kids.
Your brother Law with all my love Frank

But encourage one another daily, as long as it is called Today, so that none of you may be hardened by sin's deceitfulness. "Today, if you hear his voice harden not your hearts."
–Hebrews 3:11 and 15.

Friday November 20, 1942; V-mail

Dearest Vi,
Received your letter to-day, dated Nov. 6 and the pictures of the children. The children really look swell. Joey is much taller

and better looking. Barbara is sweet as ever. She looks like a big girl now. Wish I was there now to kiss them right now. Your letter was swell and very long, thrilling and touching too. It really touch my heart and words can't not express how happy I was to receive it. Your letters do something to me, which make me very happy. By the way honey, your letter only took about 2 weeks to get here. That's really going some, Right? They're coming lot faster now and it's like writing in the states again.

  Well Vi, how's everything with you and the family? I suppose you're still busy writing to all your brothers and brother in laws. It's great to have so many brothers in the Army all at one time. I know you're all proud of it and so are we. I haven't heard from Claude as yet but if I have time I'll write to him. Johnny wrote to me once and Frank writes often. Have you heard from Jim lately? I hope the boys get together some time soon. It would really be swell. You say Claude is in Camp Wheeler, Georgia? We have some boys from there in our company. It's a great camp. So your folks and my were down to see the boys, well that's great. How did they like it? Swell, hey? Well honey, that's about all I can write in this letter. Remember I am always thinking of you all and wishing you all the luck in the world. May God Bless You All, Merry Christmas and happy new year, give my love to the children and say hello to all.

  I'll write again soon Love, John

You did not choose me, but I chose you and appointed you so that you might go and bear fruit a fruit that will last and so that whatever you ask in my name the Father will give you.
  –John 15:16

Thursday Afternoon, November 26, 1942 Camp Wheeler, Ga.

Dear Viola,

Well today is Thanksgiving. And we should all be thankful for what we have. Even though some of us have more than others. We had a thanksgiving dinner today and it sure was swell. I guess we had every thing under the sun. we even had the day off which I didn't even expect. Our Uncle sure is good to us.

I received a fruit cake from Catherine today but haven't tasted it as yet. Because it was to near dinner. But if it is anything like the one you and Helen sent it sure will be swell. By the way do you want me to send the tin back? Catherine asked me to send hers back so I thought I might as well send yours too.

Well how's little Joe? Is he alright now and going to school? Is he still gathering scrap iron? Gosh that reminds me I never answered his letter yet. You tell him as soon as I get some time I will. But right now I have so many letters to write that I wont have time.

Is Joe still working at the muck or did he get a job some other place? I suppose he has been doing a little hunting. At least every chance he gets. Gee I wish I would be home to do a little hunting. Because that is my favorit sport. But it looks as though I won't be able to until next year. I hope.

Well Christmas is just around the corner and I suppose I better start doing some shopping. I don't think I will be able to buy you all something. But I will try to get the kids a little present. John and I went to town last Tuesday and we saw a lot of Christmas toys but it was to late to do any buying.

Well there isn't much more I can say right now so I will be closing for now.

Good by and God Bless You All. Pvt. Claude

Thursday, November 26, 1942 V-Mail

Dearest Viola,

Just received your Christmas package and honey, it was really swell, words can't express how happy I was when I received it. I'm smoking one of the cigars right now and is it good O boy! Wish I could send you folks some thing, but about all I can do is wish you all a Merry Christmas and a happy New Year and hope to see you all soon. Everything came in good shape. It didn't last long with all the boys around, but that's the way it goes in the Army.

Well Vi, How's the weather now? I bet it's getting pretty cold by now. Hope you have a good Xmas this year. I know you miss us all, but you can bet we are all thinking of you and wishing we were right there with you.

How are my two little honeys? I really miss them. How's Joe doing? Still Hunting I suppose. Are you doing any dancing lately? Wish I were dancing with you right now. Boy O boy! This letter is short Vi, but I'll write you a long one soon. I'm very busy right now. Good Luck and May God Bless You All.

Thanks again, yours with Love John

John sealed the V-mail and then sat on his bunk staring into space for what seemed like an eternity… He realized that he had been in the Army for almost two years!!! Two long years of hard work riddled with worry, not for himself, but for his family and yet, the boys of the 37th Buckeye Division had not been in even one minor skirmish with The Japanese Imperial Army. He swallowed hard to fight back the homesick feeling that always lurked nearby waiting to strike him in the gut whenever he had a day off or even a brief moment like this to himself. "That must be why the Army keeps us so darn busy," John thought. He had one other thought as he rose from his bunk harboring all of his pent up emotions, "When they do meet, those Japs are going to know what it feels like to stumble onto a hornets' nest and the world of hurt that comes with it."

Whatever you do, work at it with all your heart, as working for the Lord, not for human masters, since you know that you will receive an inheritance from the Lord as a reward. It is the Lord Christ you are serving. –Colossians 3:23-24

Sunday, November 29, 1942, 11:50 a.m., Fort Bragg, N.C. (USO stationary with the caption on the bottom of each page, "Idle Gossip Sinks Ships")

Dearest family,
I received your package sure was good candy I like it & all the boys like. I didn't see John but I hope to soon. But we are so damn busy we get all the training we can here we are in the woods all the time.
So don't mind if you don't get a letter every week or so.
I made my jump this week sure was hell. I jump from 1200 feet.
How are my kids Barb & Joey tell them I miss them all I wish would see them soon but it's War. I got a letter from John today. He wrote it Nov. 8 so don't worry about him. He send me a picture of him if you don't get one I am sending it home so you all can see him he sure look good.
I'll have to close for this time. May God Bless You with all my love Frank

Sunday afternoon, November 29, 1942 Camp Wheeler, Ga.

Dear Viola,

I received your letter a few days ago , but was unable to answer any sooner Sunday is about my only chance to write.

The Infantry is okay but it is the weather that I don't like. Here last Monday it rained all day and the next day we had to go to the woods and practice with the machine gun. They made us sit on the cold wet ground and now we all have a bad cold. And you know what kind of a cold I usually get.

Well Thanksgiving has come and gone. It was just another day for us soldiers. We just had a lot of time to think about home and how much we wish to be there instead of here. Of course we had a big dinner but that wasn't enough. Well this is the army and you can't expect any more. There hasn't been a menut passed that I haven't thought of home. I sure did miss hunting this Thanksgiving. I can remember the last Thanksgiving as plain as day. So Joe has been getting a few rabbits. Is he using the dog any? Or is he waiting for snow?

I received your fruit cake about 2 or 3 day before Thanksgiving. It sure was swell. It wasn't moldy at all. Who told you that I didn't like cookies from the store? I don't remember of ever writing any thing like that. you know darn well I like cookies no matter where they come from. And besides they were darn good. I would like to know who started all that. it makes me feel bad to think that Catherine thinks I said that.

I don't know when I will come home. I hope for Christmas. But I don't think there is much of a chance untill after my thirteen weeks are up. I suppose Johnny will be home for Christmas. He has been there longer than I. we will probably get 3 days, and that isn't enough to come home on.

Is mother and dad about done husking corn? Helen told me about the bull dad bought at the sale. Was he worth the money? Or is he like the others he has been buying. So you bought a calf? What was the idea buying a sickling? So the prices *of eggs aren't so steady? Boy we sure do eat a lot of them here. About a case every morning.*

So Joe is finally going to the mill and work. He should have been there a long time ago. Of course $100. a month isn't bad. But he should get more then that. I hear Eugene got a new job. I'll bet he doesn't last there very long. Helen told me he was about to quit already. He should get a big truck job.

I don't know how big a bonus I will get but I hope it sure is a big one. I have been trying to find out from Ted, but he doesn't know. I guess nobody knows yet. I don't know whether I will go back there or not. I made $800. plus my $450 investment so that should bring a pretty good bonus.

John Ankowski has signed up for the paratroops. He has had one examination and passed it. Of course he has another to pass whitch will be a lot stiffer. He still has to be here 13 wks. he has been trying to get me to join but I didn't think I had a chance. I guess he wants to go across in a big hurry.

So you all got to-gether and went to Cleveland. Veronica told me about it. But she didn't say who's car they drove. But I knew with out her telling. I don't care how much you drive it so long as you take care of it. Tell Joe he can drive it when ever he wants to. Did Jim put in that new battery yet? I suppose you have anti-freeze in it? Don't forget to check it once in a while. How are the tires holding out? About our heater in the car. I think there is a tube that is broke. If you haven't already fixed it you better have it done. Jim will know what to do. Well I will have to be closing for now.

So Good by and God Bless you all.
Your Brother Pvt. Claude

Chapter Five

John was feeling tough as nails and about as ornery as the family's bull back on the farm. After almost three weeks of field training, he longed for three things: a long shower, a hot meal and the comforts of his bunk under his lower back. He actually felt relief at the first glimpse of camp and now longed for nothing more than news from home.

Sunday November 29, 1942 Camp Davis, N.C.

Dear Vi,
We just got back from maneuvers. I don't know why you people worry about me so much. I told you not to expect any mail from me for some time, that we were going away. If you don't hear from me don't worry I can take care of myself. Just keep writing it means a lot to get mail when we're out on maneuvers like that.
I received your cake when we got back it was swell. It was after Thanksgiving but it tasted good anyhow, the boys really enjoyed it too. We didn't get back until after Thanksgiving. I didn't miss much because we were so busy that I didn't even know it was Thanksgiving. I'm telling you I don't know what day it is anymore. The month of November sure went by fast.
Ft. Bragg was off for Thanksgiving so we had to be on duty. But I hear we get a 5 day pass for Christmas then Ft. Bragg will be on duty. They can't leave all the camps go at one time. Frank wasn't home for Thanksgiving was he?
So Joe didn't get any pheasants yet? Tell him I'll have to

come home and show him how to shoot. I really miss hunting this year. How is my dog are the boys using him?

Don't worry about Ceil and I it doesn't make any difference to me I think it was all my fault. I really don't care for women, the army made me so tough that they don't phase me any more. Don't tell her I said this. You ought to see the letters she writes me I don't pay any attention. You know how I used to be when I was at home I just ignore her. I guess I shouldn't treat her that way but I'm just a brute and can't help it. Does she ever mention anything about it when she comes over?

Tell Joe to look after the car, truck and tractor. I don't want them to freeze up or anything like that. I suppose he knows that there is two places to drain water on the tractor. I hear you've been having cold weather up there. It's been pretty warm here lately.

I graduated from school Saturday it reminded me very much of when I graduated from school. I think I'll send my diploma home so I won't lose it it means a lot to me.

How is everyone at home? So Ruby had a girl well I wish her the best with it. I suppose they are all proud of it. I can just see Ruby taking care of it. Well I must close now. Give my love to Mom and Dad and rest. I'm writing a few words to Barbara on the bottom. You told me she felt bad when I wrote to Joey and didn't send her a picture so I'm sending her one now I hope she likes it.

Love your Brother Johnny

P.S. I'm on K.P. to-day and I'm writing in my spare time.

Dearest Barbara,
I heard you were mad at your uncle because he didn't write to you or send you a picture. I think about you kids every day and I pray for you every Sunday, I hope you do the same for your uncle. I love both of you kids and miss you very much. I hope to see you at Christmas time. Tell Joey I said hello and to be a good

boy. God Bless you both.
    Your loving Uncle John

John was outwardly the biggest brute of the two families. The ironic thing was that the harder army life made him, the more sensitive he became with regards to his correspondence home and his faith.

So that you, your children and their children after them may fear the Lord your God as long as you live by keeping all his decrees and commands that I give you, and so that you may enjoy long life. –Deuteronomy 6:2

Friday night December 4, 1942; Co. B, 2ND. BN., Camp Wheeler, GA.

Dear Viola,
I received your card today and was very glad to hear from you. I haven't been getting very many letters lately. It kind of had me worried that everybody back home has forgotten me. you know how it is when you don't get a letter every day.
I just don't know what to think about Johnny. He might still be on maneuvers. But I don't think there is anything to worry about, he can well take care of him self. He is big enough. I haven't heard from him for about 5 wks. I wrote to him last. I sure do miss him and when I don't even get a letter from him I feel so lonesome. Of course I feel lonesome for all of you, but at least I hear from you once in a while.
I haven't been feeling so well for the past few days. I have a bad cold. I got to the doctor every day but it doesn't do me any good. I thought I would never get a cold in Georgia, but found out different. when we first came here the weather was warm and dry, but now it is wet and cold. It seems as though two thirds of the camp has a cold or some other sickness. Well how is the weather

out there? Is there any snow? I hope so. So Joe can do some good hunting. Has he been doing any or has he been working every day. I suppose he has a new job by now.

I am glad to hear that my letters are enjoying to read. I never thought they would be. I am not much of a writer.

John Ank. and I went to town Wed. night to do some shopping, but by the time we got there most of the stores were closed. So we walked around and did some window shopping and then we went to a show.

Well I can't think of any more to write just now and besides it is getting my bed time so I will be closing. Good by. God bless you all.

Your loving brother Pvt. Claude.

Sunday, December 6, 1942 Camp Davis, N.C.

Dear Vi,

I received your other package the other day. The candy and cake was delicious only I have a little trouble eating candy it bothers my teeth. You know what I would like very much for you to make me instead of candy, some horns with nuts. That is if it wouldn't be to much bother and if you can get the nuts.

I got a letter the other day from John Soukenik. It was a swell letter and a long one too. I read it over several times. I was so happy when I saw it was from him. He sure writes a nice letter. Have you been getting any mail from him lately? He wants me to send him a picture of myself.

Have you been hearing from Claude any? He didn't write to me for sometime. I don't know whats the matter with him.

We are going out on a 7 to 10 day bivouac the 14th. We won't be back until a few days before Christmas. I think we will get a five day pass for Christmas. I'm comming home if we do. I'm to be acting communication sgt. On this bivouac so I want to do my best. We pick are lines up in the dark then move to another position and setup in the dark again. It is suppose to be as if we were in actual combat. It's going to be a tough problem.

Well I must be closing now cause I got a lot of studying to do also letters to write. Don't worry about me. Write often I won't be able to. Give my love to mom and dad also the kids.

P.S. thanks again for everything. Love your brother Johnny.

Tuesday, December 8, 1942 V-Mail

Dearest Vi,
I received your letter a few days ago but very busy. Have a little time today as I am writing. Yours was a very touching letter, brought tears to my eyes. How's everyone at home now? Fine? I hope so, I'm O.K. Still going on but a little lonesome for you all. Course that can be expected when you are so far away from home. How's my two little sweethearts? How's Joey? Is he feeling better, and little Barbara, I bet she's as sweet as ever, boy I miss those kids. And Joe, is he still working at the Ohio Muck Farms? And you Vi, I bet you're busier than hell, Right? How are your Folks and my Folks? I haven't heard from my Mother in sometime and I'm worried. Is she sick? Let me know. How are the boys doing in the Army? How's Claude taking it? Well Vi, there isn't much I can write about right now, so I'll close, hoping you all had a good Xmas, and thanks again for the swell package you send me. I miss you all and the family. Good luck and May God Bless you all and keep you safe. Please write and I'll try to do the same.
Give my love to Helen and family.
Love John

Thursday night, December 10, 1942

Dearest Viola,

I received your letter today and was very glad to hear from you. I got a letter from Helen the other day but just couldn't find time to answer. I don't write over one letter a nite because it takes me so long. Last nite I didn't write any because I was on guard duty from 8:30 to 10:30pm

So you finally heard from Johnny. Well I am glad to hear that because I haven't. where has he been on maneuvers? I wrote to him about 6 wks. ago and he hasn't answered yet. I didn't think there was any of us writing if I didn't get an answer. How has he been? Does he weigh 250 yet?

I am also glad to hear you are taking good care of the car. I hear the winter is perty bad out there. It is a good thing you had the heater fixed. It feels perty good on those cold days. Gosh I have been thinking when I get back I will have to learn to drive all over. Of course I never did know very well.

Helen told me in her letter about Veronica getting a job at the Packard. If she has to much trouble riding back and forth why doesn't she board there, or is it to high. I wouldn't want to have her drive every day. That nite work won't be very good for her will it?

Yes I got your candy sometime ago and it sure was swell. The trouble is I had too many friends. I also received a present from Veronica and mother, I suppose you know what I got. It all was swell it is just what I needed. And them cigars you are sending sure will be swell. I will look like a big shot with one of them in my mouth.

So you are kept very busy sending Joey to school and Joe to work. Well I guess that is a house wife's job, isn't it?

I am sorry to hear about your calf. Can't you do something for it? Feed it raw eggs or something. There isn't any use of keeping it if it is not growing. It sure makes me feel good when I hear what is going on at home. I wish I were coming home tomorrow. I sure do miss home. And I get so lonesome for you and the others.

To-morrow we go on a long hike and we have to get up 15 minutes earlier. Because we have to make up a full field pack. That pack weighs about 45lbs. but I don't mind that. I would rather do that than any other thing.

So Father Bialek misses us. Well we all miss him too. He sure is a swell priest. I get a letter from Elsie every now and then and she tells me what goes on at the church.

Well it is getting late so I better be closing for now. Goodby and God Bless you all.

Love and kisses your brother Pvt Claude

Sunday afternoon, December 13, 1942 Camp Wheeler, Ga.

Dear Viola,

I received your card and I sure was glad to hear from you. I also got a card from Johnny. I haven't received anything from him for 6 wks. there for a while I thought he has gone across. From what he tells me he must be doing alright. He said he already graduated and shook hands with a Colonel. I hear he gets 5 days for Christmas and is coming home. Gosh I wish I could come home too. But we will only get 3 days and that won't be enought.

I received your candy some time ago and it is all gone. It sure was good. I got your cigars Friday. Thanks a lot for everything.

To bad ma and dad feel so lonesome. Can't you do something to cheer them up. I think when Johnny gets home that will cheer them up.

  John A. and I went to town last nite to do some shopping. I wanted to buy Junior and Barbara something for Christmas but I just could find nothing that I thought he would like. It is so darn hard to find what you want. So I am sending some money instead and let you do the buying. It won't be very much do the best you can to make them happy.

  The weather out here is not very good. It rains about every other day. My cold doesn't seem to be getting any better. The only way I could get rid of it is by going to the hospital and I don't want to do that. because I would have to make that time up.

  I suppose you think I am getting low on paper to be using Red Cross paper. I just wasted a sheet of my own and I only had enough for the amount I was going to write.

  So Joe is going to keep on working at the Muck. I had a hunch he would. Is he doing any hunting on the muck? I suppose he gets the limit every day. Well it is getting rather late so I better stop for now. I will write as soon as possible.

  Goodby and God Bless you all. Love and kisses Pvt Claude

Thursday, December 17, 1942 Camp Davis, N.C.

Dear Vi,
  I received the box of cigars you sent me the other day. Them R.G. Duns sure taste good after smoking these Southern ropes. Ok yes! Tell mother I received the tobacco and gloves also.

  We went on a 30 mile hike Monday. I'm so damn tired I can hardly move. I feel like I'm walking on an inch of steak that's how my feet are swollen. I didn't do so bad half of the guys fell out they couldn't take it.

  Well I hope to be home soon. I can't say when for sure because things change so fast in the Army you can expect anything. So I don't want to tell you when I'm coming home then disappoint you. I think you can expect me soon I hope.

Be sure Veronica gets plenty of gas and good whiskey. Because when I get home I'm sure going to raise hell. I just can't wait till I get home to see you folks.

Well it's time for the lights to go out so I must close. I'll write more later. Hoping to see you soon. Give my love to all. May God Bless everyone of you always.

Love John

Be joyful always; pray continually; give thanks in all circumstances, for this is God's will for you in Christ Jesus. -1 Thessalonians 5:16-18

Friday nite, December 18, 1942; Camp wheeler, Ga.

Dearest Viola,
I received your letter today and thought I had better answer it right away. I also got Joey's Christmas card. It sure was nice. It sure makes me feel good to get a card from him.

You know I'm having a heck of a time keeping up on my letter writing. I have been getting cards, letters and packages. And all I can write is one letter a nite. And since Christmas is so close I will be lucky if I do that much. But I will write as often as I can.

So you want to know what guard duty is like. Well there isn't much to it. You have to walk around a certain area. You have to walk 2 hours and then you are relieved. but the heck of it is your 2 hrs may come at any time of the nite. You have to guard against fire. This isn't very plain but I just don't know how to put it into words. It really isn't hard except it breaks up your sleep. There are other soldiers around but guard different areas. There isn't any thing to be ascared of because you have a rifle on your shoulder. Yes the boys receive a lot of packages. Especially now since Christmas is so close. Johnny A. sure does get a lot of packages and letters. Of course he has two girlfriends so that would make a difference. But I'm not doing so bad either. I have 4 cartons of cigarettes, a box of candy and I still have some of your cigars. I don't know where that pipe could be. I am sure I didn't take it with me. I gave Joe the pipe I had. The gloves will be just what I need. I have a pair here but they aren't very good.

I heard from Johnny last week but it was only a card. I sent him a letter and haven't received an answer yet. I sure hope he gets to come home for Christmas.

We went to town tonight and it is getting rather late so I will have to cut this letter short because the lights are to go out in a few minutes.

Goodby and God Bless you all. Love and kisses your brother Pvt Claude

Wednesday, December 23, 1942 V-Mail

Dearest Vi,

How are you Honey? Hope you are all feeling fine. Are you having a good Xmas? I really miss those Xmas dances at St. Mary's. How are my two little sweethearts? Fine? I hope so. Hope they's got all kinds of Xmas packages. I been doing pretty good myself. I got alkinds of presents. Cigarettes to keep me for a long time. How's Joe doing? Is he still working and doing alkinds of Hunting? He should do plenty of Hunting with Johnny and Frank's dogs. I wish we could be there to do some with him. Has Johnny been home yet? He should, for he's not so far away from home now. Haven't heard from Johnny or Claude for some time. I hear from Frank often. Well Honey, I'll close and write you a long letter soon. Have a good Xmas and New Year and remember I'm thinking of you all.

Yours with Love and kisses, John

Thursday, December 24, 1942 Fort Bragg, N.C.

Dearest family

I received your letter and card to day & don't worry about me. I am not sick honey my health is good. You know me. you tell mother not to come to see me because we are going on maneuvers with the Glider. Tell her I am O.K. How are my kids Joe and Barbara?

I hope Joe is working every day. How was the turkey? We are having turkey for Xmas too. I'll have to close for this time may God Bless all. I wish you all have a good year to. Same with all my love. Frank

Whoever dwells in the shelter of the Most High will rest in the shadow of the Almighty. I will say of the Lord, "He is my refuge and my fortress, my God in whom I trust."
–Psalm 91:1-2

Chapter Six

Thursday, December 31, 1942 Camp Wheeler, Ga.

Dear Viola,
Yes, Christmas is over and a new year is about to start. I would have enjoyed Christmas if I could have been home. But as it was I was rather blue that day. I guess just about every body was. There wasn't any excitement at all. Even though it was a nice day we stayed in camp. Getting sick of going to town. The night before, John A. and I went to town but came home early because there was nothing going on.

We didn't go to midnight mass because they didn't have any so we went in the morning. Going to church here is nothing like going at home. It is so simple, it doesn't seem like you are in a church. But still it is a place to pray and that is all that is necessary.

We had a swell Christmas dinner. You couldn't ask for a better one. But that doesn't make a good Christmas. All through the day I was thinking of home and how I wished I could be there. I got plenty of presents for Xmas. I am glad to hear you all had a nice Christmas and plenty of presents to.

It sure was nice of Johnny to get a furlough right at Christmas. I bet he had a swell time visiting all of his buddies. I'll bet he was feeling good when he got back. Did he get more gas when he went to the Rationing Board? I bet he walked around rather proud of himself with those stripes, I know I would.

So Joe has been getting quite a few rabbits. There must be a lot of them around. Boy I wish I were there to do a little hunting.

75

Well it won't be long before I'll be leaving this camp. I don't know just where to. I hope it will be closer to home.

It won't be long until bonus time over at Ruetenik Gardens. I was wondering if you could find out and get what I have coming. I hope it will be big. You can bank half of it and buy war bonds with the other half. Or any way you think is best.

I got a letter from Helen today but haven't had time to read it yet. I guess I better hurry up and answer her's because I haven't wrote to her in a long time. We have been very busy lately. Going on nite hikes. Last nite we went on a 16 miles one with 65lbs on our back. So you can imagine how I feel today. We probably will be having a lot of them from now on. I don't know how I will be able to do any writing.

I will close now, I just can't think of any more to write. Love and kisses. Your brother Pvt. Claude

Excuse the poor writing.

Since, then, you have been raised with Christ, set your hearts on things above, where Christ is, seated at the right hand of God. Set your minds on things above, not on earthly things.
–Colossians 3:1-2

Thursday, December 31, 1942 New Year Eve; V-mail

Dearest Vi,
Received your air mail letter today and was so thrilled to hear from you again. Your letter really made good time getting here it was dated Dec. 14. Thanks again for your package it was swell. No the mice and rats didn't get into it, and the candy and cigarettes came in good shape. But honey, please don't send any more candy or smokes. We get all we want. Cigarettes are 60 cents a carton I know you have to pay more back home. Of course

your homemade candy will be appreciated very much. I haven't received the box you sent me yet, the one for New Year. Talking about New Year, it's just around the corner and soon it will be 1943 how time flys Right? Hope we spend the next one home together. Heard from Johnny and frank but not from Claude yet. How's my two sweethearts Joey and Barbara? Hope they's had a good Xmas and many presents. Tell them I am proud the way they are on the honor role for buying bonds. How are you doing with your dancing? And Joe with his hunting? Too bad about Jiggs my dog. Well Honey, I must close and write more letters, my candle is low and it's time for darkout so good night and Say hello to My Folks and yours and write. Love to all. John

Worship the Lord with gladness; come before him with joyful songs… give thanks to him and praise his name. for the Lord is good and his love endures forever. –Psalm 100: 2-5

Wednesday nite January 6, 1943

Dear Viola,
I received your letter and was glad to hear from you. I haven't been doing very much writing because I was rather busy.
So Johnny left already. I bet he hated to leave, and you probably hated to see him go. That is the trouble about a furlough. I hope to get a furlough soon, but I don't think I'll get one within a month. Did Johnny have a good time when he was home? I'll bet he didn't get much sleep. I know when I get home I'm going to have a good time.
Well how does Joe like his job? I bet he likes it better than his old one. Anyway he's making more money. Say, how does he stand with the army? Well I was just thinking if he wouldn't be drafted befor Spring, I mean some time after Spring, and of course he wasn't too busy, maybe he could help dad, at least do some

plowing. Because I don't think I'll be there and I don't know about Johnny.

Ask Dad about the wheat. I would like to know how it is coming along. Whether the frost hurt it any. Or is there too much snow on it to see.

I got a letter from Mr. Ruetenik today. He told me what the bonus was and how much I got. He said he sent the check to mother. It sure is swell to get that amount. He also ask me if I wanted to invest any. Well what I want you to do (if you have not already done it) is to take $150. of it and take it to Mr. Ruetenik. He will give you a note for that amount. You then take the note and put it in my safety deposit box in the bank. Ask him if $150 is the limit. If it isn't then you put the limit in. you can put the rest of it in the bank if mother doesn't need it for something.

I hope John reached camp in time. I heard over the radio about the floods they had in the Eastern States. We never get a flood around here, but it sure does rain sometimes. The weather here isn't so bad now but it sure was bad there for a while. It was rainey and cold. My cold is finally breaking up after about 4 wks of it. You said for me to rest instead of writing. Gosh I am so far behind now I don't know if I will ever catch up. I guess by the looks of my writing I better quit altogether. I was going to write to Mr. Ruetenik, but I don't think I will. so, you tell him how it is and fix it up for me. To-morrow nite we go on an all nite hike. I sure do hate to think of it. Well, I must close now because I still have a letter to write.

May God bless you all. Love and kisses.
Pvt. Claude

Wednesday, January 13, 1943; Camp Davis, N.C.

Dear Vi,

I just got back from maneuvers. I'm sorry I didn't get a chance to write sooner but I got into camp 4:00 Sunday morning. We had to pack all our stuff Sunday and I didn't get time to do anything. I would have to get back just in time for maneuvers.

We were out for seven days. It rained almost every day it sure made things miserable. I wish I could have taken some pictures when we were out but they wouldn't let us take cameras. We all looked like apes. I washed my face twice while we were out so you can imagine what I looked like. We did all our moving at night under black out conditions. The first night we traveled 50 miles in the dark. We had more damn trucks in the ditches. One truck and large gun went over a bridge in the river. That's about 20 thousand dollars lost. We were attacked by marine tanks, paratroops and snipers. Our food consisted of six cans per day. We put it in our mess kit and warmed it over a fire. It's the same type of food they get over seas. They are trying to toughen us up and get us used to short rations. I just about starved if I could have found a little pig or chicken I would have been all set but no such luck.

Well how is everyone at home? I hear you are getting lots of snow. I'm sending you a few more pictures and also the negative. Well I must close now I'll write more later. Give my love to mom and dad and all.

Love your brother John

Wednesday, January 20, 1943 Co. G 305th Infantry 77th Division
Shreveport, La.

Dear Viola,

I received your letter today and was very glad to hear from you. I have not been able to do very much writing because I have been so darn busy. We are going on maneuvers. We are leaving in a short time. I can see very plain why Johnny doesn't write. It seems as though I had a lot more time at Camp Wheeler then I do here. Boy did we work today. We had to wash the baracks in side and out. Did Johnny say where he was going on maneuvers? I suppose not, because that is a military secret.

So, Veronica took my money to Mr. Ruetenik and the bank. I am glad to hear that. I should have quite a sum by now. I really don't know how much I do have. Can you find out and let me know?

So you still have them gatherings and talk and laugh. I wish John and I could be there and help out. I am sure there would be more to talk about.

Did Dad buy a cow at Wysenski's sale? If he did he should of gotten a good one because he had them.

So you are having a lot of snow. Boy would I like to see some. Over here it is warm one day and cold the next. Boy did we have a rain storm the other day.

So you got a letter from John S. Well what did he have to say? How is he getting along? I sent him a Christmas card. I haven't heard from yet.

I am glad the wheat is covered with snow. Maybe dad will get a good crop. I hope so.

Who takes mother and dad around when ever and where ever they go? Is Veronica ever home to take them? Or do you drive them around?

So Joe would rather work in the muck. Well I think if I were home I would be there too. I made perty good money there didn't I? My bank account will prove that.

I am sending my suitcase home because I can't take it along with me. I have some of my friend's stuff in it too. Please have them take care of it for me. I will send the key to Veronica.

Well I must be closing now because the lights will go out very shortly. We will be on maneuvers for two months and then maybe we will get a furlough at least I hope so.

Good by.
Love and kisses.
Your brother
Pvt Claude

Do not send any mail to this address.
I got a letter from Helen today.
Sorry I couldn't write more.
I will write as soon as possible.

Saturday, January 23, 1943 V-mail

Dearest Vi,
I received your most welcome letter and package the other day. I was very much pleased and happy to hear from you. Vi, nothing could make me more happy then to hear from you. I didn't even eat chow that nite. I was too anxious to read your letter and open your box. In fact I read your letter over several times, it was so good. The package came in good shape, the fudge was a little spoil but I ate it anyway, it was really good. The next time you send any home made candy, send it in a can. The gum and cigars were swell and I enjoy them very much. Well honey, anyway you took a chance with the candy and I'm really proud of you for that. I know you work hard making it and with all the rationing it cost

you plenty. I got letters from Johnny, Frank and Mother today. I haven't heard from Claude yet, I wrote to him but I guess he's too busy. Veronica wrote and give me hell for not writing. I'll try to write to her soon. I have been too busy lately. Well Vi, I'll close for this time, thanks again for the packages. Give my love to all and may God Bless You All. Always yours, John

But let us encourage one another-and all the more as you see the Day approaching. -Hebrews 10:25

Friday, January 29, 1943 Camp Davis, N.C.

Dear Viola,

I suppose you wonder why I haven't been writing lately? To tell you the truth I haven't had time to write anyone. I was on (Charge of Quarters) last night. That give me a chance to catch up on my letter writing. The Charge of Quarters goes on for 24 hours straight without sleep. From 7 to 7 the next day, it is now 6 o'clock. I still have one long hour to go.

Last night I wrote 15 letters. I made a list of the people I haven't written to in a long time. Every time I got a letter written checked it off the list. My arm is about paralyzed I never did so much writing in one night since I've been in camp.

So Joey has chickenpox, I certainly hope and pray it don't hurt him in any way. I think the world of those kids. I really miss them both, give them my love. I hope he gets over it soon so he can go back to school.

We are starting a new telephone communication school in our battalion. I am going to be an instructor. Can you imagine me teaching a class of about 50 men? That's more headaches teach class all day then grade test papers and study all night.

I'm sending couple pictures so you can get an idea of some of the things I do. The big truck I'm in is a (Prime Mover) they pull the big 90mm guns. It's just like setting in heaven when you climb in one of those, they are big.

Well I must close now because I have to straighten the office up before I leave. I want it to be in good shape for the next guy. Give my love to Mom and Dad and the rest.

Love your brother Johnny

Saturday, January 30, 1943 Shreveport, La.

Dear Viola,

I received your letter yesterday and was very glad to hear from you. I was sorry to hear about Joey being sick. But again I am glad to hear he is doing well in school. I am feeling alright except for a slight cold.

When I was sent to South Carolina it sure made me feel good, but when I heard we were to stay there for only a short time it made me sick. I am perty sure I will get a furlough after maneuvers. I didn't say any thing to mother about coming home because if I told her I was coming and didn't she would be disappointed.

The weather here is warm in the day and cold at nite. We have been sleeping in tent and on hard ground. We are not on maneuvers yet but expect to soon.

I sure would like you to send me some nut horns, but I don't think you better because they would lay around until after maneuvers. Of course if you want to take a chance it is alright. I sure would like some. I haven't tasted good bakery for a long time. And that is the only kind you bake.

So Joe is working nites. How does he like it? I know I never liked to work nites, but it was not what I liked. He will get used to it just like I did. At first it was really bad but later it got better.

I am glad you like my picture. But I am sorry I couldn't

sent you a large one. Why did you sent me that money? You shouldn't of done that. I didn't want to sell it I wanted to give it as a present.

We get paid today and I am sending most of it home so after maneuvers I can send for it to come home on. That money isn't going to do me any good here any way.

Catherine wanted to come see me when I was in Camp Wheeler but I thought I would be coming home soon so I told her not to. I probably will come home some time in April.

Well I must close now because we are to have dinner soon. Please don't worry too much about me I will be all right. Goodby and God bless you all.

Love,
Your brother Pvt. Claude   Please write soon

I will not be able to write very much but will as much as possible.

Friday, February 5, 1943 Camp Davis, N.C.

Dear Viola,

How is everyone and everything at home? I'm glad to hear Joey got over his case of chicken pox as soon as he did. It didn't leave any scars on him did it? I certainly hope not! Barbara didn't get any of it did she, or did she have it before?

I'm getting along with my work alright. It gives me plenty of work and headaches though. Some of these guys are dumber then hell, it's just like talking to a stone wall. Oh well I guess I just got to have patients with them. I get a kick out of the recruits they (Sir) me all the time. They're only supposed to (Sire) the commissioned officers. They ask some of the most foolish questions. I wonder at times if I was that way when I got in the army?? It's nice to have the men respect you like they do.

You asked me what I do when I'm charge of quarters. My

duties are to take all messages on the phone. Then deliver them to the person whom they may concern in the battalion. Lots of times I get long distance calls at night. I have to get the guy out of bed or try to find him wherever he may be, which is quite a job sometimes.

I don't want you or mother or anyone to worry about me. Climbing poles isn't very dangerous. You know I'm plenty tough. I can take care of my self no matter where I go so mother not to worry if they don't hear from me for some time. Cause I try to distribute my letters to all, what few I do write. That reminds me I wrote to Claude twice and he didn't answer yet.

Well I'll close for now. I want to thank you for the card it was swell. Hoping to hear from you soon and often. Give my love to mom and dad and may God bless you all.

Love your brother Johnny

Tuesday, February 9, 1943 IV-mail

Dearest Johnny,
Received your most welcome letter some time ago, but this is the first time I had to answer it. I was in the hospital for three weeks and now I am ready to go again. Words can't express how happy I was to hear from you and to know how you are doing, for I always wait your letters in every mail call. Congratulations on your promotion to Corp. That's swell. Vi wrote and told me. Keep it up. I always knew you would make good. I received your picture, it was swell. You look wonderful in a uniform, I bet the girls really go for you. I'm sorry Johnny that I can't send a picture of my self right now, but you can bet I will when I can. I was so glad to hear that you were still in the good old U.S.A.

I heard you was home on furlough and did some hunting. Wish I could have been home with you then. We would've given them hell, Right? I bet it was really good hunting this year. Have you saw Frank yet? I hope you have. He always writes about you. You and Frank should get together before you boys leave for some other place. If you do have a drink on me, O.K.? How's Claude doing? I wrote to him, but all I got was a Xmas card. Maybe he's too busy.

Well, Johnny how's the girlfriend? Sweet as ever? I bet you really miss her. I heard from our old girl friends Lee Hicks & Annie. The times we had together are unforgettable and boy when we get back we'll do them all over again, Right? I'm so glad you keep the ring of friendship on your finger all the time, it does keep us closer together. I have a feeling it keeps us safe as well. Well kid, I must close now. I remember you in my prayers every day.

Take good care of yourself and may God Bless you always. Keep your chin up kid. I'm always with you.
Your (God Father) John

Similarly, encourage the young men to be self-controlled. In everything set them an example by doing what is good. In your teaching show integrity, seriousness and soundness of speech that cannot be condemned, so that those who oppose you may be ashamed because they have nothing bad to say about us. –Titus 2:6-8

Sunday, February 14, 1943; Headquarters Battery 320th Glider F.A. BN. 82ND A/B Division Fort Bragg, North Carolina

Dearest Family,
I had a good trip back to camp. And received your card. Thanks for it sure was a good one to get. I am sending you the stamps I said I was going to send. I'll write more next time. Every think is O.K. so don't worry about me. I got a letter from John l. today. We are going to move soon some place in Texas on maneuvers. Well may God Bless you all.   Love Frank

Tuesday, February 16, 1943, Shreveport, La.

Dear Viola,

I received your letter a few days ago but was unable to answer. I am fine except for a few things. I was glad to hear that you are all well except for Barbara having the chicken pox.

Well our first two weeks of maneuvers are over and I sure am glad of that because it was nothing but misery and from what I hear it is to be worse. I can't blame Frank S. and John S. for not saying much about them. You should of seen us after the two weeks. You couldn't recognize us. Our cloths and face were black as coal. In the two wks I got about 10 hrs of sleep. We walked about 500 miles and boy, are my legs sore.

I got two letters from John and one from John S. I answered the one from John but could find no time to answer the one from John S. boy I bet he won't think much of me, but I just can't help it. He thinks I am still in Camp W. (I wish I was).

The weather out here is warm in the day time and cold in the nite, just when you want to sleep. I don't care what the weather is like here I still would rather be in Ohio.

I got your cookies today at least I think you made them. Boy they sure were good. Thanks a lot. When you told me about getting a release from the army I sure was glad. You don't knowhow much I want to get out of this. You ask me to see if I could do anything about it. Well I don't think I better say anything because they will think I don't want to be in the army. I think you have a lot better chance. I want you to do every thing possible. Maybe Howard Ruetenik can help you out. At least give you some advice. Maybe you can go to the board. But do something, no matter what it cost. Army life wouldn't be bad if you wasn't in the infantry. I guess John has it perty easy at least that is what he tells me. I wish I were that lucky. One of the boys here from Greene told me his folks are trying to get him out too. I think I could do more good on the farm than I am here. They aren't teaching me anything here. Don't tell them anything about me wanting to get out. Just tell them Father needs me very bad on the farm.

Veronica sent me my Income Tax blanks and I can't do any thing with them out here so I am sending them back. You can have them filled out and if I have to pay any you can draw the money out of the bank.

Well I must close now because I am going to try to write some more letters. Well Goodby and Good luck.

Thanks a lot for the Valentine it sure makes me feel good to get one from you. It sure was a nice one.

Write soon as possible. I will do the same.

Love and kisses

Your brother Pvt. Claude

Say hello to Joe and the kids for me. I miss them a lot.

My total income for 1942 is $1,301.83. of course there will be some deductions. You will have to figure that out.

Chapter 7

Don't be afraid for I am with you; -Genesis 26:24

As the door to the plane opened, Frank could feel the rush of cold air enter the cabin and awaken his senses. Frank felt good about his growth as a paratrooper. The job matched his demeanor, and he loved that rush of adrenaline that swept over him as his feet left the security of the plane.

The jump started out much like the others during maneuvers with the C-47's flying in low, often less than one hundred feet. As the planes approached the drop sight marked by smoke screen, they would climb to approximately five hundred feet so that the paratroopers could make a safe jump... Frank was third behind the jump master this evening and as he felt the tether immediately open his chute he began to coordinate in his mind how his landing would go.

The gusts of wind had been picking up throughout the jump exercise and although Frank could clearly see the boundaries of the jump zone marked by the smoke, he was quickly heading toward the eastern quadrant which was littered with fox holes that looked like a pock marked face from the air. As Frank rapidly approached the ground, he tried to brace himself as he headed toward one of the holes. Upon impact, he felt his left leg hit the ground first followed by a sharp pain that shot up along his left leg, tearing at his left testicle followed by the jarring impact to his lower pelvic region. Then, everything was black!

The Lord is my strength and my shield; my heart trusts in him, and I am helped. –Psalm 28:7

Thursday, February 18, 1943; Camp Davis, N.C.

Dear Vi,
I received your package the other day. It sure was swell thanks a lot. I certainly enjoyed the bakery, so did everyone else. The boys said I should tell you to make some more.

Well how is everyone at home? Well I hope. I'm still trying to recuperate from the train ride. These southern trains certainly give you a beating. It took me 7 hours to travel 137 miles. I've never seen such terrible transportation in all my life. Mother can tell you she rode on some of these southern trains. One of the boys that went with me on the weekend pass come back a day late. I think they are going to stop the passes now. I'm sure glad I got mine when I did, maybe I won't get another chance like that.

I'm on Charge of Quarters again to night. This gives me a good chance to catch up on my letter writing. This is almost the seventh one I have written to-night. When I got back I had all kinds of mail.

We got in a bunch of new men again. One of them has measles, now we're quarantined for 10 days. Damn it, that burns me up I can't go anyplace now. A lot of them are hillbillies, they can't march at all. I guess they are so used to walking around the hill that when they get on level ground they're lost. They can all go back to the hills as far as I'm concerned.

Well, I'll be saying good-nite for now. Give my love to all.
Write soon.
Love your brother Johnny

Thursday, February 25, 1943 Shreveport, La.

Dear Viola,

I received your letter today and also those nut horns. They sure were good. I am fine except for some very sore feet. Yesterday we walked 46 miles so you can see the reason for sore feet.

I answered that letter I got from Veronica a few days ago. And as soon as I get a chance I will write again.

So they are trying to get some of Smith's neighbors out of the army. How about you and the rest of the family trying to get me out. I am going to see the Captain as soon as I can. And you do all that is in your power. But you will have to work as fast as you can. I got a letter from Johnny yesterday and he said he had a good chance of getting a release. I hope so. Don't let every one know about it. If the farm situation is so bad it shouldn't be hard to get me out. Please do all you can. Read this letter to mother and tell her I am alright. Please write as soon as you can. I can't write anymore because I don't have time. Goodby. Good luck and God bless you all. I will write as soon as I can. Don't worry too much about me.

Love and kisses. Your brother Pvt. Claude

I am sorry I can't write any more because I have so much to write.

P.S. excuse the poor writing.

Claude put down his pen and simply held his stomach for what seemed like an eternity. His chest felt like it was being stepped on by the entire United States Army making each breath a struggle, and his stomach burned like a scorching iron from the overwhelming stress of knowing deep down that the harder he fought to get released, the further away he was headed from home. He felt compelled to continue building his case that the farm could not continue to operate without him. Despair was slowly paralyzing Private Claude Lulek.

An anxious word weighs a man down, but a kind word cheers him up. –Proverbs 12:25

Tuesday, March 2, 1943;Camp Davis, N.C.

Dear Viola,
How is everyone at home? Are the kids alright? You never say much about them in your letters. I think you should tell me more about them after all I am their uncle. tell little Joey that he should write me a letter. I enjoy his letters very much. Is Joe still working in the mill?
I got a V-mail letter from John the other day. That is the first I received in almost two months. It sure was good to hear from him and to know he is alright. I'm sending it to you so you can read it (dated February 9th). Please save that letter. I hear from Claude once in a while. According to his letters he is having it plenty tough. I know what the infantry is like, it sure is hell. I really feel sorry for the poor guy. I hear Congress is fighting a bill about letting the farm boys go home. I wish you would look into that and see what you can do for him. I certainly would like to see him get home. He should stand a good chance cause he never worked any place except on the farm. It would take a lot of worries off my mind if he could go home. I told him to try to get out but you know how he is, he won't say anything. So do all you can for him.
Several of the new boys got the measles. now we're

restricted to the battalion area for 15 to20 days. It burns me up, just when some good shows are coming to camp. Oh well! I guess it's just one of those things we'll have to put up with.

Well I'll be closing for now. Give my love and regards to mom and dad and all. Write soon.

Goodnite.

Love your brother John

Wednesday, March 3, 1943; Fort Bragg, N.C.

My Dearest,

I received your letter was glad to get it. I haven't the time to write you a letter, but I will when I have a little time. The weather to day and all day yesterday was snow & cold. This is the South. Ha. Ha. So long. Will write soon I hope. Say hello to the family.

Yours forever Frank

P.S. Don't worry about me or your brother (Johnny) because we will be O.K. Good by for this time.

With love.

Friday, March 5, 1943; V-Mail

Dearest Vi,

How are you honey? I received your swell letter today and was sure glad to hear from you and family, and to know every thing is O.K. I'm feeling fine, I'm still in the Southwest Pacific and doing O.K. so tell mother not to worry about me. I been pretty busy lately so I had little time for writing. How's my little

sweetheart Barbara? I hope she's pretty big by now, and Joey, how's he doing? Still going to school I suppose. Is he still A1 in his school works? And Joe, how is Joe working? Is he going to work on the Ohio Muck this summer? And you honey, I hope you're not working too much. Did you enjoy your self at the Smida shower? I suppose you did. Right? Are you hearing from the boys lately? I hear from Frank often and once in a while from Johnny, but not from Claude, I suppose he's too busy training. Well Honey, I'll close for this time. Say hello to all for me and good luck to all.
 Your Love, John

Monday, March 8, 1943; Fort Bragg, N.C.

 Dearest,
 I received your letter but didn't have time to write so I am writing you a card. We are so damn busy from training that I don't get no time to write. I hope you all are feeling fine. I will write soon.
 Yours, Frank

Friday, March 12, 1943; The King Cotton Hotel Greensboro, North Carolina

 My Dearest family,
 I received your package from you this morning sure was glad. The cookies was so good the boys liked them. Well honey how are all of you feeling? I hope fine. I hear from your brother (John) this week. Maybe I'll see him before going sure would like to. The weather is warm this week. It rained. We are working

terribly hard for the last month but don't worry about me. I'm glad to hear that you like my picture of me. I guess you will not see me for a long time the way it looks but I will be O.K.

I hope you can read this letter because I so damn tired I can't write. I just wrote to mother. I'm so sorry for not writing sooner to you dear. I'll close for this time.
Your brotherlaw
Frank

P.S. I miss you all may God Bless you all say good by to Barb and Joey

Do not be anxious about anything, but in every situation, by prayer and petition, with thanksgiving, present your request to God. And the peace of God, which transcends all understanding, will guard your hearts and your minds in Christ Jesus. –Philippians 4: 6-7

Tuesday morning, March 16, 1943; Shreveport, La.

Dearest Sister,
I am getting along pretty good except for some sore feet and I guess everybody has them. These maneuvers will be over in another two weeks and maybe sooner. I hope so. At first I told you that we were to go to Florida well, that has been all changed now we are to go to California for some desert maneuvers. But I also heard that we are to get furlough first. Gee, I sure hope so. I want to get home in the worst way.

I saw the company CO yesterday, but he didn't give me very much satisfaction. He said that I would have to get proof that my farm work would be more important than being in the army. I guess they got a letter from the Red Cross. I told them my story and just how things are at home. They asked me a few questions.

The company CO didn't say anything about my papers that would have to be signed. Maybe that will come later. You will have to keep after them out there. I am going to see them here again. I sure hope things work out alright. Eugene, he's helping too so don't get in his way.

So Dick Cook is quitting his job and Joe is thinking of taking his place. That sure is a big job. A lot of responsibility. But I know Joe can do it. He sure can make them kids work. But if I were him I wouldn't do it for any less then Dick was.

So Johnny has to stay in because some of the boys have measles. I know that is hard to do after going out like he is used to. But how would he like to be me? out here I'm in no man's land. I haven't been to any town for two months. There are towns around but it costs so darn much to get there. And only 25% of the company are allowed to go at a time. I really would like to have gone but now I am glad I didn't. I will have more money to spend on my furlough. Veronica sent me two pictures of Johnny. They sure are swell looking. I guess he always did take good pictures. I haven't heard from him for a week or so, but he is doing alright I know it.

So little Joey has spring fever already. Boy I bet they sure do like it when the weather gets warm and they can go out and play. I don't blame them I wouldn't want to be cooped up any longer either. Say by the way, how is he doing at school? Is he doing as good as he has been? He should be he is very smart. When is Barbara going to start to school, next summer?

Well I must close now hoping to here from you soon.
Goodby and God Bless you all.
Love and kisses
Your brother Claude

Excuse the dirty paper. I had to write with dirty hands. Because the lack of water.

Claude's persistence in trying to get out of the army could have been one of the reasons why Joe was never drafted into the armed services. The Army may have figured that keeping one of a family's sons around to help with the farm would prevent a potential flood of correspondence from every farm boy that was ever drafted.

Do nothing out of selfish ambition or vain conceit. Rather, in humility value others above yourselves. –Philippians 2:3

Sunday, March 21, 1943 Camp Davis, N.C.

Dear Vi,

I suppose you wonder why I haven't written you for so long. We were out of camp for more than two weeks. We were at Ft. Fisher doing some night firing, that is about 70miles from camp. We didn't come back to camp in that time at all. When we're on the move like that it's hard to carry any writing equipment along, in fact I didn't have time to write. We're also training a lot on blackout driving. At times we have as many as three hundred trucks in a blackout convoy.

I received your cigars and I certainly appreciate them. Especially now that I've quit smoking cigarettes and you can't buy a good cigar here not even for a dime.

So you are getting plenty of rain now, we are too, it rains out of a clear sky here. I would like to get home to see the spring there but I don't think it's possible. I told you about that guy screwing up the works and now we're plenty busy too. Things must be pretty bad with all that water standing around.

Tell Joe to take the tractor down to Jim's for a check over. Don't wait until it's time to work. Have the oil changed, new filter put in, be sure all the spots are greased, check the oil in the rear end, in other words check everything. The right wheel brake is bad I think.

I am sending Joe a pair of my old shoes, they are still good, he can have them re-sold and new heals put on. That will make one pair less that I'll have to shine. Also in that box is some tobacco and cigarette papers for Dad. I'm sending the kids a box of mixed bars also. I hope they get there in better shape than some of the things I get. I wrapped them up pretty good to my estimation. I haven't heard from John since that v-mail letter. I get two or three letters from Bessie every week. Pretty good, no hey? I hear from Claude once in a while also from Frank.

Well I must be closing for now. Give my love to Mom and Dad and the kids. Take good care of yourself.
Love your brother
Johnny

Praise be to the Lord, to God our Savior, who daily bears our burdens. –Psalm 68: 19

Monday, March 29, 1943; Shreveport, La.

Dear Viola,
I received your letter the other day and was very glad to hear from you.

The maneuvers are over. They ended Saturday the 27th at about 3 o'clock in the afternoon. I am very sorry to disappoint you all, but I don't think we will get a furlough, at least not until our maneuvers in California are over with. We still don't know for sure whether we are going or not. If we do go they probably will last two months.

I haven't heard from Johnny either. I wrote to him about two weeks ago and haven't received an answer yet. He must be on maneuvers too. But I don't see why he can't write, I do.

Gosh, you know I received a letter from John Soukenik about 2 mo. ago and I haven't answered him yet. I don't know what he will think of me. I just can't seem to get down and write to him. I should have a lot to say. Do you write to him very often? In your next letter to him explain why I didn't write. I sure do miss him. He sure is a swell guy. I sure would hate to have anything happen to him.

  Eugene wrote a letter to Com. Co. and as soon as he got the letter he called me up to him. He told me he would do everything he could. He said it was now up to the War Department. He said there is a lot of red tape to go through and it would take a little time. But he said I had a good chance of a release. I have been going up to see him about every chance I got. I also wrote to Eugene and told him to write to the War Department. I sure hope every thing works out allrite. Is father doing much on the farm? If he is tell him to take it easy and sit around the house. In case the Red Cross does come around they won't see him working. I know the work isn't good for him, but he wants to work anyway. If I don't come home he can always sell out and I don't think the Government would like to see a farm like that idol (idle).

  To bad about Shirley but I don't think he will have it so bad. If he gets in as a welder. He can be sure he doesn't see much action. I don't know about Andy. Catherine never says anything about him. I don't think he would mind going, but it is the rest of them. What is the matter, don't you go over there any more? Don't you get along with them? Yes they are expecting again, but don't tell them I said so. I guess they think that is the only way he will keep out of the Army. I would like to see him get fooled.

  Glad to hear Joey is doing fine in school. I always knew he would do alright. He sure is a smart kid. But don't tell him that because it may go to his head. Say it won't be many years before Barbara goes to school. You know I have forgotten just how old she is. I have a poor memory. I sure do miss them a lot. I just can't waite to get home to see them. It seems ages that I have been home. Yes, I received all of your packages. It was all swell and thanks a lot for everything. I have received a lot of packages from Catherine too. I liked them all very much. I can't thank you *enought for all that you have do for me.*

We haven't been doing much walking the last two weeks but we didn't get much rest. We wouldn't any more than go to sleep and we would get an order to move out. Sometimes we would go two days without anything to eat, and then other times we would get so much we couldn't eat it. But that is maneuvers and that is the way it will be during action, so we got to get used to it.

Well I must close for now. Please write soon and let me know how things are coming at home. Goodby and God Bless you all.

Love and kisses to all.
Claude

Did Joe get that job as forman on the Ohio muck yet. If he did he should get plenty for it. Because that is a hard job to tackle.

A heart at peace gives life to the body, but envy rots the bones. –Proverbs 14: 30

Chapter Eight

Saturday, April 3, 1943

Dearest family,
How are you all? I just came back from Fort Knox, Ky.
Went for a Passover. Have to wait for a train for 10 hr. it's hell.
With all my love,
Frank

Thursday, April 8, 1943; Fort Bragg, N.C. 194th Field Artillery Battalion
Battery B

Dearest family,
How are all of you at home? I just came to a new place today. No more Airborne for me. will write when I can. We are going out in the woods for two weeks.
Love, Frank

Frank was fully healed from his injuries during maneuvers, but the loss of his left testicle and now chronic back problems left his commanding officer no choice but to remove him from Airborne and reassign him to a support division. His body simply could no longer take the impact of landing those jumps.

Saturday, April 10, 1943; V-mail

Dearest Sister in law,
Just a few lines to let you know how I am and to say hello. I'm fine and hope you all are the same. I rec'd your last letter dated March 12th and was very happy to hear from you. I'm sorry that I didn't write Joe a letter on his 33rd birthday. May I wish him luck and happiness the rest of his days.
Heard from Frank and Johnny and they were swell letters. Gosh I miss those kids, I sure would like to be with them. Well honey, how's everything with you all. I suppose Joey will be out of school soon and I know that makes him happy. Also, Barbara so they can play together. Right? I still have the little picture taken of them last spring. I love it. Hope Joe is working on the muck now. Suppose he will be going fishing soon. Well honey, take care of yourself and family. May God be with you all. Good luck.
John

Thursday, April 15, 1943; Camp Davis, N.C.

Dearest Viola,
I've been wanting to write to you for a longtime but can't seem to find the time. It seems that I get hell from everyone for not writing. We're not around camp much anymore. We go out for two weeks at a time. On maneuver, bivouac, or cross-country hikes. The cross-country hikes sure are hell we walk in water and mud up to our ass and I'm not kidding either. It sure is rough life but I don't mind it. I wish we'd get moved out of this camp I'm

getting tired of it 8 months in the same camp is a long time. Don't you think?

I got a V-mail letter from John the other day. I sure was glad to hear from him. Bessie has been writing me quite often but I haven't heard from Frank for some time did you? Bessie said he might come home again soon. Gee! I don't know when I'll get to come home again. The passes are all screwed up and God only knows when I'll get another furlough. I sure would like to be home for Easter but no dice.

I'm certainly glad to see that Claude got his furlough and 15 days he's lucky I think. I feel as happy as if it were my own furlough. I hope he gets to come home for the summer he should keep on trying. I don't see why he can't get out.

Helen wrote me and said Catherine is occupying all his time. I can imagine she is hanging on his neck all the time. She also told me that Catherine came over and got him out of bed. That beats everything I know of. What do you think? Sad case as we say in the Army.

So the Drabek's (Eugene and Helen Lulek) sold their little bungalow and bought a mansion in Champion. It must be a pretty nice place for that price. It was nice of Claude to lend them his money. I heard the Grahams(Catherine's family) are burned up about that. that's good, I hope they are. Claude certainly sent me the cigars in time I was all out. I sure was surprised to see they were from him.

So Dad planted some oats already. I think that's pretty good in fact I'm surprised it seems rather early to me. I don't know why. I'll bet mother is busy as heck doing all the work. I think Veronica should quit for the summer it's too much work for the folks. I'm glad to hear Joe is helping them all he can. Tell him to be sure and keep all the tools greased especially the tractor. Tell him to take the red book that shows all the grease spots on it that's very important. There are several spots that are hard to find under the tractor. Also there is supposed to be so many shots for each spot that is important too cause over greasing is harmful too.

How many days a week is he working in the mill? Tell him I said he should keep up his good work and I'll send him a box of cigars.

Well hear it is almost Easter I can hardly believe it. I'll bet you got the kids all dolled up already. Gosh! I'm certainly going to miss being with them and the rest of the family this year. It will never seem like Easter until I get home again.

Well I must close for now. I wish you all a very happy Easter. Give my love to all. Hoping to hear from you soon.

Your loving brother. Johnny

Claude and Catherine while on leave

For everything that was written in the past was written to teach us, so that through the endurance taught in the Scriptures and the encouragement they provide we might have hope. –Romans 15:4

Wednesday, April 21, 1943; Somewhere in the Southwest Pacific

Dear Vi,

How are you kid? Hope this letter finds you & family well and having a good time. Been some time since I written you and some time since I've heard from you. I don't know whether I've thank you for the lovely Valentine you send me or not but it was beautiful and swell of you to think of me. I haven't anything new to say, since our letters are censored. But I guess as long as I write and let you know I'm still O.K. you wouldn't mind. I was sure glad to hear Johnny Babinshak was home and came down to see my Mother. Mother send me a clipping about him that was in the Warren paper. I suppose you saw it too. It was quite a write up about him. I don't know whether I told you or not about Edward Wludyga going home some time ago, he was sick and they couldn't do much for him here, so they send him to the States. He's the boy that goes with Irene Verbanic. He was a good friend of mine. He hasn't wrote to me yet so I don't know where he is at the present time. The whole gang here often asks me if I've heard from him. I guess they think since he and I were such good friends, he would write to me first.

Haven't heard from Frank, Johnny or Claude for some time but I guess they're busy too. Rec'd Veronica's letter a few days ago and I will write when I have time. She sure writes a swell letter but not often enough. Well that's the way it goes, Right? How's Joe doing? Is he still working in Warren or has he decided to work at Brown? I'd sooner see him working at Brown's myself course it all depends how he feels about it. After this War is over he can go back again, Right? Mother wrote me that dad is now home and is not working in Warren anymore. I was glad to hear that, he needed a rest and now that gas is rationed it makes it hard to come & go to work anyway.

    I suppose the weather is nice back home now and Joe will be going fishing again. Gee, I miss that and can't wait till this war is over and I can come home again and do some more of it, course some of the places I've been over here would really be the places for fishing. But, there's no time for that so guess I'll have to wait till I come home.

    Well Vi, how are the children doing? I sure miss them and miss their little letters. I suppose Joey will be out of school soon and Barbara's glad of it. Right? Have you any pictures of you all that was taken lately? If you have please send me a few, I'll send them back if I can.

    Well Honey, I guess I wrote enough for this time and hope to hear from you soon. Lots of love and kisses to you all. Say hello to all for me. if I had more time I would write to all. But you know how it is.

    P.S. Don't forget the pictures. Veronica sent me a swell one of Johnny he really looks swell. Good luck. Yours always. Love John

Chapter Nine

Thursday evening, April 29, 1943; 305th Infantry A.P.O 77th Division; Desert Training

Dear Viola,
Just a few lines to let you know just what it is like out here in Arizona. Well to begin with it hasn't rained out here in about 7 years. I guess it is one of the worst parts of Arizona. And boy is it hot and dusty. Don't get angry if you don't get very many letters. I will write as often as I can.
To bad about the trouble you had with the car. I didn't think it would last much longer. So they could only find one of those tires. That is funny they told me both tires were in good shape. And both of them could be fixed. Did Veronica bring the other one back?
I am glad to hear that Johnny got those cigars and just when he needed them. It was too bad he couldn't come home for Easter. I was riding a train on Easter. Some of the boys that rode on a different train stopped in a town and got to go to church. I went to church on Good Friday and I also went to confession.
So they (people from the Army) came down from Warren. I hope they (the folks) didn't say anything they weren't suppose to. I gave that letter I had to the Com. CO. I didn't have much to say until he read it over. And a little later another officer came up to me and said the letter past and it was a matter of time now. So, I think it won't be long now. I am going to see him again very soon.
Well, I better close now because I can't even see. Boy I wish you could see the place we are in.

I will write soon. Goodby and God Bless you all. Love Claude

Excuse the writing.

And the God of all grace, who called you to his eternal glory in Christ, after you have suffered a little while, will himself restore you and make you strong, firm and steadfast. -1 Peter 5:10

Wednesday, May 5, 1943; Camp Davis

Dearest Vi,
First of all I want to thank you for that wonderful box of cigars. They arrived just in time I was almost out from the box Claude sent me. I certainly appreciate it Vi. Thank you again.
So Joe wore my brown suit on Easter Sunday. Why didn't he wear my green tweed with the brown pants that looks much more snappy don't it? I don't care if he wears all my clothes. He might as well use them as to have them lay around and rot. He's perfectly welcome to wear anything I got, what's mine is his, I really miss that guy and the good old hunting and fishing we used to do to gether. I don't think anyone could have a better brother-in-law and your two sweet kids. I really miss them too as if they were my own. So you tell him if he wants any of my clothes to go ahead and wear them anyway. They were too small for me when I left and now I weigh 210 pounds, some pile, ha! ha!
I received a letter from Veronica and Catherine to day and both of them contained pictures of Claude. Boy! Does he look swell, he's gained a lot of weight hasn't he? I sure hope he gets to come home for the summer.
I suppose you heard that I got a bald head. It sure feels good that way, one thing I don't have to worry about is combing it. I have a circus with it every time I take off my hat the guys laugh

like hell. They all call me Joe Louis now, of course I'm almost as dark as he is. I'm sure getting a swell tan or burn you might call it.

How is the gas situation now, Vi? Do you get plenty for the tractor? I want to know cause I might get a furlough around the latter part of May or first part of June maybe, I hope! Don't count on it too much cause that's just a rumor going around. Write and let me know how it is. I want to be sure there is plenty that's why I'm giving you a warning ahead of time. I really intend to go to town when I get home this time and I'm not kidding either. I want to go fishing pretty bad so tell Joe to get things in shape.

How is the farm work going? I hear you've been having plenty of rain just like last year. That's tough, all the work will be piled up for one time. I certainly hope it clears up so the work won't come all at one time or Joe will be run ragged.

How is he working now 6 or 7 days things should be going pretty strong now shouldn't they? I'll bet you're stacking up the cabbage now, ha! ha! How is the muck this year are they going to run it? I'll bet Dick can't get anyone to work now. They should be well under way by now if they are going to run it.

Well I must close for now Vi cause I want to write to Helen yet and it's getting late now. Give my love to Mom and Dad and the kids. Hoping to see you in about a month. Write soon and often.

Your loving brother
Johnny

p.s. Catherine wrote and said Joey wants to get a baldy now cause I got one. Tell him to wait till I get home and I'll give it to him, ha! ha!

7:30p.m. Wednesday, May 5, 1943; Claiborne, La.

Dearest Soukenik family,

How are all you dear folks? I hope you are fine. I was very happy to hear from you. Tonight I am in charge of Quarters. That is all the men in our HQ. Battery. That's when you're a corporal but I like it. You know me kid!

Don't work too much on the farm dear. How are the kids? Tell Barbara and Joey to pray for me if they want to see me. tell them I still love them and I'll pray for them and I love you to dear. Ha. ha.

It rained like hell to day. I have no time to write cause we are going on a 4 day trip. It's no good. I hope you can read my writing I am no good at spelling.

I have to operate the switchboard to morrow. Darn men assigned to me to learn how to operate the switch board. That's what I like. Is Joe still working on the muck? I hope so. Did he get a raise?

I have to close dear. God Bless you all.
Love Frank

p.s. tell Barb and Joey to be good kids and to pray for their uncle.

Frank realized the severity of his situation. When he was with the 82nd and the paratroopers he was kept far too busy and the men of the 82nd were too crazy to ever leave Frank with a feeling of vulnerability. He felt alive and invincible right up to that jump that landed him in his current situation. He had been reassigned to the 194th FAB or heavy artillery acting as support for his buddies of the 82nd. His role was changing but Frank still felt every bit as close to the front line. May God bless us all.

Thursday, May 6, 1943

Dear Sister,
I received your letter yesterday and was very glad to hear from you. I am sorry I didn't write to you sooner, but it seems as though I can't start. For one thing it is so darn hot and dusty that you don't feel like writing. This is the worst place I have ever been. I don't like it one bit. I sure hope I can get out of here before long. The Com. Co. got that letter some time ago and it was passed by him but it takes quite a while to get to Division Head quarters and back.
It's too bad it has been raining so much. It probably will be a late spring. It will be a darn good reason for me to come home won't it?
So Joe has a terrible cold, well so have I. the last week that I was in La. I caught the worst cold I ever had. I have had it now for 2 weeks or so and I can't seem to get rid of it. If Joe thinks he sweats a lot in the mill he should be out here for a while. You don't have to do anything at all and you sweat like a horse. I went to the doctor twice and all they give you is a few aspirin tablets. They give you the same thing no matter what ails you.
Well I suppose by now Helen is all done moving. I'll bet she will be glad when she gets settled down. How did they move the furniture with my truck?
If Eugene keeps working day & nite he should lose some of that weight shouldn't he? It shouldn't take him long to pay for the house at that rate. Did mother get her chicks yet? I sure hope that brooder stove works all rite, it should last at least one more season.
So you had a lonely Easter this year. Gosh it was too bad Johnny couldn't come home. I realy thought he would get a chance to come home. It was the worst Easter I ever had. I spent the day riding on the train. I didn't get a chance to go to Church. But I did go Church on Good Friday and also to confession. I sure

was thankful of that.

So Rudy felt sort of out of place. Well I don't blame him for staying out as long as he can. I sure hope we can all be together next Easter. I wish you could of taken some pictures with your Easter bonets on. I like to look at pictures, it keeps me from getting so lonesome. Well I must close now because we are going on a nite hike and I must get ready. Thanks for the pretty Easter card.

Goodby and God Bless you all.
Love & kisses to all.
Claude

Write soon.

I got the Easter package that mother and you sent but it wasn't in very good shape because of the hot weather we have. Please don't send anymore food unless it is something that won't spoil. Thanks a lot for everything. Please say hello to mother, dad and Veronica and don't forget the Soukenik family.

Friday, May 7, 1943; Battery 13 194th F.A.B.

My Dearest family,
I received your letter sure was surprised to get one so soon. Sure was glad to hear that you are all feeling fine.

The weather here is hot oh about 95 to 100 some days and we are so damn busy all the time. This outfit has hard work. The gun weighs 15,000 tons and fires about 15miles sure a good gun, but I just soon be over with the boys I was with.

I'll have to close it is getting time to go to work. We are going out in the field about 3 times a week, and we are going for 3 weeks from the 17th to 30th of May. Honey if you don't get a letter from me every week don't worry because I am busy. I hope Joe is *working in Copperweld tell him not to work in the muck if he don't have to. Well may God Bless you all with all my love. Frank*

Sunday, May 9, 1943

Dearest Vi,
I rec'd your most welcomed letter yesterday and words can't express how happy I was to hear from you again. It's just like a gift from heaven to hear from you. Don't write and say that you have neglected in writing to me lately, and that you haven't forgotten me. How could we forget each other, not for a moment after all the fun we had together. I know you're busy and have all the boys to write to. It makes it pretty hard, Right? Well I suppose you folks are working on the farm and have quite a lot planted already. Agnes Smida wrote that you were having some terrific weather and it seems more like February than it does April. I hope it's better now so you can get all your planting done. Is Joe still working in the mill? Or has he decided to go to work for Orwell Gardens? I hear there is a shortage of help on the farms. So I think it would be better for him to go there. Course the hours are long and you can't blame him, but with gas being rationed and all that. it would be better on the muck. Don't you think so? They just called mess so I will write more after mess.
Here I am again and I have some good news. Got a few letters, and you know what? Got a letter from Johnny and was I happy. It's the first in a long time, it was a swell letter too. Also got a dandy from Frank the other day. You know Vi it really makes me feel swell to hear from you folks. I wish I could write and answer all the letters that I get, but I haven't got the time. So if anyone should say I'm not writing to them, and that they wrote to me, please tell them how it is, O.K.? in your letter you wrote about Irene Urbanek's boyfriend. Well Honey, I wrote about him some time ago. That he left, I don't know till a few days ago when I

received a letter from him. He is now in N. Carolina in a hospital and doing fine, said he was going to have his tonsils out next week and then goes back to duty, and may come home too for a few days and said he'll try and see my folks. I know Mother will be glad to see him. Remember the fun we had the nite he was home with me last year when we went to St. Mary dances and whooped it up. Sure had a swell time alright! I wish we have a chance to do it again and then look out! Ha. Ha.

How's my two little honeys doing? Boy I miss them and can't wait till I get home to see them. I bet I'll not know them. Are they still as good looking as they were when I left home? Every one wrote that they are better looking. Well I can see why when their Ma & Dad or should I say Pa are so good looking! Tell them I said hello and that I love them more every day.

Say what is the matter with Claude is he out of ink or paper? I wrote to him and I'm still waiting for a letter, I know he's busy, but he could drop me a few lines, I love to hear from him. I was really glad to hear that he had a nice furlough and enjoyed it. I bet he looked good in a uniform. Say I bet his girl friend really loved him up when he was home. Oh boy! Oh boy! I know you all hate to see him go back to camp and I suppose he hated to leave, but that's the way it is honey. I went through that too, and it's not so hot.

I'll have to close for this time and please write again. I love it. Say hello to all and good luck. Mau God Bless you all and keep you safe. Love and kisses. John

It had been two years, full of anxiety, questions never asked because they would be answered in good time, two years of training, making ready, deployment, establishing defensive positions, waiting, more training, redeployment, establishing a new defensive position, more waiting, intensified training, two years… two long years from home… faces of loved ones slowly fading…two years…clinging to letters from home…two years…longing to complete the inevitable task at hand so John Soukenik and his men could get home…there would be no further delays. The 37th Buckeye Division, one of the best trained divisions in the United States Armed forces was about to make ready to go on the offensive. The Japanese Imperial Army had no idea what they were about to encounter in the upcoming months.

You may say to yourself, "My power and the strength of my hands have produced this wealth for me." But remember the Lord your God, for it is he who gives you the ability to produce wealth, and so confirms his covenant, which he swore to his ancestors, as it is today. –Deuteronomy 8: 17-18

Chapter Ten

Friday, May 14, 1943

Dear Viola,
I received your letter yesterday and was very glad to hear from you. I am getting along as good as can be expected and am glad to hear that everything is getting along good. Too bad it has been raining so much. That will make everything so late on the farms. I wish we could get some of that rain here. At least to settle the dust. We are having a terrible dust storm. You can't see ten ft. ahead of you. We didn't do very much today on account of it being so windy and dusty.

Well tomorrow and Sunday is our days off. I sure am glad of that. I probably go and take a shower. We have to walk about two miles to take one and by the time we get back we are just as dusty as befor. But at least we feel good while we are under the shower.

To-nite we are having a beer party. You can have all the beer you want free. Boy am I going to drink. After the party we are having a show. The U.S.O. is putting it on. Every weekend a movie actress comes from Hollywood and gives a show.

I knew dad shouldn't have sold all of that hay. It always happens that way. He should figure on things like that to happen. I guess the farmer never does have any luck if it isn't one thing it's two. Gosh when I was home Spring had really come, but I guess it could change over nite.

Yes, I heard Eugene Huntley was home on furlough. I think

Catherine wrote and told me about it. Wasn't he in some camp in Louisiana?

So Frank is going across pretty soon. Too bad he has to go across but I guess that is the only way to win this war. I heard that when we are through here we are to go to some camp in Virginia. I hope so. I wish dad could see what we have to go throughout here in the desert. In fact I wish a lot of people saw what we soldiers have to put up with.

No, we get plenty of water to drink and cook with. They have about three deep wells drilled. We carry 1 qt. with us wherever we go. A quart lasts us ½ a day.

I wish I could take some pictures out here. But I can't get a camera. And nobody wants to lend theirs. If I can get one I will have some taken. Yes, John A. is with me. He is in the 306th and I am in the 305th. I see him about once a week.

Yes, I got yours and mothers packages. Everything was all rite except the eggs. Thanks a lot for everything.

I don't know when I will be coming home. I haven't heard anything from them yet. I sure hope I get my release pretty soon.

So, Joe is still at the Copperweld. I think that is a good place to stay. Unless he can get a better job in some other mill. If I were him I wouldn't go on the muck and work. At least not this year.

Yes, I got your Easter card. I got it when I got to Arizona. You see, they sent all of our mail down here.

Mother should try to buy some more chicks. It takes too long sitting chicks. How is the brooder stove working? I hope she isn't having trouble with it.

Well, did Joe get the garden fitted and planted or did it rain again.

I'll sign off now because it is time for dinner. Goodby and God bless you all.

Love Claude

Excuse the poor writing.

p.s. I didn't get to finish the letter Friday so I had to Sat. Say hello to all.

Did mother and Joey get their glasses? I'll bet Joey looks cute!

Endure hardship as discipline; God is treating you as sons. For what son is not disciplined by his father? If you are not disciplined, then you are illegitimate children and not true sons. – Hebrews 12: 7

Wednesday, May 19, 1943

My Dearest family,
How are you all? I am fine to-day just received your letter in the hospital don't worry I am O.K. will be here for 3 weeks or maybe I get out sooner. Having a good time here with the nurses you know me I give them a line of my B.S. she likes it and boy is she a honey. If it wasn't for this war going long, I would be here for 3 months with these nurses haha.
So you got baby chicks that will be O.K. I'll come for a dinner when I get a pass O.K. with you.
How is Barb and Joey getting along? Tell them I miss my honeys, kiss them and tell them to pray for me.
Well I'll close for this time it's time for bed. God Bless you all with all my love.
Yours always, Frank

p.s. I didn't get a letter for a long time from John L. or John S. maybe get one some time this week.

Lord my God, I called to you for help, and you healed me. –Psalm 30:2

Wednesday Evening, May 19, 1943

Dear Viola,

I received your letter today and decieded to answer it right away. It took only five days for your letter to get here. I can't understand why it takes longer for mine letters than yours.

I am sorry I disappointed you. I haven't heard from them yet. They said they sent the paper into Washington and haven't gotten them back yet. I wish they would hurry up and let me know whether I get my release or not. It is getting late already. I told Catherine I expected to hear from them soon. I didn't think it would be this long. Maybe you ought to go to the Red Cross or to the U.S.B.A. or where ever those men that came over are from and have them investogate. I don't believe these officers down here. They say they will do a thing and then don't. I don't believe any of them.

I wrote to Johnny some time ago and haven't received an answer yet. He told me he was getting a furlough. I sure hope so. I sure wish I would be home so I could see him. I see his pictures but I would like to talk to him. I never thought I would miss him as much as I do.

Catherine sent me some of the pictures that you took on Easter. They sure did come out nice. So Eugene is a hard working man. Maybe he will lose some of that weight. I hope he keeps it up so he can pay me back in the near future. Of course you don't have to tell them that. You know there is a certain party I don't want to know about this.

That Betley farm must be bought and sold every wk. or so. I'll bet mother and dad could get a fortune for there place. I am glad to hear the brooder stove is working alright. I sure hope mother has good luck with those chicks. It sure takes a lot of work and feed to raise them. So you are having good luck with your *setting hens. That rooster that you got from mother sure was on the ball. To bad mother isn't having very good luck. Why doesn't she try to get ducks that will sit.*

So you have been having frost. I sure hope it didn't freze those apple trees. If they did father won't be able to make any cider this fall.

One of the boys just got word to go and see the Red Cross. They got a letter from the Red Cross in Warren. He is going to see them again today (20th) to write a letter to the com. Co. stating why he wants to go back on the farm. And if it is more important than the Army. It has to be down in black and white. Then the Com. Co. will make out a paper for his release. Why don't you see the Red Cross and see if any thing is being done. Maybe they have a letter here for me, but haven't gotten to it yet. You better go down and find out what you can. Where were them men from that came to our place? Were they from the Red Cross or U.S.B.A. try and go down as soon as possible.

Well I must be closing for now. Good by and God bless you all.

Love, Claude

P.S. say hello to Joe and the kids.

Consider it pure joy, my brothers, whenever you face trials of many kinds, because you know that the testing of your faith develops perseverance. Perseverance must finish its work so that you may be mature and complete, not lacking anything. If any of you lacks wisdom, he should ask God, who gives generously to all without finding fault, and it will be given to him. But when he asks, he must believe and not doubt, because he who doubts is like a wave of the sea, blown and tossed by the wind. That man should not think he will receive anything from the Lord; he is a double-minded man unstable in all he does. –James 1: 2-8

Tuesday, May 25, 1943 (R&R)

Hello Joe,
What ya know? Boy is it good fishing here. All I catch is catfish. I got one that weight about 8 pounds. See ya when I get home.
Frank

Friday, May 28, 1943 Camp Davis, N.C.

Dear Viola,
I received your letter to-day and was very glad to hear from you. This is going to be short because I want to get it out before the mail man goes. The main reason for this letter is to let you know that I'll be seeing you some time next week, if the plans don't change. Be sure to have plenty of gas and etc. I have to close now, we'll talk things over when I get home. I'll be seeing you soon. Love to all.
Your loving brother
Johnny

A cheerful heart is good medicine. –Proverbs 17: 22

Saturday, May 29, 1943 Hospital Ward #2, Fort Bragg

Dearest Family,
How are you all getting along? I hope you are all fine because I am feeling good maybe I'll be see you all in 2 week of

June. I hope, not for sure yet.

The weather here is the same its been hot but this week its been rain all week you would know it.

Did you get a letter from your brother John lately? Didn't receive one from him for hell of a long time, damn him. I wrote to him but didn't answer it.

The Hospital is just the same so I don't have much to write. I'll tell you everything when I get home. Is Joe working in the mill? Hope so or is he working on the muck?

Well I'll close for this time. May God Bless you all & hoping this war will be over soon so all of us boys will be home.

With all my love your brother in law Frank

Sunday Morning, May 30, 1943 Co. G 305th Infantry APO 77th Division Desert Training Center Los Angeles, CA.

Dearest Viola,
I received your letter today and was glad to hear from you. I should have gotten it sooner, but we are on a 6 day problem and it took longer to get to me.

I haven't been able to do any writing because I have been doing so much moving around. Bunch of us boys got sick the first day from the heat and not enough to drink or eat. We were so weak we couldn't go any farther so they sent us back to camp to a doctor. We are now all rite but don't know how long we will last. Boy I am telling you this heat is terrible. It's enough to kill any one. I thought the heat on the muck was bad, but it is nothing compared to this.

So you are working at the Packard. Well that is fine and good but it doesn't look as though I will be coming home. There isn't anything I can do since I am 40 miles from camp. I haven't heard anything about it. I haven't been able to see the Com. Co. for 3 wks now. why don't you see the Red cross and find out if anything is being done about it. You should have gone to the Notary Public. You don't have to be afraid of anything. Why don't you try and get an Affidavit don't know how you could go about to get it, but you could find out from a Notary Public.

Glad to hear Joey passed with good grades. Boy time does fly. It seem like only a year or so he was in the first grade I sure hope Barbara does as well or better. I guess if there's better she'd be perfect.

So Joe is still working in the Copperweld. I guess that's a darn good place to stay since it has been raining so much. I don't know what father will do about the farm if I don't come home pretty soon. Everything will be so late. I wish they would realize it and do something about it. I sure wish they would hurry and let me come home so you can keep on working. But, if it is so wet you can't work the farm anyway. Has father any corn in yet? Did you get your garden planted yet or has it to wet for even that? Are the cows out in the other woods yet? I mean the heifers and the dry cows. There should be a lot of grass out there since it has been so wet.

Well, I must be closing for now, hoping you can help me out some way. Goodby and God bless you all.

Please say hello to all. Love, Claude

Sunday, May 30, 1943

Dearest Vi,

How's my dear sister in law any way? fine? I hope so. I'm doing fine, thank you. Rec'd your beautiful Easter greeting card a few days ago and I must say it was really beautiful. The more I think of it, I sure have a wonderful sister in law. Joe is sure lucky. I bet Joe will like that. He'll say I'm spoiling you I suppose, but deep in his heart I know he feel the same as I, Right? How is he coming with the Army? Has he heard any more?

How is the fishing? Is he doing any? I sure wish I could do a little with him. Sure had fun fishing last year with the gang, Remember? Sure could go for some of that beer now. O boy! I suppose the weather is just right for fishing now, and Joe has all of his things ready to go. How's the car? Still running? Well Honey, I'll have to close for this time and will write more soon and in the mean time write when you can. Say hello to my two honeys and may God Bless them for their prayers for me. also say hello to your mother and Dad. Good nite.

  Love and kisses. John

Monday May 31, 1943 Hospital Ward #33

  Dearest family,

  I received your letter to day was surprised to hear that you are working at Packard. Do you like the work?

  Well I'm feeling fine and hope you all are the same. How are the offsprings feeling? No school for Joe? He likes that!

  Is John still in NC he didn't write to me for a long time, damn him. I didn't receive a letter from John S. for a long time but he must be write to my old address. I will get them late

  Well, Joe still working in the mill? It must be raining all the time in Ohio. Well the weather is hot here but I think it will rain here to night.

  I'll close for this time may God Bless you all and don't worry about me. I will be O.K. with all my love. Your brother in law. Frank

  p.s. Beverly work at the Packard maybe you will see her.

Written Sunday morning, June 13, 1943

Dearest Vi & Family,

Just came back from hearing mass and course it reminded me of home, each time we hear mass it brings back memories of home and how we used to attend church back home. Course it's a lot different then back home but the same feeling. Glad to hear that you made such a fine collection at our church on Easter Sunday. I know Father Bialik was pleased.

How's everyone? Fine? Hope so. I'm O.K. and at the present I'm doing M.P. duty. It's O.K. so please don't worry about me and tell Mother the same, if any thing would happen, you would be notified. I know you worry when you don't hear from me, but some times I'm too busy to write.

Heard from Johnny and Frank, they're doing fine. I can now write that I was in the Fiji Islands. I'll write more in my next letter about the Island. It was O.K. there.

I'll have to close for this time. Say hello to All for me and good luck to all. May God be with you and family. Love and kisses. John

The 37th Buckeye Division was stepping up security measures and defensive positions as the U.S. Army prepared for "Operation Cartwheel." New Georgia would be the first real test for the 37th as the division had split duties between reinforcement and perimeter security.[13]

Lift up your eyes and look to the heavens; Who created all these He who brings out the starry host one by one and calls forth each of them by name. Because of his great power and mighty strength, not one of them is missing. –Isaiah 40:26

---

[13] www.Wikipedia.org

The LORD is good, a refuge in times of trouble. He cares for those who trust in him, -Nahum 1:7

Sunday, June 20, 1943 Camp Davis, N.C.

Dear Viola,
I'm (Charge of Quarters) to-day so I'm writing to you. This is the first chance since I got back. I planned to go to the beach swimming but I got stuck with this job. Of all the days of the week to get it I have to get it on Sunday. It's so quiet and lonesome around this office to-day that I'm going batty. I finally got the radio to work that makes it a little more cheerful around here.
My suit case isn't unpacked yet and here it is Sunday already. I walked right into a 25 mile hike. I'm so tired at night that I just flop on my bed and sleep. The heat is terrific, the day of the hike it was 110 degrees, that's hot enough for anyone. I wish you could have seen us when we got back from the hike. We were a bunch of (sad sacks) if there ever was any. There wasn't a one that had a dry stitch of clothes on him. My feet got blisters the size of quarters on them. I sure got the hot foot if I ever had one, just like the pictures you see on some of the cards. About half the boys fell out or passed out.
Well how's everything at home? I certainly hope you are having nice weather. It sure was heaven to be home for that little while. I could have used 15 more days. I was having a wonderful time and everyone treats you so good, now I can't get used to being in camp again.
Well, I must close for now. give my love to all, hoping to hear from you soon.
Love your brother, John

P.S. Please send me Claude's address quick cause I lost the one I had.

Some day in June 1943 in Somewhere in the Pacific

Dearest Vi,

Here it is Sat. nite (Some day in June) I'm on duty now and have nothing else to do but answer your swell letter, which I rec'd yesterday, dated May 13. Took some time getting here. This is about the only time I have to write because as soon as I get off M.P. duty, which I'm doing at the present time, I get other things to do. We haven't any time to ourselves anymore.

First I'll let you know about the mail service. It took one of your letters about six weeks to get here. The other one came in about 10 days. That is why you haven't heard from me in some time. I'll do my best to answer them now though. Just because you don't hear from me though is no sign you shouldn't write honey. You can't do more for your country than build this soldier's morale with your letters. They are a great help too, especially today. My morale hit a new low this morning, don't know why. Just one of those mornings when you feel in the dumps.

I'm glad that you agree with me on the idea of those v-mail. We don't think so much of them either. I don't like to receive them, course I suppose they are better than nothing, but not much.

You're right honey, about all those good times we had still being continued after this is all over. In fact they have just started. At nights we sit around by candle light and make post-War plans. Do you know where Chagrin Falls is located? That's where we spend a lot of our time. One of my buddies live there. That is about all he talks about.

Are you hearing from the boys much? I hear from Johnny and Frank quite often. I'll kick the devil out of them for wanting to come across. Any one is a damn fool to want this kind of life. I guess they won't learn by other experiences though. Oh well, maybe they'll be lucky and not get into any trouble, anyway we hope not. Haven't seen Cy Young for some time. The last time I saw him was about a month ago. Heard from Eddie, saying he was over to see my Mother, said he had a swell time. I suppose Joe was kidding him about Irene. He may go back to duty soon. I wonder where they will send him.

 Just ran out of ink---

 Here I am back again. Boy I had to run about ten miles (almost) for this pen full of ink. That is hard to get around here.
 In your letter you wrote that Joe & James Sabo went fishing around one of the creek. How did they make out? Wish I was with them. Sure miss my fishing. I suppose fishing is good now. is the weather still raining? Hope not. You will not have any fruit for the winter.
 How's Joe doing? Is he still working in the Copperweld? How come he can't get transferred to a better job? I guess it's pretty hard isn't it? Well any way he has more time to go fishing than if he was working on the muck. Right? Does he work on different shifts? I suppose he does that way he can work on the farm too.
 Yes, the news from Tunisia was wonderful, the Germans and Japs aren't so hot any more. Wait till we really get going.
 So Claude is in Arizona now. I bet it's hot all right and sandy too. Well, that's good training since when they come over here it's really hot. You get used to it thou. I don't mind it any more, and what good would it do if I did. Ha. Ha. Hope Johnny got that furlough that you wrote about. Frank said he wants one too before he goes across. Hope they get them.
 Well Honey, now that school is off I suppose Joey and Barbara are helping you around the house, while Joe is at work. Joey should be able to help some. I remember when he used to come over to our place and tell frank and I how daddy has his corn in and so on. Frank and me would kid him and say that our corn

was lot bigger. Quite a boy. I bet the girls go for him now in the fourth grade already. Honey, how time flys. By the time I get home suppose they'll be out of school, if it keep on. Well it can't last for ever. Right? How's my little sweetheart Barbara? Sure miss those Sunday afternoons, when you folks came over. Better stop before I begin to cry—Surprised to hear Young Drabeks bought a home in Warren. Well, maybe it's better for Helen. When you see them, say I said hello and good luck. I wish I could write to all of them, but it's impossible. You can bet I think of them all.

So the Cleveland Indians aren't doing so hot. Well, maybe as the months go by they'll get better.

They say we can mention about being in Fiji now. it has been so long since we have been there I've forgotten most everything about the place.

Another T.M.B. I've got to check my posts.

About two hours have passed. I'm off duty now but a couple of the fellows wanted hair cuts, so I had to do that. Maybe I be able to finish this letter by to-morrow. Right?

Back to Fiji with it's beautiful mountains and rivers, there a few places and things I'll never forget about that place. One thing in particular was a native wedding. They buy their wives with so many whale's teeth. Another time we were camping by a native village and a small native child died. The rest of the village sang and hollered all night long to drive the evil spirits away. It was a weird scene but after it was over it was a great experience. Did I ever tell you about the Figians singing? They are always singing. I liked to go to their church just to hear them sing. It sounded just like an old time revival meeting.

Speaking of churches, I've never seen a more picturesque scene than Easter Sunday on this island. As I was sitting in church I couldn't help but think of the difference between here and home. Over here the fellows put on their clean overalls or if they haven't the clean ones, dirty ones are just as good. Back home everyone has to have a new suit for Easter. The church is a lot different too.

Over here the pews are logs cut and being on the ground, the pulpit is one of the stumps the logs were cut from. There's no oncers or twicers here (oncers go to church Xmas and twicers go Xmas and Easter). The fellows here go to church for the meaning of the thing.

Well Honey, I must close and will write more about Fiji Islands in my next letter. Good luck to you and family. Say hello to all for me and write again soon.

Love and kisses. John

Come to me all who are weary and burdened, and I will give you rest. Take my yoke upon you and learn from me, for I am gentle and humble in heart, and you will find rest for your souls. For my yoke is easy and my burden is light.   —
Matthew 11:28-30

Thursday, July 8, 1943 Fort Bragg, N.C.

Dearest Family,

Well how are you feeling? I am just fine. The weather is hot and rain. It rained all week but that's O.K. with me.

I was glad to hear that you have a vacation now. how is Joe working? I hope every day. Hope Junior and Barb are feeling good too.

Well Vi I'll close because I am not feeling so good to night because I worked all day in the rain and my back is no damn good.

So John is not in the Fiji Islands? I didn't know he moved from there. I got a letter from John L. to day he sure likes the hot weather.

Well good night and May God Bless you all. With all my love.

Your brother in law, Frank

Chapter Eleven

The Large Vehicle Personnel Carrier or LCVP left a lot to be desired as far as personal comforts were concerned. As a matter of fact, its overall design encouraged a soldier to rush out of the craft as soon as it reached its destination. At a quick glance, the boat which was only either side of forty feet in length, looked more like an oversized sardine can with the top rolled back most of the way.

The shape of the craft was narrow so as to make for a more difficult target as the craft approached a beachhead. The entire front of the boat was a reinforced steel ramp held secure by two ropes. With the ramp upright, the front stood roughly seven feet in height and at approximately a 70-degree angle so as to offer the troops some head on protection. The setback in design was that the pilot had to stand slightly elevated to the rear and on the left side of the craft leaving him more exposed.

The inner walls surrounding the thirty six troop payload were also made of steel and rose to a height of approximately five feet. The width of the boat allowed four men to stand shoulder to shoulder. The frame protruded an additional two feet on both sides of its metal walls to allow one of the three crew members to walk up and down the length of the craft, tie it off when needed and store extra rope. This extension along with the hull and back of the craft was made of plywood thus improving buoyancy but severely reducing protection from enemy fire.

There were two .30 caliber machine guns anchored directly behind the pilot. The original design called for them to be in the front of the boat, but they severely reduced the available space for a quick exit once the ramp was lowered. They also reduced the size of a vehicle that could be transported from a tank to only a jeep. Thus, they were moved to the rear of the boat where one of the crew would quickly drop into a shallow manhole behind a gun turret mounted on a restricted swivel and somewhat protected by a plate of steel.

The overall shape of the boat caused it to pitch side to side more readily and with a top speed of only 12 knots, rough seas made seasickness a common occurrence. Likewise, the fumes from the 225-horsepower engine along with the stifling heat and anxiety contributed to this illness.[14]

The sweat was beginning to trickle down from beneath John's helmet as the morning sun fully showed itself above the eastern horizon. There was a permanent stain along John's collar from the perspiration and he could feel his dog tags sticking to his chest. His pack felt like a lead weight glued to his back, and John would occasionally lean on the inner wall of the boat for a rest and an opportunity to regain his composure. The walls would soon be hot to the touch while the floor remained somewhat cool from the water offering a bit of relief on his feet. John preferred a spot toward either front corner of the carrier where he could set a good example for his men by being toward the front and capture an occasional mist from the waves slapping against the boat. He did not mind the smells from the craft nor the pitching of the hull because both helped him to escape to the smells of the tractor and other equipment back on the family farm or times fishing on a perpetually churning Lake Erie. He was able to find some small comfort in the occasional wafts of salt air generated by the speed and rolling of the craft. John could taste the salt on his cracked lips and feel the light sting in the corners of his eyes reminding him that he was alive!

Just as the monotonous roll of the boat once again lulled him home, gunfire erupted from the twin .30's and the salt air was replaced with burnt gunpowder from the expended rounds…

The division had two roles as they approached the shores of

---

[14] www.Wikipedia.org

New Georgia. Part of the division established defensive positions at newly acquired U.S. strongholds and two battalions were part of the reinforcements for the 43rd infantry division in the battle for the Munda airfield.[15]

Because of the Lord's great love we are not consumed, for his compassions never fail. They are new every morning; great is your faithfulness. I say to myself, "The Lord is my portion, therefore I will wait for him."

The Lord is good to those whose hope is in him, to the one who seek him; it is good to wait quietly for the salvation of the Lord. –Lamentations 3:22-26

Saturday, July 10, 1943, V-Mail

Dearest Vi,
How are you honey? fine? I hope so. Sure miss you and family and can't wait till I see you again, hope it is soon. Rec'd your swell letters, the last one was dated June 20, which made very good time, don't you think? Well honey, how do you like your new job? It's swell isn't it? But I know it means a lot more work for you and Joe.
Glad to hear the boys were home on furlough and had a good time. Gee, wasn't it swell the way they came home together? Sure waited a long time, didn't they?
This letter is short cause I'm quite busy to night. I'm doing M.P. duty, feeling fine and doing O.K. If I have more time in the next few days, I'll write you a long letter. I'll close saying good luck and good night. Say hello to all for me and be careful.
Love and kisses. John

---

[15] www.history.srmy.mil

Sunday, July 11, 1943, Camp Davis, N.C.

Dear Viola,

I certainly appreciate your writing to me as often as you do. There is nothing better when I come in at night than to find a letter from home. I hear from Veronica about once a month. Of course I know she is busy as heck but she could at least drop me a few lines.

I'm glad to hear that Dad is having good luck with his hay. Ten loads sure was a good crop for that field. Did it have any clover in it? I suppose Mother is killing herself with all the work. I thought maybe they would have a sale and sell some of the stock. If they would leave five or six cows that would be plenty to keep Dad going. Another thing Veronica should quit her job for the summer and help them out. Now that she bought that expensive fur coat she'll never quit.

Things look very good over there maybe we'll be home before we know it. I hope so, it's hell being away from your family and the ones you love. I didn't say much while I was home but I hated to leave this time more than ever. It was heaven to be home again and everyone treated me swell. That's what's tough, then when I get back to camp I can't get used to it. Sometime I think I'd be better off if I didn't come home until it's all over. The next time I come home it will probably be snowing and the Christmas bells ringing. If things run right maybe I can make it sooner although I'd rather be home for Christmas.

I went to the Wilmington City Hospital the other day to give a little girl a blood transfusion. She was in a terrible auto accident and lost a lot of blood. The mother was getting frantic the kid had to have the transfusion by six o'clock in the evening. They couldn't find anyone with the same type blood. Two of my buddies were down in the morning but their blood wouldn't match. I was called about 2 o'clock in the afternoon. By the time they made all the tests it was 5:30 fortunately my blood matched perfectly. That was quite a relief for all concerned. They took little over a pint, it's surprising how the loss of so little blood weakens a person. I hear the girl is doing very well.

I'm sending you a picture that was taken while we were on a cross country hike. I was eating dinner while it was taken. You can see a piece of bread in my hand and a mess kit on the ground.

Well Vi, I must close for now. tell the kids I miss them very much and love them more than ever. Tell Joe I said hello. Give my love to Mom and Dad and all. Please write soon and as often as you can.

Love Johnny

Do nothing out of selfish ambition or vain conceit. Rather, in humility value others above yourselves. –Philippians 2:3

Note on the envelope dated july 20, use rye bread in your lunch dad…milk ready in jar…cookies & orange in pail already…your pants are on line… thanks for the jam Helen and family

Tuesday, July 20, 1943; Some where in the swamps of N.C.

Dearest Soukeniks,
I just got done writing to Ceil and Veronica. We're out on maneuvers for a while. I hope to get back to camp soon, I'm getting so darn tired of this that I feel like going over the hill. It's almost dark now, I'll probably have to use a flashlight to finish this.

The mosquitoes and gnats are so thick here that it's unbearable. I got welts the size of a quarter all over my body. That's not the worst of it we also have the snakes to put up with, the Rattler, the Coral and the Copperhead. I can stand almost anything but snakes. Now I believe John when he said snakes used to crawl in their tents and sleep with them. When I got up this morning I turned my blanket over and found a rattler lying there. I didn't stand there very long I got my revolver and shot him. I don't know whether I'll go to sleep tonight or not. I'll probably be dreaming about them to night.

    I went to the photo shop in camp last week and had some pictures taken. I'll send you one if they come out alright. I got my fingers crossed hoping for the best.

    It's getting so dark I had to put my flashlight on. If you find a lot of mistakes just overlook them. It's pretty hard holding a light in one hand and trying to write with the other.

    How is everything at home? I see they got everything under control at the Lulek ranch, at least that's what Veronica says. How does the corn and soybeans look do you think they'll amount to anything? How is my little niece and nephew and also Joe? Still going strong I suppose. I'll bet Barbara is preparing for school isn't she? She certainly is a cute little doll. I'd like to see her when she does start.

    I'll have to quit for the time being. It's time to post the guards now. I'll have to do this all night, we change guards every two hours. Every time new guards go out I have to get up so, I won't get much sleep. Oh well! I haven't slept over three hours in the past two days any way I get used to it. Maybe it'll help me reduce???

    Give my love to all. Hoping to hear from you soon if not sooner. Love Johnny

            Sunday eve, July 25, 1943

Dear Viola,
I received your letter yesterday and was very glad to

hear from you. I was going to write to you but I kept putting it off all the time. My Co. hasn't sent me my mail yet. I probably would have wrote a long time ago if they had sent me your mail. I never write unless it is to answer a letter. I have been thinking of you and the family although I haven't been writing.

I have been in the hospital for about a month and a half. I don't feel much better than I did, but I didn't feel too bad when I went in. my stomache was bothering me so I thought it was a good time to find out what was the matter with it. They have taken X-rays and different kind of examinations and still they haven't found out any thing. I still have the same pain as before. I have been hoping they would send me home, but if they can't find anything wrong they won't. The only thing I can do is keep complaining. I would like to get back to my company because they will be giving out furloughs. I will probably be one of the last ones to get it.

I wish I could be home just in time for the pickles. I hope mother has a good crop of them. They should bring good money this year. How are they, do they look pretty good? I hope the weather is just rite for them. If you have to quit working at the Packard you can always get a new job. What do you intend to do with the kids? Yes, I remember the time we went to Market and when we got home Joe was there. I remember just as if it happened yesterday. I always liked to go even if it was tiresome at times. I'll bet Johnny is going to miss going to the market too. I think it was fun and still we made money at it. I sure hope we can be home by this time next year. Things have been looking rather good but still there is a long way to go. I read the papers every day just to see how the Allies are getting along.

I sure am going to miss thrashing this year. I never liked it when I was home, but when I am away from it I miss it. Let me know how much wheat father thrashes out. Gee but I miss the farm. It's hard work on the farm, but it is a lot better than the army. Glad to hear the corn is doing well. At least you will have one good crop.

So Mrs. Betly was weeding my Christmas trees. I hope she

does a good job. But I think she will. Gee I can't wait until I get home to see them. I knew there would be some to transplant. Has mother got the shading on them? A lot of them are still small and they would die in the hot sun. Did Mrs. Betly get her tan or did she get a sunburn? She should come out her and get a tan. It wouldn't take her long. I'll bet mother was glad to have her help. She should help her out to help pick pickles too.

So Rudy, Veronica and Ceil had a good time in Middlefield swimming. I sure miss the times Frank, Johnny and I had. We would always go alone (well most of the time) to the lake or some other place. We always had a darn good time.

You must be making darn good money if you are working 6 days a week. I suppose at that rate you will be buying a bigger place. Or moving to the city like Helen did. By the way how is she doing? I haven't written to her in a long time. I suppose I better get busy and write her letter. I got a letter from Veronica the other day and she told me mother was to have a vacation and stay at Helen's place. I think she need one alright. It sure would do her good just befor pickle time.

How is Joe doing? Is he working every day? I hear Jim Sabo went to Canada fishing. I'll bet Joe wishes he was with him. Has he been fishing anywhere lately? I suppose he has been to busy for that.

Catherine wrote and told me about Leo Owen drowning. It sure is too bad. He went to Cleveland with me for our Examination for the Army. He was rejected because he had three fingers cut off and he had a bad lung.

I better be closing now because I can't see how to write very well. I had my eyes tested and I need glasses. I didn't get them yet. I won't until I get to my company. I am going to hate to wear them because I look bad enough without.

The hospital here is made of tents. They are long ones and I sleep on the end where the opening is . Every nite I look out at the moon. It sure is beautiful. I think it is the same moon as you *have in Ohio. But I would rather see it there then here. Please write.*

Love and kisses. Your brother Claude

P.S. Say hello to Joey and Barbara of course don't forget Joe. Excuse the poor writing.

Hope deferred makes the heart sick, but a longing fulfilled is the tree of life.   –Proverbs 13:12

As water reflects the face, so a man's heart reflects the man. –Proverbs 27:19

Sunday, July 25, 1943; Hospital #3 Ward 367 Fort Bragg

Dear family,
How are you all feeling? I am just fine but back in the damn Hospital. Well maybe I'll be a M.P. or working in the Hospital. Will write went I get out of the Hospital. Till then I'll be in the same Hospital.
Love yours, Frank

Evening, morning, and noon I cry out in distress, and he hears my voice.   –Psalm 55:17

Wednesday, July 28, 1943 Camp Davis, N.C.

Dearest Soukeniks,
I appreciate your promptness in answering my letters. You'll never know how much your mail means to me. I only hope you keep up the good work. Don't disappoint me keep them

coming as regular as they have been. I'll try to answer every one if it's at all possible.

I'm going to get my big pictures to-day. They didn't come out very good at all, these photographers here don't know anything about taking pictures. I'm sending them all home, you and mother pick out the one you want and then give one to Helen and Irene Drabek. I'm sending Ceil one from here. I know you'll be disappointed in them but what can I do about it now. There will be an extra one or so so do what you want to with them.

So Leo Owens was drowned at Pymatuning lake some time ago. What happened was he swimming or what? I couldn't believe it at first I had to read it over twice to make sure my eyes weren't deceiving me.

So you folks don't believe I shot that snake with a revolver? When we're on maneuvers I always carry a revolver on my hip. It's nothing to shoot a snake at close range. I didn't take time to look for a club for fear he would get away. That's one thing we have plenty of is snakes. Then we have the jiggers they're murder. Do you remember the jigger bites John had on his legs when he was home on furlough? They get in under your skin and die there that leaves a big open sore. I have them all over my legs from my ankle up to my hips. The funniest thing about it they're so small you can hardly see them. I'll be the happiest man in the world when we get out of these damn swamps.

It seems they thrashed wheat early this year or is that my imagination? Sixty bushels is very poor but I guess that's better than nothing. How was the straw this year do they have plenty of it? I wish I could get home for a few days to see everything. How is the corn, pickles and potatoes doing? Write and tell me all about it. I'll bet father's got his hands full running the farm and helping the neighbors thrash. What does mom plan to do with the pickles this year? She isn't going to the market is she? That will be a big job for her again I don't know why she planted them again this year.

I got a letter from John the other day and there is a change in his address he asked me to pass it on so I'm sending it to you and I want you to pass it on to the folks at home, if they don't already have it.

I'm sending you a few negatives that I couldn't get developed down here. I wish you would get them developed immediately and send them back. I would have sent them to Veronica but I can't depend on her. She hasn't sent me the pictures we had taken while I was home (you see what I mean). I'll close for a while hoping to hear from you soon. Give my love to all.

Your loving brother, John

My new address-

Cpl. John Soukenik

A.S.N. 35006996 M.P. Co, Service Command APO #709

c/o P.M. San Francisco, Cal.

When you write home please pass on my new address. O.K.?

Wednesday, July 28, 1943; 51st Evac Hospital Ward 10

Dear Viola,
I received your letter today and was sure glad to hear from you. I am feeling as good as can be expected. I am glad to hear that you are all well.

I have been in the hospital for a month and a half. They still haven't been able to find out what is the matter with me. I sure am having a good rest. But I guess that isn't winning the war. I know of a lot better way but I can't make them think so. Did I tell you I need glasses? I had my eyes tested and the Dr. said I need glasses. As soon as I get back to my co. I am to get them. I haven't been able to read very well. I couldn't even see to write. My eyes would hurt and blurr.

    The wheat crop sure must have been bad. Gosh I expected more than 60 bushels out of that big (peace). It looked pretty good when I saw it in April. The rain sure must have fixed it. Are they going to have 60 bu. Of oats? Well maybe it's better they didn't have more. They would be able to take care of any more. I sure hope the corn crop will be better. You see what happens to the farm as soon as John and I leave. ha.ha. if the corn doesn't ripen and make good father will have to sell some of his stock or buy feed. He can't feed them just hay and expect to get lots of milk. By the way, how many cows is father milking and what is he getting for milk? I wrote a letter to Veronica yesterday. I should have asked her, but I suppose you are over more often than she is at home. The way she writes she is a busy girl. She told me about that fox fur she got. She must be up in the bucks. Does she make as much as you do? It sure must be bad since they are taking so much out in taxes. You figgure you have so much made and when you get paid you don't have that much. I guess that would make anyone mad. Can't you get that job or another after the pickles are over with? Mother could watch the kids and when they go to school they could go from our place. So little Joey working in the muck? He should be he is big enough. Say what are you going to do with all that money? I don't know why I am asking that since living conditions are so high. I guess I am just jealous I am not in a position to make a lot.

    So watermellons are a $1.25. well pickles should be at least 3 or 4 dollars a pk. Shouldn't they? Don't forget to have watermellon when I get home on furlough. When that will be I don't know yet.

    You and Joe should make out darn good. You work for cloths and living expenses and all Joe makes you can save.

    I sure would like to see mother's Victory Garden. She must spend a lot of time in it. I don't see how she can find time since there is so much to do. But leave it up to mother, she always finds *time for everything.*

The reason I haven't been writing is I have been moving around from one hospital to another. Everytime I moved to another hospital the address would change. So I thought it would be better to wait until I got settled down before I wrote.

Catherine is sending me a package with cigarettes in it so you don't have to bother. The Dr. told me not to smoke very much. And they would only dry out in this California heat. Thanks just the same.

Well I guess I better close I can't hardly see to write. It is only about 7:00 o'clock but we have the sides of our tent down and the sun is shining in. The boys are all groped around playing cards. They do that every day to pass the time away. Goodby.

Love and kisses, Claude

P.S. Say hello to all.

Thursday, July 29, 1943

Dearest Vi,

Another morning rolls around once more, but it isn't one of those blue morning 'cause I rec'd two letters from you in the last week, which is really swell. I could kiss you and no kidding.

Well Honey, how is every thing? fine? Hope this letter finds you in the very best of spirits- as for me- well- I feel like doing some somer soults. I do feel tops. Maybe I 'm feeling younger.

Hope you're enjoying your job at the Packard and not working too hard. How's Joe doing? Is he doing any fishing? Boy, I wish I was home, so I could a little my self. How's Joey and Barbara doing? fine? I sure miss them and can't wait till I see them again. Well close for now keep your chins up and keep smiling. Remember, I'm thinking of you all the time, and pray that

we will be all together soon-
   Love and kisses, John

Friday, August 6, 1943; Hospital Ward #3

   How are you all getting long? I am just fine so don't worry about me my back is the same.
   The weather is hot just like hell. It look like rain to-night. I hope so maybe it will cool a little. Did you get a letter from John L. late? I didn't get one since two week go. I glad to hear that you are working in Warren. Are you going to work all year? Maybe it will be hard for you when the kids go to school. I hope Joe don't have to go to Army this year.
   Well dear I'll close for this time may God Bless you all with all my love.
   Your brother law, Frank

   P.S. Tell the kids to praye for me.

Sunday, August 8, 1943; Desert Training Center California

   Dear Viola,
   I received your letter today and was sure glad to hear from you. I always am glad to hear from you and I answer as soon as I do. You know those letters you have been sending to my co. well, I haven't gotten any of them. I think you will get them all back. Because Catherine sent me a bunch of letters that came back. I guess the mailman in my outfit did not know where I was at and was to lazy to find out. So he just sent them back.
   I am feeling pretty good today for a change. I am supposed

to get some glasses but don't know just when.

You don't have to worry about me not staying in the hosp. I know when I am well off. I have been in the hospital for two months now. They still haven't found out what is ailing me. the way he talked he was going to send me to another hospital. It's to a General hospital. If I go there I will be all sat. they either cure me there or get rid of me. even if I get in another outfit I would be satisfied. My own outfit is having 6 more weeks of maneuvers. I sure am glad I am going to miss that. Maybe I better keep my fingers crossed. I think that is why they cancelled all furloughs.

I wrote to Johnny a week ago and as soon as I get an answer I will write to him again. I haven't received a letter from him yet either but I now understand why I haven't. my co. probably sent them all back.

I don't blame Frank for going to the hospital. If there is something wrong with him it is alrite to go. I guess there is because he was always complaining at home. I don't think he is going to the hosp. because he don't want to go across. At least he didn't talk that way at home.

I will write to Johnny as often as I hear from him. I would sooner write to him and home than any other place. Because I miss him as much as I do anybody else. I wrote to Helen quite a few times a while ago but they all come back. I didn't have the rite address. I got a letter from her today with the rite address so I will answer it as soon as possible. I would like to write to John S. but I just don't know when. I didn't know he was an M.P. that is a darn good job if you like it and I think he should.

So you are having a hard time to make ends meet. Gosh I didn't think it was that bad at home. I know there are a lot of taxes and things are very high, but still the wages are high.

It sure is too bad about the pickles. We didn't mean to worry that much about them. I sure hope you get some rain so they come out all rite. Isn't that just heck once it rains too much and then it doesn't rain at all. I guess it is because there are too many bad people in the world.

  Is father figguring on replacing them two cows he sold for beef? He should at least buy one good one. You know they are going to ration milk in California. It must be a darn good price here too. We sure do get a lot of milk here at the hospital. I have been drinking about 2 qts. A day. I should be getting fat, but I'm not.

  Helen said peaches and other fruits are scarce and the prices were high. It just reminds me we had peaches today for dinner. They were the most beautiful peaches I ever saw. We get an afull lot of fruit. Apples, plums, peaches, pears and etc. of course this is an Army hospital. And they usually get the best.

  Well I better close for now. love and kisses, Claude

  Please excuse the poor writing <u>Say hello to all.</u>

  Wednesday, August 11, 1943

  Dearest Soukeniks,

  I certainly was glad to get your letter to-day. You know I think it's been more than a week since I heard from you. It seems like ages. For a while I thought maybe you were angry with me.

  You certainly have your hands full now don't you? I feel sorry for you with all that work. I know how it is when you don't get much sleep. Then too working in the mill and doing all that work at home.

  You sure are having funny weather. Once it's to wet and now it's to dry. Maybe it's better that way mother won't kill herself with the pickles. How is the corn doing do you think it will do any good? How was the hay this year was the barn full?

  So Baldy Smith got married. Ha. Ha. First he runs the farm to beat the draft now he gets married. That's pretty good. I saw him at the Greene School dance when I was at home. He is ignored by everyone nobody talks to him. I'd rather be in the army any day then to be in his position.

I'm glad you like the pictures. They're not very good but there the best I could get made down here. I should have had some taken while I was home but you know how it is to (busy). I'll send them pictures back because I have no place to keep them we're very crowded now and I have no place for anything. I got some more pictures and stuff I'm going to send home. I'd love to keep them all but we're always on the go and I have no room.

I'm still hoping to get home pretty soon. I'm still waiting impatiently for the right time to pull a few strings (if you know what I mean).

I wish you wouldn't tease me with apple pies. My mouth is watering and my tongue is hanging out. Helen pulled the same thing on me last week. You girls don't how much I suffer when I hear the word apple pie.

So you can't get R.G. Dunns? Try again and if you can't get them get San Fileca, El Verde or Donalda. What I'm after is a darker cigar.

Well how is my sweet little niece and nephew? It won't be long they'll be going to school again. I really miss them very much often times I lie awake on my bunk thinking of how I used to play with them. Vi, it hurts being so far away from them and for such a long time.

Well Vi, I will close for now. say hello to Joe for me. Give my love to Mom and Dad and the kids. Please write soon.

You loving brother, Johnny

Friday, August 13, 1943

Dear Viola,
I received your letters that you sent me. you know the ones you sent to my co. and they sent them back. I still can't understand why they didn't send them to me. I also got a letter from you to

day. I sure have been busy reading those letters but I sure did like to read them. There was a lot of things that was news to me.

I haven't been feeling to good the last few days. Oh I haven't been so sick that I couldn't get around but I have felt a lot better. I am going to stay in the hospital until I am well or send me home. The Dr. said they are to send me to another hospital. I don't know when I will go or where. I will be darn glad to get out of here. I have been in this hospital for 6 wks. Now. I want a different scenery to look at. One thing nice about it here and that is, it is nice and cool here. Way up in the mountains. A nice cool breeze coming in from the ocean.

That was a nice picture of Johnny. Only if it was a little larger. What kind of an outfit is that that he is standing by. I never saw anything like that before.

I wrote to Johnny about two weeks ago but haven't received an answer yet. I sure would like to hear from him. I would like to know how he is getting along.

So you still haven't had any rain. That sure is too bad. I have been expecting a good crop. Since the other crops failed I thought at least the pickles would make good.

When I read about those apple pies you made it sure made me hungry. I can't remember when I had my last piece of pie. I always did enjoy your pies no matter what kind they are.

So Richard Smith is getting married. Yes I know him very well and I think I know the girl but not very well. I would probably know her if I see her. How did he manage to keep out of the Army? That chicken farm isn't that emportant, is it? I guess if I had of paid the draft board I could have been home too.

I am going to miss them fairs this year. I always liked to go. I guess they are only for kids now. At least untill this war is over with.

Well there isn't much mor I can think of to write just now. I should have a lot to write but I can't seem to think of anything just now. please say hello to kids and Joe.

Love, Claude

Saturday, August 14, 1943

Dearest family,

How are you getting long with world? I didn't hear from you for a long time. Maybe you are busy that O.K. I know you are busy.

How is the kids getting long when you are all working do you think you have to go to the Army this year? I don't know why you could because you have to kid.

I am feeling good. I am getting heat treatments everyday. Maybe I'll get out of the hospital soon. Tell mother not to come down because I am O.K. I'll close for this time I am going to mass to night and everynight. I'll pray for all of you till next time may God Bless you all.

With all my love, Frank

P.S. I didn't hear from John or Johnnie for a long time.

Note written on envelope, "Dad, Turn off the meat please", "Joey cut hair tomorrow Babs get hers combed", "Cook yourself some potatoes and slice cucs."

Sunday, August 22, 1943

Dear Viola,

I received your letter yesterday and was sure glad to hear from you. I got a letter from Johnny last week. I sure was glad to hear from him. He was telling me that he might come home if he gets a three day pass. He and his buddy are supposed to come home in his car. It sure is a nice picture of him. He is darn lucky to be able to come home so often.

  I am still in the same hospital. I was supposed to be moved to a Gen. Hosp. but don't know for sure. I sure hope they decide something pretty soon. Of course, it isn't so bad here, but I am getting tired of the old place. They aren't doing anything for me. they haven't given me any medicine for two wks. now. I guess they didn't expect me to be hear that long. I guess it is pretty hard to get transportation.

  Well how did mother and Joe make out with the pickles? Did they sell out? Have you been having any rain lately? I hope so or they won't have to worry about the pickles any more. I bet the ground is plenty hard to plow. That is if it hasn't rained lately. I remember what a job I had last fall. The ground was so darn hard I spots you couldn't keep the plow in the ground. Has the plow got new points on? If it doesn't it would be a good idea to put a new set on. But Joe know what it is all about.

  It is bad the oats didn't turn out very good. Didn't the upper end of the field turn out either? Since it is much higher I thought it might.

  So you went to the lake. Don't tell me it was too cold to go in. Joe should have gone fishing or can't they fish in the lake any more?

  Yes, I need glasses but I haven't gotten them yet. I don't know what they are waited for. When I do get them I am only going to wear them when I read or write. I hope I get them pretty soon maybe I can do a better job when I read the daily paper.

  I went to church this morning. It sure was a nice mass. They even had a choir. They didn't do a very good job but this was the first time thay had a choir so I can't blame them.

  Well I must close for now. it is time for dinner and I don't want to miss that.

  Goodby and God bless you all. Love and kisses. Claude

  P.S. Please say hello to all. Excuse the poor writing.

Wednesday, August 25, 1943

Dear Viola,

I received your letter yesterday glad to hear from you and too learn that you got my package. I have been wondering what shape it was in when you got it. I didn't expect it to be in very good shape since it was such a weak box. I don't think they were hurt any though (cactus). I think they should grow but don't give them too much water. Tell Joey and Barbara that I don't know just how tall they will grow. But I don't think they will grow very tall. Maybe a foot or so at the most. I don't think they are like the large ones that grow out here. You don't find very many in Calif. At least I haven't seen any large ones. They grow in Arizona and New Mexico.

$30 wasn't bad for the first was it? The first pickles never does bring very much. Just so you get a little rain once in a while so the vines don't dry up.

Yes I know just how you feel about quitting the mill. There you meet all kinds of people and get acquainted with them. But the work at home is just as important. Such as the kids getting ready for school. I can just picture them looking like two little dolls. I'll bet Barbara will be tickled when she goes to school. She always did like to. I wish I was in my school days again.

I have been feeling perty good but still not the way I should. I am still at the same hospital. I am suppose to go to the general hospital soon. I haven't seen a Dr. for a week now. I guess they don't care weather we live or die. You see all the ones that are to be transfered to the general are put in separate wards. I am in ward 64 now but you write the same address as you have been. I will let you know when to change.

Yes I know Johnny is to come home if he gets a pass. (And I bet he gets one too). I got a letter from him the other day and he told me they are to drive his buddies car out. Gee isn't he lucky though. I wish I was half that lucky to be able to come home so often. I don't know when I will be coming home but I hope it will be soon. One way or the other. Johnny also told me what a swell time he had on his furlough. It sure made me lonesome when I read his letter. I answered his letter the same day I got his so I should hear from him again soon. Yes it won't be long before it will be a year that we are in the Army. It seems more like 5 years though doesn't it.

So you are to get $.76 an hour. That isn't bad for three months. that is if you didn't have to work very hard. You probably will think twice before you quit since you got a raise. But I guess you have to quit there isn't anything to do but quit. You sure will have it easy once the kids go to school. I suppose you will be with mother most of the time. It will be rather lonesome for both of you if you don't.

Well, I must be closing for know because I have another letter to write and you know how long it takes me.

Love and kisses. Claude

P.S. <u>Say hello to Joe and the kids and tell them I miss them a lot. Excuse the poor writing.</u>

Thursday, August, 26, 1943

Dearest Vi,
I hope you'll excuse me for not writing sooner. We are now getting our advanced training. Believe me it's plenty hot in this damn hot hell hole. If it wasn't for the heat I would take anything. I'm suffering with the heat rash , it's driving me crazy.

The other day we went through the (infiltration course). I don't suppose you know what that is so I'll try to explain it a little. We begin with a tough obstacle course. The first obstacle is a large hole filled with water, logs and brush. We plunge into that and struggle like hell to get out without getting to wet. The water is deep and the guys come out dirtier than pigs and wet up to the chest. Then there are other obstacles such as low barbed wire we crawl on our stomachs under that through mud about six inches deep. I won't go on to explain the rest I think you have a fair idea of what it's like now. don't you? There are all sorts of obstacles like that. When we finish that we go to the infiltration course.

Now a little about that. There are two machine guns mounted thirty inches above the ground and they shoot over our heads. We crawl on our stomachs for a hundred yards under fire of machine guns. They also have land mines planted through the area as you're crawling they blow up in your face. Then to they shoot rockets and other high explosives to assimilate battle conditions. I had a land mine blow up in my face and I'm still eating dust. The purpose of it is to get the men used to it. Also to teach the men to keep close to the ground. Believe me I kept my head down plenty low. That hundred yards felt like a mile on top of that they shoot smoke bombs they almost choke you. They wouldn't let us take our gas masks. I guess they want to see how much we can take.

Enough of that stuff now, how is everyone at home? Well, I hope. I don't know if I'll get a chance to come home or not but I'm still trying.

So you're going to quit your job pretty soon? I think that's the best thing the kids do need you at home. After all what's money if you don't have your kids. I miss them more and more every day. I'm praying for them every Sunday. I'll bet the weather is nice at home now isn't it?

It doesn't seem like the kids will be starting school to me. down here it's hard to tell what season it is. I can't imagine Barbara going to school. She still seems like a baby to me. I wonder how she'll like it?

I got a letter from Claude about a week ago. I also heard that Frank joined a new outfit. I guess he isn't feeling very well yet.

    I read about the Johnson Rubber fire in the Warren Tribune. One of the boys gets it and I get it from him that keeps me up on the home news pretty well. That was quite a big fire it says a $100,000 damage in the paper.

    Well Vi, I must close for a while. Give my love to Mom and Dad and kids. Please write soon. Don't worry if I get shipped out. I can take care of myself.

    Love to all. John

Keep your lives free from the love of money and be content with what you have, because God has said, "Never will I leave you; never will I forsake you." –Hebrews 13:5

Friday, August 27, 1943

Dearest family,
    I received your letter so I am answering it to-day because we are going on maneuvers for some time so if you don't hear from me for some time don't worry because I'll be OK.
    How are you & all the family getting long? Bar & Joey are going back to school soon. I hope Bar will like to go I did. ha.ha. some B.S. did you hear from John & Johnie? I didn't hear from them for some time. I wish John S. would write because I can't send him a letter no address so next time you write send it to me.
    I received 6 letters to day so I have to answer them all. Winnie wrote to every day. She's O.K. Beverly didn't write for she's mad because I don't write. You know me don't have the time. Well I'll close for this time.
    May God Bless you all.
    With all my love. Your brother law Frank

Chapter Twelve

Monday, September 6, 1943; Battery A 793 F.A.B. Ft. Bragg, N.C.

Dearest family,
How are you getting long? Just a line to let you know that I am O.K. & that I am in a new outfit again. Write more when we get back from the woods.
Love Frank

Tuesday, September 7, 1943

Dear Viola,
I received your letter yesterday and was very glad to hear from you. I got five letters yesterday and it sure is keeping me busy answering them.
I am still at the same hospital that I was in but expect to be transffered to a general hosp. most any day now. I have been waiting for four weeks to be sent to the other hosp. but I don't mind waiting if they don't. it makes 85 days that I have been in the hosp. they soon will have to do something with me. I sure am rested up. All I have done is eat sleep and do a little K.P. since I have been here. I am getting offul soft. A hard days work would kill me rite now. I don't expect to do any work for a while yet either. At least not until they fix me up or otherwise.
So you are soon to quit working at the Packard. Yes I suppose a lot of girls will be quiting the mills. Especially the

married ones.

I suppose it would have been alrite to work there, but just for that reason. I don't think I would be much ahead in the long run. I still think Ruetenik's is better for me to work for. You know they are getting $.73 an hour and a bonus. I got a letter from Ted yesterday and he told me about everything that was going on. He told me about Howard trying to get me out. He said he thinks Howard has a good chance. But I don't know wheather it will or not. I hope so. Howard wrote to me for the commanding officer's address. But I haven't heard any more about it.

I wrote a few cards to Viney but they were greeting cards. I suppose I should write a letter but I don't know I can explain why I didn't write sooner. Anyway I find it hard to write as much as I do.

Well I suppose the kids will be in school when you get this letter. You will have a lot of time to your self. You now can go bumming around to the sales etc. you say you haven't been to market yet. That isn't like you. I thought maybe you would stay home from work just to go to market. If you don't go pretty soon it will be too late. Or maybe it is already. I sure did miss the market this year. I wish I could have been home to go at least once.

So Joe and Joey went fishing. And they caught some large ones. I bet he will go more often now. I hear Jim went to Canada fishing. I bet Joe would have like to go with him. But I imagin he has just as good a time fishing around home.

Well I must close for now. I have to shave and wash up a little. I look like a hobo. Goodby.

Love and kisses. Claude

In their hearts humans plan their course, but the Lord establishes their steps. –Proverbs 16:9

Wednesday, September 8, 1943 (New Outfit) Fort fisher, N.C.

Dear Veronica,
Just a few lines to let you know that I was transferred to another outfit and to give you my new address.
This place is right on the ocean and is much smaller then Camp Davis. There are no hard roads here and the sand is ankle deep. I'm having a hell of a time getting around in it.
Well Veronica I'll close for a while cause I'm pressed for time. Give my love to all. In case you can't read my address from the envelope I'll put it on the back here it is.
Cpl. John Lulek
A.S.N. 353 20 990
Hq. Btry. 557th A.A.A.
Auto Wpns. Bn. Mobile
Fort Fisher, N.C.

John Soukenik never thought he would be happy to see Guadalcanal again but as the ship approached land, there was a rushing sense of relief that came over him and the rest of his men as they sensed for the first time in two months a small measure of safety. There was great joy pent up in the men in anticipation of some well-deserved R&R.

Wednesday, September, 15, 1943

Dear Viola,
You know I haven't heard from you for over a week. I suppose you're busy as heck with the fall coming etc. I know I haven't written to you for sometime either cause of this moving

around and stuff.

Well how does Barbara like school by now? it leaves you home all alone now that the kids have started school. I'll bet you're pretty lonesome without her aren't you? I'll bet Barbara is a knockout all dolled up in her best, probably the best dressed kid in school if I know you, which I think I do. Joey is in the 4th grade isn't he? Gee! How time flies it just seems like yesterday that he started school. Pretty soon he'll be a big man it's hard to believe.

I'm going to send some more of my stuff home in a barracks bag. I have to much stuff to lug around and we're crowded in the barracks too. I'm sending a pair of over shoes that Joe can use. Later I'll send him a pair of shoes if I can get the old ones salvaged. When you move from place to place it's hard to lug all that stuff around.

This place I'm in now is right on the beach and it's much smaller than Camp Davis. The barracks are small only fifteen men to a barracks. They're well hidden in the brush if you go out at nite and come back when it's dark you can't find your barracks. Then too being right on the coast we're blacked out most of the time. There are no hard roads, the damn sand is ankle deep, it sure is tough to walk in.

Well Vi I'll close for a while. Please write soon. Give my love to all.

Your loving brother. Johnny

Sunday, September 19, 1943

Dearest Family,

How are you all? I am getting long just so the weather is hot it look like rain to-night. We are in S.C. this week the maneuvers are hell. Will write a letter soon as I can.

With all my love. Frank

Endure hardship with us like a good soldier of Christ Jesus.
-2 Timothy 2:3

Sunday, September 19, 1943; Someplace in S.C.

Dearest family,
I received your letters that you wrote to 203. Just got it. Well how are you all getting long on the farm. I hope you are all feeling fine.
The weather is rain to day we are on pass for Sunday. i am going to town and getting some ---? Viola my back is not so good but don't tell mother or dad please. I am worry about my back. I didn't know that Claude is in the Hospital please send me his address.
We are going to have maneuvers for 3 or 4 weeks more. Maybe I'll get to come in camp soon. I hope that Joe don't get lay off. Did you know that Beverly and I are not know more. Well did you hear from the Johns? I didn't hear from one of them this month or last month. I hope everything is O.K. well I'll sign off as it is time to go to Church for mass.
May God Bless you all. Tell Bar and Joey to pray for me
Love always. Frank

But for you who revere my name, the sun of righteousness will rise with healing in its wings. –Malachi 4:2

Monday P.M., September 20, 1943; Camp Callan, California

Dear Viola,
I received your letter today and thought I better write before I let it go to long.
So Joey has been over sleeping at our place. Well you tell

him to sleep there a lot. I want those springs to keep limbered up. I may want to use that bed again and I don't want a hard bed to sleep on.

We listen to the raido a lot here but all we can get is the news. Yes I remember the program Truth or the Consequences. I think I heard it last Sat. afternoon. I don't remember the other program. (You Top This). There is three radios in the ward. But the heck of it is they are all playing at the same time or none at all.

So the frost finished everything. Well that is all the farmer needs to make it a perfect year. Too wet to dry and now a frost. To bad something else couldn't happen to the crops. Did it hurt the other crops any? I mean besides the corn. You don't need very many canned tomatoes do you? Joe doesn't like them anyway.

The Roscoes have quite a family started haven't they? What is it one every year?

No I didn't faint but was surprised that you went to the market with so few pickles. Of course it payed for itself so that is all that matters. It sure is too bad the pickle crop failed or you could make some good money.

If that cow turns out to be a good one he (dad) should keep the calf and raise it. That is unless it is a bull or that he is short of milk.

I haven't heard from Johnny in a long time. He must be darn busy. Or he would write. I don't think he will go across yet but you never can tell. If they need his kind of an outfit in a hurry he will go. Of course he can take care of himself no matter where he goes. I bet Mrs. Huntley don't like the idea about Eugene going does she? My outfit is suppose to head for new York to before long. I guess they are getting ready for a big drive.

I knew you would miss those big pay checks. But you can't eat your cake and have it too. Yes Ruetenik is paying his men well and I wish I was there rite now. I sure hope he can help me. I haven't heard anything about it so I don't know what to think.

You just aint kidding it is getting tiresome. I have been in the hospital for just about 3 ½ months. if I stay in much longer I will go crazy of course I am not going out unless it is the way I want to or they forse me. if they would give me an easy job that would be different. But the infantry that is out as far as I am consered.

It sure would be swell to spend a vacation in Canada. I came darn near going a few years ago. Ted and I was supposed to go on a fishing trip. But he backed out. He got married instead. Maybe that was a better idea. At least it worked for him.

Well I must be closing for now. I have another letter to write. And you know how long it takes me to write a letter.

Goodby and God bless you all. Love, Claude

P.S. say hello to Joe and the kids for me.

Please excuse the poor writing.

Thursday, September 23, 1943

Dearest Family,
How are you all getting long? I'll write to you all next week. We are so damn busy I got 12 letters to day don't worry about John he will be O.K. till next time.
May God Bless you all. Love, Frank

But seek first his kingdom and his righteousness, and all these things will be given to you as well. Therefore do not worry about tomorrow, for tomorrow will worry about itself. Each day has enough trouble of its own. -Matthew 6:33-34

Friday afternoon, September 24, 1943

Dear Viola,
Just a few words to let you know that I am going back to my outfit in a few days. They haven't been able to find anything wrong with my stomach. I had a talk with the Dr. and told him I wouldn't be able to do duty. He said he couldn't do anything about it since nothing didn't show up in the x-rays. So I guess there isn't anything to do but go back and if I can't make it I just will go back in the hospital.

My outfit is suppose to move out east before the first. Maybe I won't even go with them. It doesn't look like Rueteniks help did any good does it?

Boy Johnny sure is lucky to get home so often. That makes the fourth time he has been home. I don't know how he does it. I sure wish I was home having a good time with him. I got a letter from him the other day and he didn't say he was expecting to go home. I sure hope I get a furlough, but I wouldn't want one from out here unless I got enough days.

I am glad to hear you had good luck with the corn binder. Oh it is bound to work good if the corn is nice and straight. You should know quite a bit about the machine by now. I suppose you was able to show Joe a lot of things? I sure did like cutting corn but the trouble with me I would get angry as soon as we would have trouble. I sure do miss farm work. I can't wait till I get back to it.

We just had mail call and I got 3 letters and a package. It's a cartoon of cigarettes from Catherine. It sure makes me feel good to get all of these letters. But I have a hard time answering them all.

I am glad to hear that Barbara likes school. I always thought she would because she always wanted to visit before she *started. You know that is a good idea. They get used to the school and they don't get afraid when they do have to go.*

Well I can't think of anything more to write so I will close for now. Maybe you better not write for a while. I will let you know as soon as I have my new address. I don't know for sure where they will send me yet. If I go to my outfit I won't be there very long. So just wait untill I get a perminate address.

Goodby and God Bless you all.
Love and kisses, Claude

P.S. Excuse the poor writing.

Friday, September 24, 1943

Dearest Family,
I received your letter but didn't have time to write to you all. Did you get the card I send you? We are come back to camp this week and something came. I don't know for sure but I think it no good maybe over seas?

How are you and the family getting long? Is Joe working every day? I hope he is. I hope he don't have to go to the Army. I am sure glad I didn't go with the 82nd Division. Some of my pals were killed and one of my Sgt. From Warren was killed.

The weather is fine to day but it sure was hell last week it rain all the time and cold.

Well I'll have to close for this time. O yes, did you hear from John or Johnie this month? I didn't hear from them for over a month. I know everything is O.K. but I sure like to her from them. Well how does Bar. Like school? Tell her that if she wants to be my girl she will have to like school.

Well Viola I'll close this time for sure. Till next time may God Bless you all with all my love and kisses.
Your brother law Frank

P.S. Please write when you have time. I hope I can come home befor I go over sea.

Sunday, September 26, 1943

Dearest Family,
 How are you all? I see that John L. was home last week and so was Jim did you see him? How is he looking good? We are so busy I can't get much time to write to know one. I wrote to mother to day maybe I'll get time to write you a letter this week. Take good care of yourself and the family. May God Bless you all. Till next time.
 Love Frank

Friday, October 1, 1943; Battery A 793 F.A. Bn.

Dearest Family,
 How are you all? I received your letter but don't have time to write to night. We are so busy all the time. I'll write when I can. Maybe I'll get a pass some time in Oct. I hope so may God Bless you all. Till next time. Love Frank

Sunday, October 3, 1943

Dearest family,
 Well how are you all getting long? I hope that everything is fine with you all. I am just so. I am taking treatment all this week in the Hospital. Maybe I'll get a pass some time in

October. I hope so.

Well how is Joe is he getting all the work he wants. I hope he don't have to go to the Army. Tell him not to get in it if he can.

How are my kids getting long. Is Bar. And Joey good? Do the kids like the school I hope everything is OK.

I hear that John L. is not feeling so good is that right? I don't know because he don't write to me for a long time.

I'll close for this time may God bless you all till next.
With all my love.
Your brother law. Frank

Make it your ambition to lead a quiet life, to mind your own business and to work with your hands, just as we told you, so that your daily life may win the respect of outsiders and so that you will not be dependent on anybody. -1 Thessalonians 4:11-12.

Sunday, October 3, 1943; Fort Fisher, North Carolina

Dear Viola,
Yes, I made it back to camp alright but I haven't recovered from my furlough and the trip as yet. Those train ride sure do knock the hell out of a guy. Trying to sleep on a train seat ain't very comfortable. Then too I didn't get much sleep at home as you know. No remarks either! When I got back we started packing our stuff getting ready to move. Here I thought I'd have Saturday afternoon and Sunday off but I didn't we worked all the time. You can't imagine how much work there is to moving. Although now that we are here I don't regret it a bit.

I met a pretty 2nd Lt. nurse on the train. Boy! She was alright. You ought to see the other soldiers look at me a corporal with a 2nd Lt. nurse. Their eyes were popping out. She had beautiful black hair and dark eyes and what a shape she had Wow! I wished I had more time I would have stopped off with her for a while. We could have had a swell time. Now don't get me wrong. She gave me all kinds of hints but I told her I had to be back at camp.

We got up at 2 O'clock Tuesday morning and left Fort Fisher at six. I got three hours sleep that night then had to drive all the way down here. The trip was 225 miles and it's plenty tiresome driving in a convoy. The speed limit is 25 miles per for a convoy as you can imagine how long it took me to get here. We had a hundred and ten trucks in the convoy stretching over eight miles of road. We had police escorts lead us through large towns. The people all run out to see us go by you know they don't see that many trucks very often. One thing about the Army we stop for nothing.

The camp (Camp Jackson, S.C.) really is beautiful compared to the other two I've been in. I really like it here the days are hot but at least the nights are cool so one can sleep. It's on high ground not in the swamp like Camp Davis or fort Fisher. It's a very large camp too it can house 120 thousand soldiers. Next to Fort Bragg it's the largest in the U.S. we have almost every branch of service in this camp Coast Artillery, Field Artillery, Infantry, Engineers, Cavalry and many others. It's easy to get lost in a place like this. I still don't have my bearing.

So Dad lost another calf he sure is having tough luck with them lately. How is the silo filling, getting along, is he almost through with them?

Well Vi I'll have to close for a while cause I have so many letters to write. Give my love to the kids also Mom and Dad. Say hello to Joe for me. please write soon.

Love to all. Johnny

Thursday, October 7, 1943; Fort Bragg

Dearest Family,
I hope everything is O.K. with you all. How are the kids? Tell them to be good. I am just fine so don't worry. I got a letter from John to say he is O.K. but is so damn busy all the time. I know how it is that's the same thing with me. well I got a letter from John L. to day he is in the same camp I was in last month. I send him some good addresses of some gals! ha.ha.
Well maybe I'll get a pass next week I am not sure. Till I see you or write you may God Bless you all.
Love your brother law Frank

P.S. I hope you can read this. I didn't have time to write. We are going out to night boy it sure is cold.

Sunday, October 10, 1943; Private Frank Maygar, one of approximately a dozen different servicemen that corresponded with Viola and Joe; Fort Hayes Columbus, Ohio

Mr. & Mrs. Joe Soukenik & Family,
This Army life isn't so bad as I thought it was. I really like times and then it's pretty tough at times.
I don't know what I'm going to be as yet or where I will be sent. I expect to find out today or sometime this week. Will write you as soon as I get there.
Best of luck, Frank

Encourage the young men to be self-controlled. In everything set them an example by doing what is good. In your teaching show integrity, seriousness and soundness of speech that cannot be condemned, so that those who oppose you may be ashamed because they have nothing bad to say about us. –Titus 2:6-8

Sunday, October 10, 1943; Camp Jackson, S.C.

Dearest Vi,
This is going to be rather short cause I have a lot of letter writing to do.
I'm sending some more clothes home. Don't be alarmed cause I am not moving or anything like that. It's just that I have too much stuff around and it's hard to take care of especially for inspections it don't look good. I've got an outstanding record for neatness and also clenliness so I don't want to ruin it now. lots of those clothes I don't use and I think Joe can use them. I think I told you about it while I was home. I'll send the shoes later I'm having them repaired. The sweater and scarf you can put away for me at home. That toilet article case is to small it won't hold all my stuff so I got myself a larger bag for that stuff.
I know it seems funny to have a change of address and go to a new place after being there a year and two days. I really like this place it's ever so much nicer than Davis or Fisher. I wish Mother and Veronica could see this place. Frank was here a short time ago. He sent me an address of a nurse in Columbia. I'll have to look her up. We're six miles from Columbia and the bus and cab service is swell. This place is heaven compared to Davis and Fisher I wouldn't mind staying here for the duration. We're living in 5 men huts I like it much better than the large barracks. You can keep a small place like this spotless especially if you have a pretty good bunch of men with you.
Leave it to me I got the boys on the ball. You know me I always did like to keep things clean. One has to be very

particular when so many men are living to-gether.

The Yanks certainly are doing alright. I get the paper every evening and read about it. We also have a radio in our hut so we can keep up on the latest. I suppose Joe is rooting for the Yanks. I'm betting on them too I lost a little dough on that game they lost.

I was worried to hear that the potatoes weren't very good after putting all that work in them. Oh well! I guess you have to take the bad with the good. No hey? Here I worked like hell trying to get ours in and it turned out for the worst.

There is one show I wish you would take the kids to see in fact there is two of them they are "Thank Your Lucky Stars" and "This Is The Army." I thought they were very good and I think the kids would enjoy them.

So Babs is up to 100 already, that's very good. Tell her to keep it up. Tell them their Uncle John is praying for them every chance he gets and that he loves and misses them very much.

Well I'll have to leave you for a while. Give my love to mom and Dad and all. Please write soon and often.

Your loving brother Johnny

Sunday, October 17, 1943

Dearest Family,
I received your letters and was so glad to hear from you and the family. Was good to hear that the family is feeling good. I am just so.

We are going on maneuvers next month November 15 maybe. I'll see Johnie because he said that he was going to. I hope he going on maneuvers in Tennessee. That's where we are going. Well how is Joe working this week tell him not to work to hard because I am that's all I do is work ha ha. Oh yes we have a dance last week, boy. 3 girls want me to come to their home 2 of them have a man but he is over sea <u>get it</u>? just what I like ha ha. I wish Johnie was here to help me get some. Some B.S.

I hope to get a pass before going on maneuvers if I don't I'll not get one till we come back if we come back. Well dear I'll close for this time. May God Bless you all till next time with all my love always, Frank

P.S. Tell the kids to be good like <u>me.</u> Did you see Hank?

Monday, October 18, 1943 Fort Jackson, S.C.

Dearest Soukeniks,

Received your letter to-day and was very happy to hear from you. I received six letters to-day so you can see how much writing I have to do to keep up on my correspondence. Fan mail, you know. All kidding aside it's really funny, maybe I won't get any mail for two days then when it comes it all comes at once. That kind of puts me on the spot. It's hard to answer six letters in one day.

I don't know where Helen got the idea that I needed some cash? I really don't need any unless I get the chance to come home again. If I do I can borrow some off my buddies. I don't think there is any danger of that right away or for some while now. We're suppose to go on maneuvers soon for two or three months. Won't that be swell, I hate to think of it during the winter months especially. I won't need much if I'm out in the field.

Yes I really like this camp and wouldn't mind staying here for a while. You know how it is good things don't last long. Oh well, I guess I can't have everything. I've been pretty lucky in the past with furloughs and all that stuff.

Mother shouldn't go out in the woods to make wood. After all there is a limit to everything and she's getting to old to work that hard. I know how she is you can't stop her no-how. So you can't get coal now things sure are getting tough aren't they? You have some coal aready, haven't you? It certainly will take plenty of wood to cover you through the winter without any coal.

Have you heard from John lately? You know I haven't heard from him in months. I heard Frank heard from him last week. I wrote to John some time ago but haven't received an answer yet.

Frank gave me the address of a nurse in Columbia. He says she's alright I guess I'll have to look her up one of these days and see for myself. I kinda go for nurses I don't know why.

Did Claude come home yet? I certainly hope he gets his 15 days. I'd like to get home in the worst way but I guess that's out of the picture. It's been almost 14 months since I've seen him. How the time flies doesn't it? I'll probably be an old man before I get out of the Army. You know I'll be 23 years old in two months getting to be an old man already. No hey?

So Andy left without saying good-by that's pretty good. I wouldn't lose any sleep over it if I were you. The less I see those people the better I like them. They're probably sore cause I didn't stop over on my furlough. You know I haven't written to Catherine either. I'll bet she thinks I'm a hell of a guy but who cares.

I got a kick out of where you said you ought to crawl in bed with Joe but "poohy on him"! you ain't getting to old for that are you? I wish I had some one to sleep with now. ha! ha! it's getting plenty cold here at night.

Let me know when you get the package. I'll probably send the shoes this week I hope they come in to-day.

I'll leave you for a while. Give my love to Mom, Dad and the kids. Say "hello" to Joe for me and tell him a nurse is all wrapped up and tied with a pink ribbon. Ha! ha! Goodnite.

Your loving brother Johnny

Sunday, October 24, 1943

Dearest Family,
How are you all/ I hope everything is O.K. how is the weather back in Ohio? I wish I was there know. I hear from Johnie to day. He is going on the same maneuvers that I am. Maybe I'll see him there I hope we will go out and have a hell of a good time.
Did your brother come home on furlough? I hope he did. How do he feel? Tell him to write to me. he didn't write to me since he went to the Army. Well how are my kids getting long with school? I hope everything is O.K.
Well Viola how is Joe? Is he working everyday? I hope he don't have to go to the Army. I'll be close for this time to day I am on C.Q. sure am busy.
May God Bless you all. Love Frank

Sunday, October 31, 1943; Fort Jackson, South Carolina

Dearest Vi,
I'm sorry I didn't get a chance to write sooner but we're rather busy lately. Getting ready for the maneuvers you know. We work until late at night on the equipment getting everything in top shape. That is besides our regular duties during the day so you can see how much time I have to myself now. I'm C.Q. to-day so this gives me a chance to write and catch up on my letter writing.
I made it back in plenty of time in fact I had to wait for my train in Youngstown and also in Washington. I was back in camp at midnite Wed. and I really didn't have to be in until six in the morning. I didn't meet any babe on the train this time cause I was

sleeping most of the way and didn't care to look around. there were plenty of good lookin prospects but I was to tired to do any good in fact I couldn't keep my eyes open. You know I didn't have any sleep for about three days. Staying out all nite on Monday nite finished me off. We were at the "Hollyhock Gardens" and the (Singh G.). Wow! What a nite. We were drinking most of the nite and I'm not used to that. The kids wanted to stay out all nite and celebrate like we used to before we went to the Army and we did. That's why I want you to tell "Ma" to keep things straight in case the Old Man should ask. You see they called up and told him they had trouble with the car and that they were staying over our place for the nite. If he knew we didn't have trouble with the car and stayed out all night he would raise hell with the girls. So don't forget to tell Ma to keep the end of the story up.

  You weren't kidding when you said I was here to-day and gone to-morrow. Gee! How the time flies it all seems like a dream. Doesn't it? I hated to leave but I guess I was pretty lucky to get home even for that short time. I probably won't see you for several months now. Maybe in Feb. or March after the maneuvers are over. I'll probably get a furlough then.

  I'll send the kids the gum one of these days. I'll go down to the P.X. and talk to my (boy) I'll give him the business and he'll sell it to me. if he don't there are other ways and means of getting it. Just leave it up to me and it will be taken care of. Don't worry about the money part either, where I'm going I won't need money. I know it cost me a lot to come home this time but I don't care it was worth it. After all what's money mean if you can't get home and have some fun??? I get paid to-morrow of course most of it will go to pay off the boys but that's nothing I won't be needing much money from now on and I can manage on what I got. If I ever need any more the boys are willing to let me have it. My name is good for any amount so I have no worries.

  As for the clothes they weren't much and I was more than glad to give them to him if he can use them. As for the shoes they didn't cost me cent and I don't want any money or anything for any of that stuff. Oh well! You could send me some nut filled horns when I'm out on maneuvers they'll probably come in handy. I'm just one step ahead of the supply men and every chance I get I screw them out of something. When I got these shoes the supply man couldn't understand how I had one pair size 8 ½ and one 12 ½ the ones I gave to father. I just laughed in his face and told him I used the size 12 ½ when my feet was swollen from a hike. If I get a chance to do them out of something else I will and send it home. There is more than one way to get things in the Army and I know quite a few of the angles which I have taken advantage of already.

  I suppose mother is still sore at me and I'm terribly sorry now. although I think she understands when a guy comes home he wants to have a hell of a time and doesn't spend as much time at home as he should. It seems a fellow doesn't realize it until he is gone and then it's to late. I'm in a rather tough spot with Ceil living so far away. I wish she lived closer that would make everything much better. Maybe I shouldn't have a girl so far away but I can't help it she's the only one that ever really appealed to me. I suppose you know that by now.

  Well did your cow come in yet? I know it's tough without milk and butter. How are you set on feed for her this winter or are you going to keep her at our place?

  Well Vi I'll have to leave you for a while cause I have so many letters to write. Give my love to Mom, dad and the kids. Say hello to Joe for me and tell him to take it easy. Please write soon and God Bless you all.

  Love to all Johnny

      Monday, November 1, 1943

  Dearest Family,
  I received your letter but did not get time to write we are so damn busy all the time. So John was home again. I wish I could

get home to but it look like I will not. I think my outfit going over sea soon. Next week we will be in Tenn. My address will be new I'll send it to you soon.

How are my kids? Is Joey and Bar. Good kids tell them to be good like there Uncle ha ha some B.S.

Well I'll be close for we are busy all the time. To day we are going out in the field for 3 days. Some men from Wash. D.C. are here to see if we can go over sea. I know damn well we will be going soon.

With all my love, Frank

P.S. Is Joe working every day I hope so.

Wednesday, November 3, 1943

Dearest Vi,

This is going to be very short cause I haven't much time at present.

The main purpose of it is to let you know we're moving out early Sunday morning. We're going sooner than we expected so you can see how we're pressed for time. You will get my new address from Post Hq. in Fort Jackson. They will send a card home notifying you as to what it will be. No one is to know where we are going. You know things in the Army can be changed so quickly. One minute you're going one direction the next minute the other.

I don't know whether I can get the gum yet or not cause they didn't have any lately but I'm still watching. If they get some in I'll get it you can be sure of that.

I'm also sending my old suitcase home with some stuff. Joe can have the khaki suit if he wants. Give Dad a pair of gloves the new ones cause they're larger. The flash lite leave at home in our car and that mosquito net might be used at home when I come back. There'll probably be some more small things too so let them at home I may need them some time. I'm undecided on some of the stuff I should send so you won't know what to expect in it. I'm only allowed to take two bags with me so I'll have to figure something out quick.

  Well Vi you probably won't hear from me for a little while until I reach my new home which probably will be a fox hole. Don't worry cause I'll write as soon as I get there.

  Don't forget write as soon as you get my new address. I'll leave you for now. Give my love to Mom, Dad and the kids. Say hello to Joe for me. So long.

  All my love, Johnny

Chapter Thirteen

Sunday, November 7, 1943

Dear Viola,
Well here I am back at camp. I got back Thursday morning just when I expected to. Just as I got back they told me I was a day ahead of time. I could of stayed home until Thursday nite. Boy did that make me mad.

Boy did I hate to leave Wednesday. The darn time seemed to go so fast I didn't get to do half the things I wanted to do. I wanted to spend more time with the kids. They are sure two sweet kids. I hated to leave them.

I wish Johnny could have been home longer. I didn't get to see him much at all. Well maybe we will see each other again before long. Maybe for good this time.

Tell Joe to get in touch with Mr. Betley and see what can be done about getting me out. Joe said he could get me out. I sure hope so because I can't do much here. Not with the Commanding Officer I have. He is just mad because he didn't get out.

I still didn't get my barracks bags. By the way it looks I won't too. I had a lot of things in them I wanted. I sure hope they turn up before long.

Those horns you and mother made sure were swell. Thanks a lot. The boys and I ate the last of them last nite. Helen gave me a nice box of cookies too.

I got one of your letters you sent just before I came home. I am sorry I didn't write to you since I have been here. I have been so darn busy that I can't find the time to do much writing. I will try and do better from now on. At least I will try an answer all I get from you. Your letters sure build up my moral. It makes me feel good to get letters from home. If only I could write better and more often.

Well I will close for now. I just can't seem to think of anything to write. I will write more often when I hear from you.
Goodby and God bless you all. Claude

P.S. Tell Joe I said hello, and the kids too. I miss them so much.

As the 37th buckeye Division landed on Bougainville, all John could say as his boots hit the sand was, "You gotta love those Leathernecks!" The beachhead was only half a mile at its widest point before being abruptly met by the densest jungle that John had ever seen. They were only a week behind the Marines, but what lay before him was evidence enough that every square foot of beach surrounding Empress August Bay was fought for and won. The sand was littered with makeshift foxholes and expended shell casings while the woods line looked virtually untouched with the exception of several freshly cut swaths extending into the dark moisture soaked foliage almost like fingers trying to grip something that continued to elude capture.

The U.S. Army's goal was clear secure the captured perimeter, reinforce the area with defensive patrols and commence construction of roads, bridges and an airfield within the six-mile objective on Bougainville. With the deepest port captured and the strategic airfield in place, there was no reason to lose time or men hacking across the impenetrable jungles of the 250-mile island. The dug in Imperial Japanese Army would not realize this strategy until the late winter and early spring of 1944 when they would try to go on the offensive.[16]

---

[16] www.Wikipedia.org

Wednesday, November 10, 1943; Tennessee Maneuvers, "Somewhere in Tennessee"

Dear Viola,

I received your wonderful letter last week but didn't have time to answer it because we were moving.

We traveled about 500 miles by truck convoy through S.C., Ga., and Tenn., where we are now in the maneuver area. It was a nice trip although one can't enjoy it driving in convoy and also driving a truck, which I did. I drove the mess truck all the way. I usually don't drive that truck but it required a good driver over the mts., so they gave it to me. I'm not bragging but one has to be careful with that truck cause they cook meals on the run. When we stop the food is ready and we eat and then travel along in a short time. It only takes an hour to feed a hundred men and then move on. I think that's pretty fast don't you?

The mountains through Northern Ga. and Tenn. are really beautiful. I would like to make that trip by car after the war is over and really enjoy the wonderful scenery.

Well we're here now and it looks plenty rough. It snowed a little the other night and believe me it's plenty cold sleeping on the ground. I sleep with my clothes on and I have four blankets but it's still plenty cold. I hate to think of what it will be like in December and January when there's six inches of snow on the ground.

I'm glad to hear that Joe got a new job. I'm sure he'll make good at it and get more money. If he sticks with it he might get a good job, I certainly hope he does, he deserves it if anyone does. Tell him I said to stick with it and if I know Joe he will.

I think I'll have turkey for Thanksgiving cause I've spotted ten of them to-day. If no one beats me to them I'll have one of them you can bet your life on that. This cowboy won't starve as long as there's turkeys and pigs running around. also tell Joe there are a lot of rabbits around here. Gee! I get homesick every time I kick one out and wish I had a shot gun with me.

I hope you had a nice time at the chicken dinner the other night. You did go didn't you?

How are the kids? I hope Barbara wasn't seriously ill, as you told me she was sick. I miss them very much.

I suppose you are having snow by now aren't you? I hope you don't have a tough winter.

I imagine you got my new address from Veronica by now. Please write soon and often cause it seems I haven't had any mail for months. That's all I have to look forward to now out in the field. I'll need plenty of it to keep up my morale now. It's going to be tough being out in the field during the holidays but I guess there is nothing I can't take.

I'll close for a while, give my love to Mom, Dad, and the kids. Say hello to Joe for me. Goodnite.

All my love, Johnny

P.S. My letters probably will be short and few now but don't worry about me I'll be alright.

I was just wondering if you got my packages yet or not. I sent the kids some gum and there was a pair of gloves in that box give them to dad and that flashlite I want for our car cause they should have one in it for night travel. My suitcase had a pair of khakis which Joe can have and that old pair of gloves which are very good yet.

Oh yes! I forgot to tell Veronica in my last note and I don't know how soon I'll be able to write her again. I want this as soon as possible that is a hood. You've probably seen them they cover all over your head and neck the only thing showing is your face. I would like to have one as soon as possible cause it's cold. They're made of brown wool and just come down to the shoulders. I tried to buy one in Columbia but they didn't have any. See what you can do and send it as soon as you can I certainly would appreciate it.

I certainly hope you can read this. I'm writing it by flash light and all crouched up in my pup tent, it's not vey comfortable but that's the best we have out here.

I didn't take a bath for a week and boy, do I feel crummy. If I find a river I'll dive in ice or no ice. I'll be able to eat nails when I get off of these maneuvers I'll be so tough.

Once more I'll close for a while. I'll write as soon as I get another chance so don't worry. Please write soon. Goodnite.

All my love again, Johnny

So be strong, show yourself a man, and observe what the Lord your God requires. Walk in his ways, and keep his decrees and commands, his laws and requirements, as written in the Law of Moses, so that you may prosper in all you do and wherever you go,… -1 Kings 2:3

Sunday, November 14, 1943; Battery "A" 793rd F.A. BN.

Dearest Family,
I received your letter to day out in the woods. We are have a hell of a time out here. I think maybe I'll see John out in the woods some place he said he was going to. But you said that he was going over sea I hope not.

Well Joe is working days that's fine I hope he likes this job. Tell him not to work to hard. I'm glad to hear that the kids are O.K. & working in school good tell them to be like there Uncle Frank ha ha.

The weather here is cold and rainy & a little snow this morning. Yesterday it rained all day it's hell but maybe I'll be O.K. I hope so. my back is giving me hell but I want to go with the outfit over sea this outfit will go in the next 2 mo. some time in Jan. or the last of Dec. but don't worry I'll be O.K. pray for me & God will help me.

I'll close for this time because it's cold and I can't write much. O yes, is Claude in Indiantown Gap?

Well good night may God Bless you all take good care of yourself and the family.

Always Love Frank

Sunday eve, November 14, 1943; Indiantown Gap Military Reservation Pennsylvania

Dear Viola,

I received your letter a few days ago and was very glad to hear from you. You know a letter from you means a lot to me.

I am sorry that I haven't written to you. They have kept us so busy that we even haven't had time to sleep. For a week straight we have been working 18 hrs a day. We work like hell all day then at nite we go on problems.

Well we won't be here much longer. We are going on maneuvers to Virginia and West Virginia. They won't be very long and I am glad of it. Because I hear they are to be tough.

So you have been hearing quite often from Johnny. I am glad to hear that he is well. I wish I had more time to write. So Johnny talks as though he may go across soon. Well I don't suppose it will be too long before my outfit goes places. But there isn't much you can do about it. A fox hole isn't a very good place to spend the winter. I can think of a lot better places to be.

I wish I could send things home for the kids and Joe. I have been trying to get some clothes to send home but haven't been able too. That supply room of ours doesn't have anything or I don't know how to get it. I still haven't gotten my clothes back from the hospital. I have been asking about them every chance I get. I sure hope I get them soon.

The reason I returned a day ahead of time was because I

didn't understand my furlough paper. They didn't explain just how it was. Well I will know better the next time.

Have you heard from John Soukenik yet? I am sure he is all right though. At least I hope so. I sure would hate to see him get hurt or something. You don't find swell fellows like him every day. He certainly deserves every break in the world.

Yes I know Mr. Hopkins. But I didn't know he was sick. When I saw him last he looked pretty good. Things sure do happen pretty fast don't they?

Well is Joe and Dad still making wood? They should have quite a pile by now. I wish I could have had help them more. But I had so many things I wanted to do. Maybe the next time I come home it will be for good. How is Dad getting along with the corn? I hope he gets it all husked before the rats and mice do.

Well how does Joe feel? I hope his cold is better. That is one thing I can't keep from getting. I have had one two thirds of the time that I am in the Army. I don't feel very bad rite know but if I do I go rite on sick call. That is one place I am not afraid to go.

I must be closing for now. it is time for the lights to go out. I will write more later. Goodby and God Bless you all.

Lots of love and kisses, Claude

P.S. please say hello to Joe and the kids.

So I say, walk by the Spirit, and you will not gratify the desires of the flesh. For the flesh desires what is contrary to the Spirit, and the Spirit what is contrary to the flesh. They are in conflict with each other, so that you are not to do whatever you want. –Galatians 5:16-17

Monday, November 15, 1943

Dearest Vi,
This letter will probably come as quite a shock to you, but just hang onto something solid may be you will pull through. I have been rec'd your letters and also the swell pictures (more about that later). Right now I want to know about you and family. Hope you are all feeling fine and enjoying the winter weather. Say! I wish I had some of it right now. It's pretty warm over here.
Heard from the boys lately? I mean Johnny and Frank. I'm still waiting to hear from Claude. I guess he is like me too darn busy to write. Sure is good to hear from them once in a while. It would be swell if I'd run into one of them over here. I keep looking for there outfit. I have ran into a few boys that I know from Ohio but very few. I'm glad to hear that Johnny & Claude got together on their last furlough. That was really swell. I bet they really whoop it up, I don't blame them. I wish I could have been there with them, I would've drank them dry. Say, it's been a long time since I had a good drink of good old U.S.A. whiskey.
I suppose you wonder how I am and how I am doing. I'm fine and doing O.K. we are now permitted to say that we have been in Air raids and Bombings, but we are always in a safe spot at the right time. I hope so! Ha. Ha. Outside of that, I haven't much more to write about, but remember I'm always thinking of you all and now is a good time to wish you all a Merry Xmas and a happy new year. Take care of yourself and family. Say hello to Joe, Joey, Bab, and all your folks. I'll write more when I have time, I'm very busy at the present time. Thanks for the pictures they're swell.
Love and kisses to all. John

Let love and faithfulness never leave you; bind them around your neck, write them on the tablet of your heart. Then you

will win favor and a good name in the sight of God and man.
 —Proverbs 3:3-4

Wednesday, November 17, 1943; Tennessee Maneuvers

Dearest Vi,

I was very happy to receive your letter and I'd like to have more of them.

I'm glad to hear that you finally received the packages. I put them up so fast that I didn't know whether they'd get there or not. As you said about the gum I tried to get it when I got back but they didn't have any. Then finally before we left for Tenn. I found some at one P.X. and I bought all I could and sent it.

About my address you people worry to much. Don't worry about me I'll be alright. You know me I can take care of myself I always did. As for going across it will be a long time I think.

I haven't met Frank yet but I hope to before it is all over. You know when there are 100,000 soldiers it's hard to make contact. I wrote him a letter and hope to find out where he is. So far he didn't give me any information as to where he is but I know he is here somewhere.

Betley won by a large margin, it's funny you didn't get it in the paper.

I'm sure glad you got the heifers in without any trouble. Remember the time we had several years ago?

I must leave you for a while. Give my love to Mom and Dad and the kids.

Write soon and often. Goodnite. Love, Johnny

Wednesday, November 17, 1943

Dear Viola,

I am sorry I haven't been writing as much as I should. I have been so darn busy I just could not write. You know I wouldn't forget you. Just what kind of a brother would I be to forget the ones I love. If I don't write it is because I wasn't able to. I am thinking of you even if I don't write.

I hate to disappoint you but we are leaving the Gap to nite for West Va, on mountain maneuvers. They are to last about 14 days. I sure do dread to go because they are going to be plenty tough.

I went to the dentist to day and had 4 teeth pulled out so you can imagine about how I feel. I also had two plates put in. now I have a full mouth of teeth.

You don't have to worry about that hat. I know it was hard to sew it back without looking at another hat. I bought one as soon as I had a chance.

I have enough socks. I just got a supply that ought to last for a while. I can't think of anything that I need. I ought to be sending things home like John is. I have a lot to send but I don't know how I am going to send it since we are going on maneuvers. Maybe I will be able to later.

You can send me anything for Christmas, but make it small and don't pay to much money. Please don't expect anything from me because I will be unable to get where I can buy something. I sure wish I could though. At least for the kids. I am pretty sure that John S. is getting your mail and packages, but probably hasn't had time to write. I wish I would have written to him. He is just like a brother to me. And I miss him as one.

So you had a thrill in your car the other day. I know that just how it is. I had many of them the same way. You just have to be darn careful on those icy roads.

Yes I sure will miss my hunting. Well Joe can do my share

this year. And maybe I will be home for the next hunting season. At least I hope so.

So Shirley was able to get home. I bet he is glad to get home. He sure has seen a lot of the world hasn't he? Of course I would rather see it in peace time. Did he come over to see you and the folks?

Well I must close for now I have to get a hair cut yet and a good nite sleep for tomorrow's ride. I would like to rite a lot more because it will be some time before I will be able to write again.

Good by and God Bless you all.
Love and kisses to all. Claude

P.S. Please say hello to Joe and the kids and that I am thinking of them all the time.

Thursday, November, 18, 1943

Dear Vi,
Just a few lines to tell you not to get that hood that I mentioned in my previous letter. I bought one in town the other day so don't bother if you haven't already got it. Of course if you have send it and I'll sell it to someone or you probably can take it back and exchange it for something else.

I'll close for now. give my love to all and write soon. Goodnite.
Love, Johnny

P.S. I wish Joe could see all the rabbits that are here he'd have a picnic. I never saw so many in a short distance in all my life. If they don't feed us we can always go hunting and have rabbit.

Saturday, November 20, 1943

Dearest Family,
I received your letter to night & was so glad for you to hear that everything is fine with you all. I writing this by candle in my tent. It sure is cold in this tent but I am getting warm with all my blankets. We have 4 of them for one man.
I hope to see John L. to day he is 25 miles from me. I am thinking of going to Nashville to day if I can.
Well dear I'll close say hello to my dear Bar. and Joie may God Bless you all. Love Frank

Friday, November 26, 1943; Battery "A" 793RD F.A. BN.

Dearest Family,
I have received your letter to day was so glad to know that everything is O.K. with you all and to know Joe is working every day.
Tell Bar. and Joie to be good because Xmas is coming. I hope I can get them something for Xmas but we will be out here till Jan. if I don't I'll get them something when I get a pass if I get a pass if not I'll take one. I didn't see John this week but maybe I'll see him to night. I am getting a pass for 8 hrs. so maybe I'll see him in Nashville. We are so busy all the time to day we went for a walk 18 miles just a little one ha. ha. Next week we will be busy all week if I get 8 hr. sleep all week it will be fine. Well I'll close for this time may God Bless you all say hello to your Mother & the family for me.
Love, Frank

Monday, November 29, 1943

Dearest Family,
I received your letter and was so damn glad to hear from you so soon. How are you all getting along back home it's pretty cold here.
So you got your letter from John. I am glad to know that he is O.K. I wrote him a letter to day. I didn't write for a long time because we been busy all the time. I did not see John this week. I was in Nashville this week I hope to see him soon. I don't know if I can go to Nashville because just 5 per the Battery go in one week and I was there so maybe next year I'll get a pass. How are my kids Bar. and Joie getting long in school? Tell them to be good when I get home I'll see what kind of school grades the kids have. I hope as good as mine. ha. ha.
Well Viola I don't think I'll get time to write this coming week because we will be busy all week. I'll write more when I can.
With all my love. May God Bless you all. Your brother law Frank

Sunday Eve., December 5, 1943

Dear Viola,
Well here we are in Camp Pickett and in barracks again. It sure is swell after being out in the woods. It sure was tough out there but not too tough for me. I did a lot better than I thought I would. Yes it was cold at times but that didn't bother me as much as the pack we carried. It weighted a ton but when nite came we were glad to have it with us. We had a sleeping bag in this pack and was it nice and warm. When I get out of this Army I am going to have one of them.

You know Viola we went rite through Davis, West Virginia when on maneuvers. But we were on a truck and it was nite so I couldn't see much. It sure made me want to stop and visit the Pachosas.

Well how was Joey's and Barbara's report card? I sure hope they are as good as they have been.

I have hoping for a three day pass but I don't know wheather I can get home on such a short time. The buss service isn't very good. It takes so darn long to get to a town to catch a train. If I can get a pass and can make it home I am going to try and get home for Christmas. But don't plan on it because I may not make it. It sure would be swell to be able too. That would be the best Christmas present I could get. Just to be home for that day.

I wish I could get something for the kids at least. If I get a chance to come home I will be sure to bring them something. I just can't do enough for them. I think so much of them.

Gosh I didn't even know just how old you was or when your birthday came. It doesn't seem like you are 30 yet. You know it won't be long befor I am that old too. I feel like 50. This Army isn't helping me any. Yes Johnny will be 23 this December. It seems like just last year we celebrated his 21st birthday doesn't it?

It sure will be tough if Joe has to go, but I don't think he will. If he doesn't go before Spring he won't go at all. I think there will be a lot of changes before then. You said it Mother would have too much to do. She has too much rite now to suit me.

My teeth feel much better then they did. I am not quit used to them yet. My gums are still sore where the 4 teeth were pulled out. Now I only have 9 of my own left. The dentist at home told me I would have to have them pulled out. I mean all the top ones so I wasn't surprised when they wanted to pull them here. My new ones look good thank heavens.

So Joe got a bird already. Does he get a chance to go very often. I sure miss hunting. I think it won't be long before I do some hunting, of course it will be a different kind of hunting.

I got a letter from Helen today. She told me about being sick and how hard it is to get a Dr. It is to bad that she can't have a Dr. when she needs one but it is a good thing she is near the hospital. She told me about going to California. I think it is a good idea. The air is much dryer and that is what she needs.

I got your package that mother and you sent. It sure was swell. It couldn't have been any better. I ate every bit of it my self. It came just after the maneuvers were over and was I ever hungry. That is the trouble out in the field we never get enough to eat.

Well Viola I must close for now. It is time to go to bed. I wanted to write in the day time but was put on detail. I would like to write a lot more because I don't get to write very often. I will write more as soon as I get a chance.

Goodby and God Bless you all.
Love and kisses, Your brother Claude

Chapter Fourteen

Tuesday, December 7, 1943

Dearest Vi,
I have a few minutes off to day, so I thought I'll drop you a few lines to let you know that I am O.K. and in the best of health and hope this letter fines you and family the same. I know you are disappointed in me for not writing more often. I know you appreciated the letters I used to write and I certainly used to love to write them to you, but we been busy around here lately. I can't tell you what we have been doing but you can take my word for it that we haven't been laying around any. This is the first slack time I have had in the last three months. I know you realize the hardships we soldiers endure, and we know that you folks back home have it plenty hard too. Well, may be soon this nightmare of war will end and we can all be together again. Any way we hope so, Right? You said in your letter that your Mother dreamed of me coming home. I wish that was truth, but I am afraid it will be a long time before I come home, course any thing can happen. It could be possible. I sure miss you folks, and wish I was coming home soon. I've been away too long to suit me.
Vi, have you been hearing from the boys lately? I've heard from Frank and John, but not from Claude. I guess he don't know my address. I hope they're still in the states. I really don't like to see them go over sea. It's no fun.
I heard that Agnes Smida got married to Whitey. Well she got a swell fellow, Whitey will make her a good husband. Course I felt bad about it at first, but after I thought it over it made me

happy. Agnes was one swell kid, but when a fellow is over seas, it's better if you forget about women. Don't get me wrong, I like to hear from them, but I do not want them to wait for me. you never know what may happen.

Now for a little news about this place. We've really been busy and have little time to our selfs. We did have a swell Thanksgiving. Turkey for supper. That is a little out of the way! (We usually have spam). Oh yes we had ice cream too. First ice cream in over nine months. it was really good too some thing like the kind you use to make. All in all I've had a good Thanksgiving.

I suppose the weather is pretty cold up home now. Boy, I wish that we could keep some of it here. We aren't allowed to talk about the weather, but you can imagine what it's like in the tropics. It is plenty hot. I suppose Joe is doing a little hunting now. Is he getting any thing? Or is he still shoting around them? How's my little honeys? I bet Joey and Babs are still as sweet as ever. I sure miss them.

Well honey, I'll have to close now, but I'll write again soon. Merry Christmas and a Happy New Year to all say hello to your folks. May God Bless you all.

Lots of love and kisses, John

But those who hope in the Lord will renew their strength. They will soar on wings like eagles. They will run and not grow weary; they will walk and not be faint. –Isaiah 40:31

Tuesday, December 7, 1943

Dearest Vi,
I'm sorry I didn't get a chance to write you sooner but circumstances won't permit. I'm so darn busy I hardly have time to breathe.

We have four days of maneuvers then we go to a bivouac

area or so called (<u>rest camp</u>). I don't know why they call it a rest camp cause I work harder there than I do on maneuvers. We have all of our equipment to clean besides our own personal stuff such as trying to wash clothes in a gallon of water. They expect you to keep clean and they won't get you any water to do so. We were lucky once our bivouac area was near a river. I went in for a swim that day and boy was it cold. It felt darn good after I came out though I felt like a million dollars. It's surprising how much better a little water makes a man feel.

    I haven't received your package as yet. I can't figure what's delaying it. I certainly hope it isn't lost! It's been on its way for nine days now. My tongue is hanging out every time I think of it and I wait for it every mail call but no package. After this don't tell me when you send a package. I suffer to much thinking about it. Here I am eating cheese and jelly sandwiches or sometimes nothing. I'll let you know as soon as I get it. I hope it's soon!

    I was glad to hear you had a nice Thanksgiving. We had turkey but I couldn't enjoy it under such conditions. Oh well, I guess it was as good as could be expected out in the field. I don't mind it anymore I am getting used to it now. We've been out in the field for more than a month now. I feel like a cave man and probably look like one too. I'm starting to raise a mustache, now don't laugh! I'll let you know how it comes out later, (after a few weeks).

    I haven't met Frank yet, we had plans of the sort more or less but I've been to busy week ends and couldn't get into Nashville. It seems this radio section never will catch up on work, 24 hours a day seven days a week that's us.

    I want to congratulate you on your 30th birthday, I hope you have many more of them and may they all be happy ones too!

    I wanted to send you a card but I think you know how it is out here. I haven't been in a town for four weeks now so I don't even know how the outside world live any more.

    So the boys went out hunting and didn't get any thing! ha!

ha! I guess I'll have to come home and show them how to hunt. I certainly miss my hunting this year, every time I chase out a rabbit it makes me homesick. There certainly is a lot of them up here in the hills, if I only had my gun. I tried to sneak up on them with my club but they're to smart and run out.

It seems hard to believe that Charles Jackson is going so soon. I still think of him as a kid although we have some smaller than he in our outfit. I also hear Walter Wysenski went for his blood test? I suppose Ann is crying and don't know what to do. Oh well, maybe this thing won't last to long.

What did John have to say? You know I haven't heard from him in about 4 months. I wrote him several letters and don't know whether he got them or not. Of course I know he's plenty busy and probably don't have time for writing. I'm judging by what we do out here and we're on this side. I very seldom have a moment to myself.

How is everyone and everything at home? Are the kids well? Tell them I said they should keep on praying for me cause I haven't been in church or heard mass for two weeks or more. We don't have a chaplain anymore cause I guess there is a shortage of them.

I was captured last week by the red army forces and didn't get anything to eat for two days. I told Veronica that we were at an outpost last week well, the next morning we were captured. It was a good experience, they tried to make things just as real as possible. They made us take all of our stuff out of our pockets and they questioned us to see what outfit we were with but they were disappointed none of the boys would talk.

Well Vi, I must leave you for a while, I'll write as soon as I get another chance. Give my love to Mom, Dad and Kids.

Love your brother, Johnny

  P.S. tell Joe I'll show him how to hunt when I get home.
   ha. ha.

Monday Night, December 13, 1943

Dear Viola,

I got your letter a few days ago and was very glad to hear from you. I thought maybe I could have answered sooner then I did but have been rather busy. I try to write at least one letter a week but am not doing a very good job of it. As to my where abouts you need not worry. It will be at least 2 or 3 more months before I leave the States and maybe longer.

Yes, we are through with maneuvers & now we are training for beach landing. This training is rather tough too. They are really trying to toughen us up. Yesterday, we had a force march. We made 3 miles in one half a hr. and eight miles in one hr. & thirty eight minutes. You should have seen the boys tongues hanging out. The heck of it is we have another tomorrow and Thursday.

It sure would be nice to come home for Christmas. I have been hoping they would give out passes for Xmas but I don't know yet wheather they will or not. I know that Johnny is a good and fast talker, but he isn't in my outfit and that makes a lot of difference. Yes, this outfit is due to go places. It is an old outfit and it is about time something is done with it. I shouldn't be saying all of this but I trust it will not go any farther than you.

I am glad to hear the kids are doing so well in school. Of course I am not at all suprised. They have what it takes. So they are having a Christmas play. I wish I could be home to see it. I sure like to see little kids reciting poems. They are so cute on the stage. I bet you already have new cloths for them. That is why I always liked Christmas. I always new then I would get new cloths and lots of nice things to eat.

So Dad finally bought his buss rig from Metz. For a while there I thought he wouldn't buy from him I don't think he would of gotten a better deal from anyone else. It wouldn't pay Metz to cheat father out of anything. Not after the way we have been *buying from him. I sure wish I could come home to try it out. I like to buss wood. Especialy if you have a good outfit. Tell Joe to take care of it and everything else.*

I am glad to hear that mother is getting her citizen papers. I wish father was getting his too. They sure did a lot of running around but it was worth it.

Gosh you know I haven't gone to church for 2 Sundays. It seems as though every Sunday I am put on a detail. I don't even know when the Holy Days of Obligation are. That is what I hate about this Army. You can't go to church every Sunday. I suppose I could go long as I was in a camp but I would have a lot of trouble getting permission you see we get one Sunday out of three off. This isn't like Camp Wheeler where we had every Sunday off. This is the 77th Division.

I got a letter from John the other day. I wrote one to him the same day. I suppose I should have wrote long ago but I have been just to busy to write very much. He told me how tough he is having it. well, I know just how tough maneuvers are. I have been on three of them. I sure wouldn't want to go through them again.

It sure is to bad they don't have more corn. But that is the way it is. If you have one thing you don't have the other. Eggs aren't worth much if you have to buy all the feed.

Don't you know what detail means. I thought you knew. It means a job that has to be done that doesn't pertain to your training. Such as K.P. or work in the supply room etc. Just odd jobs that has to be done. Just the Pvt's get these details.

Well I must close for now. I must get some rest if I am to make the force march tomorrow. Goodby. And God Bless you all.

Love and kisses to all, Claude.

P.S. A sleeping bag is a bag we sleep in during maneuvers. It is a long bag that you get into. I just don't know how to describe it. all I know is they are darn warm and I wish I had one. It is so darn warm in one you can sleep rite out in the snow. I already did just that in West Va.

Sunday Night, December 19, 1943

Dear Viola,

Just a few lines to let you know I got your beautiful Christmas card. It sure makes me feel good to get such nice cards from home.

I am all right except for a cold, but I always have one so it isn't anything new. I am sorry I haven't written to you very much lately. But you know how it is when you are busy and besides having a cold. When I get home from a days work I just don't feel like doing anything. It sure is too bad about you and mother being down with a cold at the same time. I bet there isn't much done at home. That Is the heck of it with two old people on the farm. You just can't tell when they will become sick. But you can't tell these guys anything.

I am expecting a pass this wk. but don't know for sure. Some of the boys got theirs this weekend. I didn't want mine because of the weekend rush. If I get one this wk. it will be either Monday or Thursday. It is only a 3 day pass so I won't be home very long.

It's too bad about Mat Smida's death. She must of took her husbands death pretty hard.

I didn't get your Christmas package yet. I sure hope I get them before I leave for home. Hard telling what it would be like by the time I got back. I am sorry you had to work so hard to get them ready to send. You should have had Veronica help you pack them. I am sure she would have had a little time.

Well I must close for now. I must get to bed and get some sleep. Goodby and God Bless you all.

Love Brother Claude

Monday, December 20, 1943

Dearest Soukeniks,
I received yours and mothers package about two weeks ago but didn't have a chance to write. It took 20 days for it to get here and much to my disappointment the belongings was spoiled. I think it would have kept if it wasn't cooked. I don't know what took it so long to get here. The horns were delicious and they certainly came in handy. We all dove into that box like wolves so you could imagine how long it lasted. Thanks a lot Vi I really appreciate it.

I suppose you people are all disappointed in me this year but it just can't be helped. I'm rather low on money this month cause I lost my coat or someone stole it and I had to buy a new coat. By the time these maneuvers are over I won't have any clothes or they'll all be ruined. I wanted to go to Nashville to at least get some cards but couldn't. I haven't been in town for three weeks. I was in Lebanon but it's a small jerk town and you can't get anything there. I know the kids and mother especially will be disappointed but it's just one of those things that can't be helped. I thought I could at least get Mother a large card like I used to but I couldn't.

I hear you've been having some pretty cold weather lately. Well it hasn't been to pleasant out here either the other morning it got down to 4° below zero. I'm getting used to it now I'm so damn tough that I don't feel a thing anymore. We only have another month of this if it don't get much colder I think I'll make it out alright.

I got a letter and also a card from Claude last week. I wrote him first and got an immediate answer which surprised me. It seems I always have to write first or I'd never hear from him.

I didn't hear from Frank for some time now. Bessie wrote and told me his back is bothering him again. I can see why, this weather out here isn't helping him any. Have you heard from John lately? You know I haven't heard from him since July.

You said the kids were having a good time sliding, I'll bet they enjoy the weather like that even though it is cold. I wish I had my skates here I could go for a little skate myself.

So Joe isn't getting many rabbits or pheasants this year? I know it's hard for one guy to hunt. Is he using my dog or isn't he any good? I guess I won't get a chance to do any hunting this year unless I get a furlough and hunt after the season is over, which I will if I do. We might get furloughs after these maneuvers are over. I hope!

I think Ceil and the family are going to be out at the farm for Christmas. At least that's what she said in her last letter.

I'll have to leave you for now. I hope you all have a good time, have a few drinks for me. I'll be thinking of you.

Give my love to all. I wish everyone of you a very Merry Christmas and a Happy New Year.

So long. Love, Johnny

Wednesday Night, December 22, 2943

Dearest Sister,
Well Viola first of all I better tell you something I wish I didn't have to. That is that I won't be home for Christmas. Christmas will be probably be over with by the time you get this letter but in case I don't get to send a telegram you will know I am not coming home. I have been hoping and praying I could get a pass it didn't do any good. Just a few of the married boys are getting passes and they have to be close to camp. The rest of us are to get them after the next phase of our training is over. That will be in about 3 or 4 weeks.

I am sorry I haven't been writing home as often as I should, but I don't feel very good. I am down with a cold and after working hrs. I have been going rite to bed. You know what kind of colds I get. Well I have one now and it isn't very pleasant. I am going on sick call in the morning & see what they can do for me.

Don't worry if I could only get a pass I would get home alrite. I would get there one way or another. But just get a pass. You'll never know how much I want to get home. Well maybe I'll be home for good by this time next year. At least I hope so.

I got your package and in good shape to. The cookies were swell and everything else was too. Thanks a lot for everything.

Catherine told me about Julius's house burning. I can't see how you got a chance to save so much. It is such a small house you would think it would burn down awful quick. You sure have had a lot of things happening around home. Deaths, fires etc.

What the heck happened to the calf price? I thought meat was awful high rite now? you should of at least gotten $20 for it. How is the cow? Is she giving a lot of milk?

Well did you get a Christmas tree from Ruetenik's? I imagin they are high. They always are around Christmas. I wish I was still working there maybe I would get a big bonus. I sure do miss that 2 hundred or so extra that I have been getting the last few years.

Well I better close for now. I feel so darn bad I can't even think straight. Gosh I wish I had a 15 day furlough coming rite now. So I could go hunting with Joe. I sure do miss my hunting days.

Goodby and Merry Christmas & a Happy New Year to all. Lots of love & kisses. Your brother, Claude

Do not be afraid, do not be discouraged. Be strong and courageous.   –Joshua 10:25

Chapter Fifteen

Tuesday Morning, January 4, 1944

Dear Viola,

I received your letter the other day but didn't have time to answer any sooner.

I am sorry that I disappointed you all by not coming home for Christmas. I tried to get a pass & I would of if they had continued giving them.

I didn't have a very nice Christmas this year at all. I was very lonesome because I didn't get to come home. There wasn't any place to go. I had a nice good dinner and all the presents I wanted but still it didn't seem like Christmas at all.

You can't blame Johnny for not writing or sending anything. It is tough out there on maneuvers. I know how it is. I have been on three of them since I am in the Army. You can't go to town or you don't have time to do anything. I am glad to hear that he is to get a furlough when the maneuvers end. Maybe I'll get one later on. At least I hope so. They may give us passes after our Amphibious training is over with. We are having this training on the Chespeak Bay. We are staying at Camp Bradford, Va. That is near Norfolk, Va. I won't be able to write for a while because we are to go out on a boat and stay for a few days. I don't know where we are to go from here but I hope it is to home.

I am glad to hear you had a good Christmas. You sure got a lot of nice presents didn't you. I am glad that the kids got a lot of gifts. I wish I could of gotten them something.

I got all I wanted for Christmas. Every time I ate a cookie or smoking I was thinking of who sent it. Everything was just swell except that I wasn't home to enjoy all the nice things I got. Maybe next Christmas I will be home for good. I sure do hope so.

I went to Midnite Mass on Christmas Eve but didn't get a chance to go to confession.

So they are to appoint new counselmen. Did Joe get put out? He sure has been in there a long time. But they don't come any better then he. I guess they all realized that or he wouldn't be in as a counselman.

We went out to the beach this morning but we didn't go on the boats because the water was too rough. The navy is in charge of us and they don't work if the weather is too bad. If it was up to the army we would probably go out anyway. Boy you ought to see the big waves beat up on the beach. It would be suacide to go out there in this big wind.

Well how is everybody and everything at home? I sure hope everything is alrite I mean that nobody is sick. You know it doesn't take much to get sick at this time of the year. I have one of those long lasting colds I get every winter. It never seems to fail that I get a terrible cold about the middle of the winter. I have been taking cough medicine but it doesn't do any good. What I need is a little rest to fix me up but I can't make them understand that.

I suppose Joe is working every day. I heard they are closing a lot of mills down because they have too much material on hand. I mean war goods. I haven't read a newspaper for a wk. so I don't know what is going on outside of camp. I used to get a paper every day when I was at Camp Pickett. A paper boy would come in the barracks every morning.

We are leaving Bradford on a short maneuvers. I guess that is what you would call. We will be on the water more of the time. They probably will last until the middle of the mo. At least that is what I heard.

Boy one good thing about the navy is that they feed good. I never ate such good food since I am in the Army. What I don't like is that we have to walk a mile or so to the mess hall. We have to get up at five and we don't go to work until 8. The eats is the only good thing about the place. We can't go to town anymore & the shows are so crowded you can't get in half of the time. Of course I wouldn't go anyway because of my cold, but if I were feeling good I'd go. I'd do or go any place to get out of these huts we live in.

Well I must close for now. it's almost time to go chow and I wouldn't miss that for anything. They call me a chow hound but I don't care I am going to eat while I can.

Goodby and God Bless you all. Love, Claude

P.S. Excuse the poor writing. I seem to get worse every time I write.

Wednesday, January 5, 1944

Dearest Family,
I received your box & sure was glad to get the candy & cookies was sure good you sure can make good candy & cookie the boy said so & so did I.

The weather is hell here it been rain since Xmas. Boy I don't like it. Did you hear from John L. I did not get to see him. This Battery D of this outfit was with us this week but not HQ damn it. I hear from John S. this week he is O.K. he wrote it the 18 of December. I got it today. I hope you hear from him.

How are the kids getting long? Say hello for me tell them I still love them. Tell them to pray for me. Because my day is come soon. We will get back to N.C. soon & then? You know.

Well honey I'll have to close for we busy & it rain all the time. May God Bless you all.

Your brother law, Frank

P.S. How is Joe in the Army I hope he don't go.

Saturday, January 15, 1944

Dearest Family,

Well how are you all to day? I hope everything is fine with you all. I am just so we just came back from Tennessee just 6 of us boys to get things for the Battalion the Battery will come next week. If you get a letter from John L. tell him to write to me so I know where he is please. We will not be here long just two months then you know where we are going but I think maybe I'll get to come home for 5 days I hope so. boy the weather has been raining since we came from Tenn. and still raining but we have a good bed to night so that will be something.

Well how are my kids get long? I sure would like to see them before I go over sea. I miss them so much how is Joey getting long in school good I hope. Is Barb doing good to? She's my honey.

Well how is Joe & you getting long what know kid ha ha. Is Joe still working in a mill? I hope he is I hope he don't have to go to the Army. Well dear I'll close for we got to work like hell for the next 2 mo. Like we didn't work at all the last 2 mo. The hell with them.

May God Bless you all. Love, Frank

Monday, January 17, 1944

Dearest Vi,

It's been a long time since I wrote you or anyone else. In fact it's been about a month since I wrote a letter. Now that maneuvers are over I promise you that you'll hear from me once a week. I know everyone is angry with me for not writing but I can't help it, if only the folks at home could realize what the conditions are like out here.

At this time I want to thank you for the wonderful package you sent me some three weeks ago. It really was swell and came in very handy. It certainly made me homesick when I opened it. All sorts of thoughts went through my mind at that time. There I was helpless everyone sending me packages and I couldn't send any in return. I know there were a lot of disappointed people and I hope to do better next time.

I didn't get to see Frank at all although we passed his outfit on the road twice while traveling in convoy. In one position one of our batteries was giving one of their units air support and were only about 500 yards away from them. It's hard to find someone you know when there are so many soldiers out there. I thought I'd meet him in town but I only got to go twice and then it was late and he was probably out with a girl at that time. There were plenty of beautiful women in Nashville and if I know Frank he did alright.

So John is a Sergeant now gee! That's swell he certainly does deserve it. I would like to see him now.

It wasn't so long since I wrote to Claude. I don't see where he gets the two months. I'll write to him this week probably.

Well we are now in Camp Stewart Ga. and it's a hell hole. I thought Davis and Ft. Fisher were bad but this place beats all. We're only staying here for (two) weeks and I think I can stand it that long. We are here to fire all our large guns and we are to clear this camp by the 1st. I don't know where we're going from here. I hope it's up North or out West somewhere like California. I'm damn tired of this South.

It took us four days to get here. Our first stop was at Camp Forrest, (Tennessee) that is where I got the stationary. The next nite we stopped at Ft. Oglethorpe Ga. that is a W.A.C. camp you should have seen the W.A.C.S. holler, yell and jump up and down when we pulled in that evening. First night we went to the Service Club and P.X. in our dirty clothes but they didn't mind. They are worse then the men in a camp when the boys see women. Everyone had a W.A.C. that nite they were fighting to buy us beer etc. Wow!

What a place I wouldn't mind staying there. The following evening we stopped at Ft. McPhearson Ga. That was a nice place only two miles out of Atlanta Ga. Coming to this Ft. we went through Atlanta. We had 13 motorcycle cops taking us through town. All the people were out on the porch girls waving and the older folks waving flags at us it was quite a site. We had 120 trucks in the convoy so you can imagine how long we had the traffic tied up there.

Our last stop was near a small town named Cochran. We bivouacked there near a small college for the nite. No excitement there at all, all small towns. Then our last stop was this moldy hole of Camp Stewart. Oh well! It won't be long and we'll be moving out again.

The people out in the maneuvers area were swell to us. They gave us eggs, milk and water. In one position the farmer's wife baked me a wonderful blackberry pie. I really thought that was swell of them. They also invited us in for meals and also to sleep in the house in the bad weather. That's one thing we couldn't do cause if we got caught it would be tough for us. We weren't even supposed to take food from them but we did that one on the sneak. The purpose of these maneuvers is to make us tough and to go without food, water and sleep out in the mud and cold. I don't know why those people did all this for us it certainly was nice of them. I guess they felt sorry for us or something.

It was remarkable how my health held up. All I had was a few light colds. I must be getting damn tough or something. Considering the weather conditions I think I was very fortunate to get by so easy.

There were epidemics of flu and pneumonia out there too. The farmers were amazed the way we carried on in such terrible weather. Many a nite I would have given anything in the world for a dry piece of ground to sleep on. My clothes and bedding were wet most of the time.

We have 74 men in Hq. Btry. and 19 of them were in the Hospital with flu or pneumonia or something. The btry. has to *function whether these men are here or not and when they're gone that puts all the more work on the rest of us. As in my case I'm a radio operator now and we had to keep our radios on the air 24 hrs. a day seven days a week.*

In addition to taking my shift on the radio I had to lay wire cause the telephone communications Cpl. was in the hospital for a month. They picked on me cause that used to be my work and I certainly had my hands full. I think I can safely say that I never got over 5 hours of sleep a nite and many times I was lucky to get that. Oh well, they're all over with now and I can't say I'm a bit angry.

We spent a rather rough Christmas and New Years. It started to rain Christmas Eve and rained for about a week straight. We were in mud up to our (ass) over the holidays. The week after Christmas it took us two days to get our trucks out of the mud for the next problem. We had to call an engineer unit with large tractors to pull us out (what a mess).

I wish you'd tell Veronica to get my two (khaki) shirts dry cleaned in case I get a furlough or pass so they'll be in good shape. Have her do that immediately will you?

Well Vi, I'll be closing for the time being. Give my love to the kids, Mom and Dad. Tell Joe I'll go hunting with him if I get home if it's out of season or not. May God Bless you all. Again, I say thanks for the wonderful package.

Love, Johnny

P.S. Please write soon and often.

Keep on loving each other as brothers. Do not forget to entertain strangers, for by so doing some people have entertained angels without knowing it. –Hebrews 13:1-2

Friday, January 28, 1944

Dear Vi,
Received your letter to-day and decided to answer it immediately cause I might not get a chance for a few days. I wrote one letter every night to someone. I've been trying to contact my buddies of the 411th but haven't had any luck yet. I heard they're on their way across. I certainly miss them boys, a finer bunch of fellows will never be found. They all seemed like old time buddies of mine. The one that sent the picture of me is a Polish boy from Chicago and a Prince too. He'd do anything for me. He says he wants me to be best man for his wedding. I always kid him and tell him when his girl sees me that will be the end for him. I'd give anything to be back with those boys. I'm darn sorry I ever asked to be transferred. Oh well, live and learn, which I did at my own expense.

Well we'll probably be moving out of here early Tuesday morning if nothing else happens. There's an epidemic of (Scarlet Fever) in the battalion and I'm afraid we might be quarantined that might hold us up here some time, I hope not. I've got my fingers crossed also toes for good measure. I don't want to be stuck here any longer. This place is a cemetery with lights and I'm not kidding either.

I think we'll get furloughs shortly after we hit our new home. I figure any time next month that is if nothing turns up again. We're attached to the 12th Corps which is on maneuvers now and I heard we might join them. That don't sound very good does it? I wouldn't mind it after we get a furlough. All we can do is hope and pray that I get home first.

I was very happy to hear Claude got to go home even for a few days. I hope he can do it more often. I don't see why it can't be done he's fairly close isn't he? It's too bad he and Frank couldn't see each other, I was hoping they'd meet before he went back. Frank sent me a telegram asking me to try to get home but that was impossible at this time. I wrote Claude an eight page letter yesterday. Maybe he can get home when I get my furlough (I hope)!

So Dad sold the big cow? Gosh! The herd won't seem the same without her she was the best cow we had. I know she's getting old but we've had her so long that it seems funny without her. That wasn't a bad price he got for her though. How is our herd now have we got any good ones left??

The weather here is exceptionally warm now, very typical of our May weather at home. The weather is very changeable though we may have a few days of beautiful weather then it will start to rain and get cold. One day I put on my long (handle undies) then the next day summer, one doesn't know what to expect. How is the weather at home? I want to know what to expect when I get there.

I don't remember what I said in my last letter. If I said any thing I shouldn't have I'm sorry. I know I should be more careful but sometimes I forget myself. I'll try to see that it don't happen again.

You weren't kidding when you said they're (angels). I really miss them and love them very much. I carry a picture of the kids in my wallet and I look at it every once in a while so I won't forget what they look like. I also have that picture that was taken of me before I went to the army. The one with Barbara, Ceil and I standing by the car and I'm holding Barbara in my arm. I got most of the guys believing that she's my daughter.

How many days a week is Joe working now? Is he still at his job on the furnace? And how does he like it?

Well Vi, I guess I'll have to close for now. Give my love to the kids, Mom and Dad. Keep on writing even if we do move. Your letters will catch up with me in a day or so. Goodnite and may God Bless you all.

Love your brother, Johnny

Friday nite, January 28, 1943; Service Club Camp Pickett, Virginia

Dear Viola,

Received your letter today and was very happy to hear from you. I know I should of written sooner but just couldn't get around to it. I was rather busy getting things straightened out. There is always a lot of work to be done when one gets back from a pass. The next morning when I got back (which was Sunday) I was on K.P. So you see I didn't have much time to do any of my own work.

I sure hated to leave for camp. But I think I will be home again before very long. At least I am hoping we do. I heard we may get a short furlough in Feb. or March. But that is only a rumor.

I say it is too bad I missed Frank. I wanted to see him in the worst way. That is the way it always happens though. We were so close and still we were far. I wish he had of stoped at the club. We could have had a hell of a good time. As it was it was dead. No excitement at all. I haven't seen Frank for more then a year and a half. So we would have a lot to talk about. I sure hope Johnny gets home in time to see Frank and go out with him. Johnny wouldn't like anything better. I can just guess where Johnny would head for. So Frank is fat. I guess he and Johnny found a home in the Army. I can't seem to get fat here. No matter how much I eat.

No Viola we aren't under the navy now. we were under the navy at Camp Bradford because that was a navy camp. I sure wish we were under them though. It was swell. Good food and everything. We are just reviewing what we already have had. It really is boring to go over the same thing again. I heard we may go to Florida or to Panama for some jungle training, but that is also a rumor. I never believe anything until I see it is being done.

I am glad to hear those candles were of some use. Maybe I should have brought home more of them. I'll try and get some to

take home the next time.

 I went to the dentist yesterday to have my plates adjusted. I told the Dr. they made my mouth sore. He looked in my mouth and said no wonder, they don't fit. He gave me heck for not coming sooner. I think I'll get a new set out of it. At least that is the way he talked. I hope I do. Then I can send my old ones home. You know a set of teeth cost a lot of money in civilian life. Today I had my eyes tested. I don't think I'll need glasses, but I am just going to have them treated.

 Well how is everything at home? I hope fine. How is the weather out there, very cold? Boy we're having some swell days here. It's just like Spring. Everybody is running around in shirt sleeves. I sure hope it stays this way. I suppose just as soon as we go out on problems it will turn cold. That's the way it usually turns out. But I don't care I can take it. Well I must say Goodby for now. Goodby and God bless you all.

 Love, Claude
 Say hello to Joe and the kids.

Thursday, February 3, 1944

Dearest Family,
 How are you all getting long back home? I am just fine my back is not so good but I'll make it I think. Did you hear from John L. maybe he will come home. I hope he comes home before going over sea.

 The weather is fine but it look like rain to night. It so cold when I came in this morning. How are the kid getting long with the school work? Tell them I miss them so much & you too. Did mother take it hard I hope not.

 Well honey I'll be closing for the time. I been on C.Q. one night. To night I am on Guard. We are sure working like hell.

 I think we are going places soon. In the next month but

don't worry I'll be O.K.
May God Bless you all. Till next time.
With all my love, Frank

It is God who arms me with strength and makes my way perfect. He makes my feet like the feet of a deer; he enables me to stand on the heights. He trains my hands for battle; my arms can bend a bow of bronze. You give me your shield of victory; you stoop down to make me great. You broaden the path beneath me so that my ankles do not turn. -2 Samuel 22: 33-37

Sunday, February 6, 1944

Dearest Family,
How are you all back home? I hope everything is fine with you all. How are my kids getting long with school. Tell them to be good till I get home.
How is Joe getting long with his job? Tell him not to work too hard, it's no good. I know because see what that work did to me ha ha. One thing this Army don't worry me. The damn Captain is sending me to school for 2 or 3 weeks, some over sea school. So maybe my day is coming. I don't care. Did you hear from John or Johnie. Tell John L. to write or the hell with him.
Well I'll close for this time. May God Bless you all.
Pray for me.
Love to all. Your brother law, Frank

P.S. if I go over sea take good care of mother & dad for me please.

Chapter Sixteen

It had been two months since John last wrote Vi and the family, but the 3rd Marines and the 37th Buckeye Divisions were involved in extensive jungle warfare training. The Americans knew that it was simply a matter of time before the Japanese figured out their defensive strategy and attempted to infiltrate the perimeter of the severely outnumbered Americans. So, everyday that passed without an attack was one more day to train and prepare to hold the strategic hills that dotted the perimeter of the airfield and the port. Without this airfield, B-29 Bombers would not be able to land and eventually advance to the Philippines and God willing, Tokyo.

John never knew his assignment, but based on the elevation and view from Hill 700, he realized the importance of the rigorous training that he and his men found themselves in, daily. Spring was about to come in like a lion and the battle that was to come for Hill 700 would be the straw that broke the Japanese Army's back.[17]

I pursued my enemies and crushed them; I did not turn back till they were destroyed. I crushed them completely, and they could not rise; they fell beneath my feet. You armed me with strength for battle; you made my adversaries bow at my feet. You made my enemies turn their backs in flight, and I destroyed my foes. They cried for help, but there was no one to save them- to the Lord but he did not answer. I beat them as fine as the dust of

---

[17] www.Wikipedia.org www.historynet.com/battle-of-bougainville-37th-infantry-divisions

the earth; I pounded and trampled them like mud in the streets.
-2 Samuel 22: 38-43

Sunday nite in the S.W. Pacific, February 6, 1944

Dear Vi,

How are you and family? Fine I hope so. Rec'd your swell letter to day and was so happy to hear from you. Sorry I haven't been writing as often as I used to. But I know you'll understand we are busy. Course I'm thinking of you folks all the time. I heard from Frank that he was home for a few days also Claude. And still they can't get together . hope Johnny got to come home too for a few days. Frank said he was going to call him up and let him know he was home. Hope he made it. I was so glad to hear Babs and Joey were doing so good in school. I'm mighty proud of them. Well I suppose Joe is getting ready for the spring fishing. If things go right I may go with him some time this summer. Any way I hope so. Well honey, I'll close for this time and write again soon.

Good luck to you all and May God Bless you all.

Love-John

Thursday, February 10, 1944

Dearest Family,

I received your letter and Valentine sure was glad to hear from you & and the family. The weather is cold to day and we are working like hell. We are going over some time in April for sure. I hope I make it but boy my back is giving me hell.

I will not tell them because if I can I want to come home and work on the farm and be a (T. 7) like Hank ha ha.

How is Joe feeling to day? I hope he will be O.K. soon. I received 5 letters from the girls back home but I don't feel like writing to them. All the girls like me so much ha ha. I'll give them some of Soukenik you know? You should. Did you hear from John S. this week? I heard from him to day and mother wrote me to.

Well honey I'll be close for this time if I can I'll write more later. Take good care of the family and say hello to the kids for me. I miss them so much.

May God Bless you all.

Love Frank

Monday, February 14, 1944; Hq. Battery 557th AAA Bn.

Dearest Vi,

First of all I want to thank you for that beautiful Valentine.

We've been pretty busy lately. There's a full month of hard training ahead. In the past few weeks we've been firing all our guns and I mean firing we stop for nothing. The weather hasn't been very pleasant lately we've been getting a lot of rain. Firing goes on through rain or shine and we haven't had much of the latter. I've laid in mud and shot my gun many times.

Well we won't be getting furloughs this month but they promised for March. I don't know how good their promises are but I got my fingers crossed. It seems that every outfit that participated in the maneuvers got furloughs already.

Oh yes, Wednesday or Thursday we go through (Nazi Village). I'll tell you what it's like in my next letter.

You asked what the letters in my address meant. Well here it is Anti Aircraft Artillery Automatic Weapons Battalion Mobile. Does that answer your question? If not say so and I'll see if I can do better.

Yes I think the 411th and all my buddies have gone over. I'll see them when we all get back. It'll take me a long time to visit them all and do a little celebrating. I'll have to go as far as Chicago and visit my Polish buddy. When I meet him I'll probably never get out of Chicago. I'm sorry I ever left those boys but it's to late now. I learned a lesson at my own expense.

The reason I left the 411th was I thought I'd get in a new outfit that was just activating and I'd have a good chance for a promotion. Well things didn't work out the way I figured as you plainly see. I would have stayed in the 411th as a Corporal but I thought I'd do better some where else well I didn't. I guess it's just one of those things we have to meet up with in our army career.

I didn't leave the outfit cause I thought they were going over seas. I'd rather have gone with them than with this outfit.

How is Joe getting along? I certainly hope it's much better. It seems to be rather serious. Tell him I got my fingers crossed for him and am wishing him the best. I'm sure everything will come out alright.

Well Vi, I must leave you for a while. Give my love to Mom, Dad and the kids. Please keep writing even if I don't write very often. May God Bless you all. Goodnite.

Love your brother Johnny

P.S. I got three v-mail letters from John last week. How do you like that isn't it swell?

Saturday, February 26, 1944

Dearest Family,
Just a few lines to let you know that I received your letter was glad to hear from you and to know that Joe is feeling much better & to know that Babs was a page girl. I sure wish I would of seen her.

I did not her from Johnie for so long I didn't know if he was in the U.S.A. damn him he should write to me but I guess he's busy to. I sure have all the work I can do. Is Joe working now I hope he is. The weather is still raining one day next day it's O.K. Today it is raining and getting cool to night we have to work 7 days a week. I think are day will be here some time in April but don't worry I'll be O.K. I don't feel so good to night. We had a 15 mile walk in 3 hrs. it made my back give me hell.

    Please excuse my writing because I don't feel like writing. I'm so damn tired but just have to write to you all.

    May God Bless you all. Love to all. Frank

Thursday, March 2, 1944

    Dear Viola,

    Was very happy to hear from you although I must say you're slipping. I used to get a letter at least once a week from you and I don't feel right if I don't. I know you have a lot of writing to do now but don't forget your brother.

    I got a letter from John Satsko yesterday. I was surprised to hear from him. He asked me all kinds of questions about the army. I'd like to see him in his uniform. Good ole Johnny, we sure had some swell times to-gether.

    So Claude was home again, gee that's swell I'm very glad to hear that. I hope he can get a furlough when I get home.

    Vi, maybe Veronica ought to file my income tax this year. Tell her about it and see if she'll do it.

    I hear Walter Wysenski kinda likes the Navy. I'll bet Ann was thrilled when he came home, I can't blame her. Ha! ha!

    Right now my arms are sore as heck. I got four shots the other day two in each arm.

    Well Vi I'll close for now hoping to see you in the near future. Give my love to all. Goodnite.

    Love, Johnny

Friday noon, March 3, 1944; Company G 305th Infantry

Dear Viola,
I just received your letter and decided to write while I had a little spare time.
Yes I am settled down to army life again. It don't take long to do that. It sure is tough to get home and have to hurry back so quick. But even if I get to stay home for one hour I would be satisfied.
I wish I would stay here at Pickett and be able to come home once in a while. But that is impossible because we are moving in a week or so. I don't know where but it won't be close to home you can bet on that.
I certainly enjoyed those cookies and cake you made for me. I ate all the way to camp and had plenty left when I got there.
We have been having some swell days out here. the whole winter has been farely well. I sure hope it stayes that way the rest of the time we are here.
To bad about Joe's good job going to heck. Why don't he try and get in some where else? Where they pay more money.
I got back to camp alrite, but just to find out I could of stayed another day. The orders were changed about every one being back on Sunday. I have had the worse darn luck on my furloughs and passes. I am always getting back to darn early. I wish I had of called up and found out what the score was. Well, I'll know batter the next time.
Dad has had the worse darn luck with his cows. There must be something wrong with the whole darn herd. If I were him I would sell the whole bunch of them. I wish this darn war would soon end so John and I could come back and run the farm. I bet we would soon fix things around there. That is if father would let us alone.
Don't worry, I will keep on writing as often as possible. No matter where I go, I may not write very much but you will hear

from me. you know I didn't write to Johnny yet. I got a letter from him just before I went on pass. I better get busy and write or he will wonder what is wrong.

You don't have to tell me that you served a good dinner. You always do. I ate at your place enough I out to know. I bet the Wysenski's never ate a better meal.

I had a class E. allotment made out. Mother will be getting $90 a month starting from April. I may be over by then and everybody has to have one before they go. Money isn't going to do me any good there. There won't be anything to spend it for. That is the only way you can send money across.

I got my glasses the other day. I got two pair of them. They don't look too good on me but I can see a lot better with them. The only time I wear them is when I read or write letters.

Well Viola I must close for now. I can't think of anything more to write about.

Goodby and God bless you all.
Love Claude

P.S. Say hello to Joe and the kids for me.

<u>Please excuse the poor writing.</u>

Sunday, March 12, 1944

Dearest Family,
I received your box and in good time everything was O.K. boy the cookies was so good all the boys liked them and so did I. The weather to day is raining & it's getting cool to. Well how is John? Good to be home. Maybe I'll get a pass for next week for 3 days. I am not sure it's hard to get in this time because you know.

Well here I am older to day I feel like 30 because it's raining and my back gives me hell when it rains.

How are the family getting long? I hope everything is fine. How is Joe working? Do you think Joe will go to the Army? I hope he don't.

Well dear I'll close for this time because we are not to write to much about the work we are doing. I'll close maybe see you this coming weekend. I am not sure so be good.

May God Bless you all & keep you all safe.
Your brother, Frank

P.S. Did you hear from John this week? I hope he get home soon.
Love, frank

Chapter Seventeen

Wednesday eve, March 22, 1944; new P.O. San Francisco

Dear Viola,
Received your letter today and was very glad to hear from you. It was about time you got my new address. I was beginning to think the card weren't even sent out. All the letters that I got so far had my old address.
I can't tell you where I am exactly. All I can say is that I am on the west coast and I do not know how long I will be there.
I got a telegram from John the other day saying that he was home on a fifteen day furlough. He sure is lucky to be able to get home so often. I just can't see how he does it. I have one coming in April but since I am so far from home I probably won't get it. I sure wish I could be home rite now. It sure would be swell to see John for the first time in two years. I hear he suprised you again. By coming when you didn't expect him. I bet mother sure was glad to see him. It's too bad he couldn't come home a little later. Maybe he could help father out a bit on the farm. He is going to need it if he expects to run the whole farm. Unless Joe is going to help him.
I haven't seen John Ankowski for a long time. I went to see him but he wasn't in. I guess he goes out every nite. You know how he is. He likes to have his good time. He and I had a swell time when we were together at Camp Wheeler. I sure miss them days. Of course I have Kalas with me but he doesn't like to run around very much.
Well I suppose I better close for now. I can't seem to think

of any more to write about.

Goodby for now and writ soon.
Love, Claude
Tell John to take it easy on my car.

Friday 6:00 A.M., March 24, 1944

Dearest Family,
How are you all feeling? I hope you all are O.K. by this time I made it back O.K. just the Captain said he wants to see me as soon as he gets back.

The weather is fine and I have been fine this morning it's raining like hell. See I am writing this letter in the morning because I couldn't last night see I am on C.Q. to day.

Is Joe working to day? Tell him not to get in the Army that's know place for him. Did Johnie go back? I sure miss him and all of you. Boy I wish I was home when he was I sure have a good time with him.

But it looks like not till the war is over. Well I guess this will be all for this time. I hope you can read this letter.

May God Bless you all & keep you all safe.
All my love, Frank
P.S. Tell the kids to pray for me & you two because I'll be on my way soon.

Friday, March 31, 1944

Dear Viola,
I was very happy as well as surprised to get your letter today. I know I should have written sooner but I was just to run down and tired to write. I've been spending my evenings and nights in bed lately.

I made it back alright and everything turned out ok. I wish I could have stayed longer. It seems every time I come home it is worse for me to leave. The two weeks I was home seemed like a day. I was having such a wonderful time too. Now it's hard to get used to the old grind again.

I was sorry to hear that you had such bad weather going home. If I'd have known it was going to be like that I could have taken a train from Warren. Oh well you made it alright and it's all over with now so I guess that's all that counts.

The train ride from Washington to Columbia was plenty rough. I'm still trying to get the cinders out of my eyes. I think it was the roughest train I ever rode.

How is Joe's boil getting along? I certainly hopes he gets rid of them, it must be very painful. I can imagine how he feel with it. tell him for me that he should take a good (diddle) and maybe he'll get rid of it. Ha! Ha! I don't know if you remember or not but he used to kid me about pimples and said a good (one) would fix me up.

Well Vi, I'll have to leave you now. Give my love to all and may God Bless every one of you always.

Goodnite.

Love, Johnny

Word had it that the first port for the 77th Division 305th Infantry was to be Hawaii for intensified amphibious assault and jungle warfare training. Claude had resolved that he was not going to get back to the farm until this war was over. There was no looking back. There was, however, a glimmer of hope that maybe, just maybe, Claude and the 305th would somehow eventually join up with the 37th and a brief reunion with John.

Tuesday, April 4, 1944; Claude overseas

Dear Viola,

I suppose you will be surprised to hear from me. But I am sorry that I couldn't write any sooner. I mean to write a lot sooner but something always came up. But now that I am settled down for a while maybe I can write a little more. At least I hope so.

I suppose you are wondering where I am at. Well I am somewhere in the Pacific. I can't tell you just where but I haven't seen any action yet so you don't have to worry about that.

Have you heard from John S. lately? I suppose he will be coming home before long. He should be after being in action for two years. I think I will right to him if I get a chance.

We are having a good time out here, playing ball and swimming. We didn't do any swimming yet but we intend to later on. We are also getting a radio to listen to. So it really won't be bad at all.

Well how is everything at home? Is Joe still working in the mill or did he go to farming? He should try and farm his dad's place. I bet he can make some good money at it. This war needs a lot of good farmers like him.

I must close for now because my paper is getting short. Goodby and write soon.
Love Claude

Thursday, April 6, 1944

Dear Viola,
Received your letter yesterday. And it sure was good to hear from you. I don't blame you for not writing any sooner. Because of the excitement of Johnny being home. I sure wish I

could write a lot better. I would do a lot more writing then I do.

Yes, Johnny sure was lucky to be able to get home so often. He came home at least seven times since he's been in the Army. I bet he was darn glad he got to see Frank. Too bad he didn't have a long furlough. They would have had a real time together. I am surprised John helped father as much as he did. Father is going to have a hard time keeping the farm going if Joe goes to the Army. Well if he can't take care of it the only thing for him to do is sell out and quit farming. There isn't any use of kidding himself. You know he isn't as young as he used to be.

I didn't expect John not to drive the car, because I did plenty of driving when I was home. The only thing I was thinking about was you have a car to runaround with. I'm not worrying about myself. When I get back and there is no car. I'll hitch up a horse and buggy like the olden days.

It's too bad about Joe's boils on his neck. I bet it sure is painful. I've never had one but I can imagine what it feels like to have a hole in his neck as big as he had. Well if he gets in the Army they will cure him or kill him.

We are suppose to get passes to town before long. I sure hope so. I would like to go down and see what it's like. It gets awful tiresome staying in camp all the time. Doing the same kind of work all the time. We had a beer party last night and had a pretty nice time. Something like that is a darn good moral builder.

I went to Church last Sunday for the first time for quite awhile. I could of went on the boat, but it seemed that every time there was mass I had to be doing something else. I am going for Easter too. I might even go to confession. I hope we have a nice Easter this year because I didn't enjoy the last one very much. Even the best wouldn't be as nice as the Easters I've spent at home.

If you care to send me packages be sure it is something that won't spoil. The weather is warm and it wouldn't take much to spoil it.

Well I guess I better close for now. It is getting late and I

must get a little sleep. Please send me some of the kids pictures when you have them taken. Goodby and God Bless you all.
    Love, Claude
I will write home as often as possible.

The Lord is my shepherd I shall not want…Even though I walk through the valley of the shadow of death, I will fear no evil, for you are with me; your rod and your staff, they comfort me. – Psalm 23: 1, 4

April 1994; Change of address Cpl. Frank Soukenik Btry. A 793 F.A. BN. Postmaster

New York, New York

Easter Sunday, April 9, 1944

Dear Vi & family,
First I want to say I am sorry for not writing sooner and hope you will forgive me. Something came up and I could not write for a time, but I will make up for it now. I'm now in Ser. Comm. Hq. Co. when I got here I had about a hundred letters from the folks back home boy! Was I happy. I guess I'll have to write all v-mail for a while. I was sorry to hear Joe had a carbuncle on his head. Vi I know what it is. I had one on my back and you can still notice it. it happened a year ago. Boy! it was terrible. How's my honeys doing. I sure miss those kids. Tell them I sent kisses and my love. I saw a show the other nite "Lose Angel" and it reminded me of Bab and Joey. Vi if you can see it, it's really good. I'll write you a long letter when I have time. Heard from Johnny or Frank? Sure miss them. I'll close. May God Bless You All. Love & Kisses, John

Saturday, April 15, 1944

Dear Vi and Family,
Rec'd your swell letter yesterday and was sure happy to hear from you, and to know the family is O.K. No I'm not sick or any thing like that. I was just too busy. I can't say why or what I been doing, but you can take my word for it that I was really busy. I'll have plenty to tell you folks when I come home. I hope it is this summer some time. Yes, some of the boys from the _____ went home all ready. I may be called some time soon. You see they only take a few at a time and then it may be five or six months before I'm called. Here's hoping it's soon. I hope the boys will still be home when I come. I sure miss seeing them. If they're still there when I come, I'll sure go down to see them. Yes, and have a few drinks with them. Boy I sure miss those days when I use to come home on week end passes. Yes, I remember May 1942. You bet we'll go out fishing and have a few little outings like we had then. I could go for some of that beer, coke and potato chips now. O Boy!
Vi I was sorry to hear that maybe by the time I come home Joe will be in the Army. I was hoping that we would do a lot of fishing together, I sure remember the nigt s Joe and I used to go to the lake. Course you gave him hell now and then, but it was fun any way. I don't think they'll take him anyway. I hope not. I was sure glad to hear that you All got together when Johnny and Frank were home on furlough and went to Youngstown and had a good time. That's swell. I still haven't heard from Claude. You say he may come this way. I hope not, but if he does I hope he looks me up. I may be able to help him. I know Vi, you hate to see him leave and I do too. But all we can do is pray that God will bring him back to us. It's no use worrying over it. That will not help. I know he can take care of himself. Just keep your chin up. Write to him often. Give him the news around home, course just the good news. See that his girl friend writes often (course that's some

thing I didn't have to worry about, was girl friends Ha). but letters really help so write often.

Well Vi, I'll close for this time and tell my sweethearts Joey and Bab I still love them too and we'll go fishing when I come home. How about a line or two from Joey and Bab? I'd love to hear from them.

Good luck and love and kisses. John.

Chapter Eighteen

The Battery A 793 Field Artillery Battalion was now in England and Frank had no idea of their final objective other than field and anti-aircraft artillery training in England and later Scotland. Plans for Operation Overlord were in full swing and with a little over a month before D-Day, personnel, equipment and training needed to be in place. Frank and the 793rd would eventually act as artillery support for his old buddies in the 82nd Airborne.[18]

Frank had a way of either appreciating or cursing and persevering through the very moment he was in. Fulfill the simple needs whether it was the sensual, euphoric feeling of the small of a woman's back at a dance hall, enjoying a brief stretch of mild spring weather in the U.K or working through the seemingly endless hours of training all the while thinking about family and being back home once again. Let's take care of business and get through this war that was the only objective Frank cared about. The Army's plans, they were finite in Frank's mind regardless of the number of problems or missions. It was simply a means to an end with the prize being home!

Thursday, April 27, 1944

Dearest Family,
I hope this letter finds you all feeling good. How are the

---

[18] www.793rdfieldartillery.hometead.com

kids getting long? I am some place in England. We had a good trip over. I sure like it here the place looks good to me

Joe would like the farms in England the weather is fine.

Will you write when you have time & tell me everything that's going on back home will make me feel good to hear from you once a week. Will close for this time. May God Bless you all. Take good care of yourself & the family.

Love, Frank

Friday, April 28, 1944; Camp Davis

Dear Viola,

I suppose you're wondering why I didn't write for such a long time. Well we moved out of Ft. Jackson Wednesday morning and pulled into Camp Davis Wednesday nite. Things happened so fast that we were all running around like mad getting ready to move.

I never expected to see Camp Davis again but here we are much to our sorrow. We aren't going to be here long ten days or two weeks and then I think we'll go back to Jackson. I hope! You see we came here for a refresher course in firing. This darn place hasn't changed a bit it's still the same old hole. They have German prisoners in our old area that's about the only change I could see.

We're sleeping in tents about two miles out of camp. Boy are the mosquitoes and gnats rough here. I'm covered with bumps from head to toe.

When you write to me use the same old address cause I'll get your mail a day later anyhow. By the time you start writing we'll probably be back in Jackson anyway. If we should happen to go some where and not back to Jackson I'll give you my new address as soon as possible.

Well how is everyone at home? I hope you're all feeling

as good as I am. Did the weather break yet so Dad and Joe could do some farming? We've been getting an awful lot of rain lately it hasn't missed a day since I've been back.

Well Vi I'll have to close for a while. Give my love to all and write soon.

Goodnite. Love, Johnny

Monday, May 1, 1944, England; Btry. A 793 F.A. Bn.

Dearest Family,

I received your letter and was glad to know that you all are fine. I hope you get all my letters I send you (this one was returned once because the state of Ohio was omitted from Vi's address).

The weather is beautiful in English. I sure like the place.

I went to a dance last night. Sure had a good time with all the English girls. The girls are O.K. Some of them are good dancers. All the girls went for me ha ha.

If you write to John L., tell him my address so he can write to me. I don't have his. I lost it.

Well honey I'll be closing for this time because nothing to write about.

May God Bless you all. Take good care of yourself and the family.

Tell Joe not to get in the Army if he don't have to.

With all my love to all.

Always, Frank

Tuesday, May 2, 1944

Dear Viola,

I received your most welcomed letter the other day. I am sorry I didn't realize it has been so long since I wrote to you.

I am now in the Hawaiian Islands. I have been here quit some time. It was a wonderful trip. I enjoyed it all the way. No, I didn't get sea sick at all, but I sure thought I would.

I received the package that mother sent. I didn't get it in time for Easter, but it didn't make any difference. I sure was surprised when I got it. I found it laying on my bunk when I got in from the days work. And it didn't take us long to dig in to it either. No matter how much we have for chow it seems that we are still hungry.

I can't very well send you bananas or coconuts but will try to send something else. You can't tell where John or Frank will go. But wherever they do go I am hoping for the best. I sure do miss them and I hope it won't be too long before I see them again.

It's too bad the Spring weather is so bad. I was hoping it would be a nice Spring for a change. It is hard enough to raise a good crop when it is a good year. I sure hope father has good luck even though it is a wet Spring. I just can't wait to get back to that good old farm.

I am glad to hear that you had such a big crowd in church on Easter. I attended services here in camp. I didn't go to communion because I didn't have a chance.

We are going to town tomorrow. We are to spend the day in Honolulu. It is a nice little town. But there is too many service men to have a good time. We went swimming all day today. I am learning how to swim. I should of knowen how a long time ago. I used to go to the beach a lot in civilian life. But I guess I didn't go at it the rite way.

Well Viola I must close for now. It's getting late and I must get a little sleep. Tell Joey and Barbra that I miss them a lot.

Goodby and God bless you all. Love and kisses to all. Brother, Claude

Tell Joe I said hello

For the past two months John felt oblivious to time. One day blended into the next sometimes moving almost in slow motion during the most intense moments of a firefight and other times feeling as if he merely blinked and wiped his bloodshot eyes as he stared at his watch realizing that he was asleep two maybe three brief hours. Even if he had an opportunity for more sleep, a foxhole was hardly a place to settle in and get a good night's rest.

When he wasn't battling one of nearly a dozen attacks during March and April, John was battling the elements. His whole body was perpetually soaked in sweat to a point that he felt parts of his clothing were rotting right off of him while other parts were metamorphosing into the earth and underbrush he spent so much of his down time removing or repositioning for some slightly improved vantage point before the next wave of attacks.

Tuesday, May 2, 1944; S.W. Pacific

Dearest Vi,

How's my honey today? Fine? I hope so. That goes for the whole family. I received your letter dated April 17th yesterday. It was so nice and long. I enjoyed every bit of it. Keep the good work up honey. It's letters like that, that help keep our morale up. I hope you are writing like that to all our brothers. A letter from home means a lot and when you don't hear from any one for a while, it makes you feel quite low.

Gee, I hated to see Claude and Frank go. I was hoping on seeing them, when I came home. I hope Johnny and Charles stay for a while yet. Vi, do you write Charles often? I hope so. The poor kid, has only us to cheer him up. I heard when he was home on furlough, his father never talked to him all the time he was home. Art should be ashamed of himself. Don't worry, I'll not forget it. I been through hell and high waters since I left home, but I can't say I ever came home and no one would talk to me. I know how the kid felt when he left home. It's a shame.

Let's talk about something more agreeable. Say, that was quite a Easter Sunday Collection. You must have had a wonderful crowd. I bet Father Bialek was sure surprised.

How did Eugene Drabek do in his Army examination? By the way, how's Helen doing? Is she feeling any better than when I left? When you see the Drabeks say hello for me. I haven't got their address, or I'll drop them a few lines. Yes, I wish I was there to see the dam, and Joe and I could do a little fishing. Dam this pen, it willn't write, I'll get another.

So Joey goes to first Holy Communion on May 14th. I hope this letter gets there in time to congratulate him. I wish I could be there to see him go, but as it is, my thoughts will be with him and also my love. How's my little sweetheart doing? I bet Babs has plenty of boy friends. I know Joey has cause he had one when I left home. Remember how mad he use to get when I ask him about the girl across the street? Ha.

In your letter you ask why I haven't been writing before. Well, I had some work to do and I couldn't find time to write. I'll tell you about it when I get home. I can't mention it in my letter.

I suppose by this time Joe & Joey are doing a little fishing. I wish Joe could see some of the fish I saw the other day. Big as a cow. There's plenty of fish around the Islands. If I had time I could caught some but I'll sooner caught smaller fishs back home and be there. You ask if I have been taking any snapshots of different Islands and scenery there. I have some, but I don't know whether I can take them home with me. I hope so. I suppose our Mothers and Dads are quite worried now that the boys are leaving. All they can do is sit tight and pray that God will bring them back to us. This War is no fun, but the sooner it's over the better. And all you can do is write and cheer the boys up. Maybe they'll not *see a girl for months I know I didn't, and things like that. It gets quite dull some time, but when a letter comes, you feel much better. I'll close and say good night. Write again soon, I love to hear from you. I'll drop you a V-mail now and then.*

May God Bless You All and take care of you. Love & kisses. Say hello to your folks for me. John

Act with courage and may the Lord be with those who do well... The priests and the Levites stood to bless the people, and God heard them, for their prayer reached heaven, his holy dwelling place. -2 Chronicles 19:11; 30:27

Monday, May 8, 1944

Dearest Family,
I received your letter and was so glad to hear from you all. This is just a line or so to let you know that everything is O.K. with me, and hope you are the same. Did you receive all my letters I send you, I sure was glad to hear you received John's letters OK! Yes, I sure like the films if you want to send them to me. if you wish so send me anything. Please send me gum and hard candy as we are unable to obtain these luxuries. If you want to tell Mother if she is going to send me some thing to send the same. Hope my kids are getting long, tell them to be good for me & to pray for me.
Well honey, I'll close for to day don't for-get to be good. With all my love may God Bless you all till next time. Good night with all my love, Frank

Sunday, May 14, 1944; Ft. Jackson

Dear Viola,

You people got me going now, one writes that the weather is nice and the other writes just the opposite. I certainly hope it's favorable for farm work so Dad and Joe can get the crops in.

I imagine you are all busy as heck now. I was surprised to hear that the oats was in and that the corn was ready to be planted. It seems I was just home yesterday and nothing was started. I sure would like to get a furlough now but that's out of the question for a while. I probably won't know the place when I get home. With new wall paper and venition blinds it must look pretty sharp no hey?

We got a new priest in north camp now. He's a swell guy just came into the army. He's from Albany New York. He certainly tries to help the boys out and get them to go to church. I went to communion to-day cause it's Mother's Day! I'm sending a card I want you to give to Mother.

Say if you're planning to plant stuff on the muck Joe will probably quit the mill won't he? Little Joe will be able to weed now too and maybe Barbara too. No hey? Remember how we used to work for "Christmas" at that age. Those were the days weren't they? We didn't do much work but we had a lot of fun.

I went swimming to day in a little pond at the fort. The water was nice but a little dirty.

We're going out in the field to-morrow so you probably won't hear from me for a few days. We're going to be out there until Sunday.

I'll have to be going now Vi cause I have to roll my pack yet to-nite. Give my love to all and Goodnite.

Love, Johnny
P.S. Write soon.

Sunday, May 14, 1944; Mothers Day; V-Mail

Dear Vi and Family,
I have a little time today and being Mother's Day, I thought it would be nice to drop a few lines and let you know I am okay and hope that you and family are the same. I still haven't heard from Frank, Johnny, Claude or Charles since I last wrote to you. I don't know whether they are too busy or if they just forgot me a little. I guess it's their too busy.
I suppose our priest had a swell speech on Mother's Day. Our Chaplain did, I really enjoyed it. there's no one like your Mother, He said, we shouldn't only think of her on Mother's Day, but every day, and he was right.
I suppose the weather is really nice now with summer almost here. I bet the children love it now. they should be out of school by now.
I'll close Vi, with Love to all good night and May God Bless you all. Say hello to all.
Love & Kisses, John

Sunday, May 21, 1944

Dear Sister,
I received your most welcomed letter today and it sure made me happy to hear from you. I am sorry to know that you have not heard from me for so long a time. I do write every chance I get. We just got back from a three day problem and couldn't write during that time. We are going on some more of them so I don't suppose I will be able to do much writing for some time. But I will write as often as possible.
I am getting along fine. Except that I get lonesome for you

238

folks at home but I guess I always be that way. We have it pretty good out here. When we aren't working we either go to town or go swimming. We got to Honolulu once in two weeks. I guess we are going again this coming week.

I got all of your letters that you sent. That is unless something happened to them on the way across. You don't have to worry about your mail it isn't censored. You can ask me anything, but I can't say what I want.

I am glad to hear that you have been having some good weather. I began to think that you were going to have a wet season again. Now that dad has his oats in the next worry is the corn. But I guess that is the farmers life one worry after another. Veronica told me about her trying to plow with the tractor. I can emagin what kind of a job she done. It is quite a job which she probably already found out. I sure hope she is taking care of the tractor the way she should be. You better have Joe keep checking it over. I was hoping Johnny would be able to get home for a short time, but I guess there any use of thinking about that. well the only thing dad can do is do the best he can.

Yes 83 degrees is warm for May but that is just what you want for good growing weather. We have been having hot weather ever since I am here. I don't know just how hot it gats, but I know I have been sweting like a horse every day.

Helen told me about her helping mother do Spring cleaning and planting my Christmas trees. I am glad that you had a chance to help out. I know it is hard work and it takes a lot of time but I hope it will be worth it.

I am sure glad that Barbara and Joey are going well in school. It makes me feel very proud of them. Joey will be a man before I get back. I won't even know him. I sure do miss those school doings. I used to like very much to attend the Graduations every year. Well, maybe it won't be very many years before I can again. At least I hope so.

Well I must close for now I want to write another letter before it gets too dark. There is a show on tonite if I have time I want to go.

> *Good by and God bless you all. Love and kisses to all.*
> *Brother Claude*

Please excuse the poor writing.

> Sunday, Time 2300, May 28, 1944

> *Dearest Family,*
> *Just thought I'd drop you a line while I have a few minutes befor I go to bed. We had a hard day to day worked all day. 7 days a week. Just came back from Church. We go to church in the night because we work all day.*
> *How are the kids getting long since school is out? I know how glad the kids are when school is over with. I sure was. I did not hear from John S. or Johnie L. for some time. I know the boys are busy but Johnie would write. I don't know why Johnie is not writing. He stil in U.S.A.? or did he go over seas to. I hope not.*
> *When you send me a letter send it V mail or air mail because if you don't it takes a long time to get here.*
> *Well dear I'll be closing for this time. I got 35 letters this week & have to answer some of them if I can but boy am I busy. I sure wish this war was over with soon. I miss you all so much. Tell the kids to pray for me every night because the day is coming soon.*
> *Well good night may God Bless you all.*
> *Love always, Frank*

> *P.S. How is Joe working good I hope. And is he feeling good? Tell him not to work to hard at night it will get him ha ha. goodnight.*

It was as if he was whispering to himself as he finished the letter home, somewhere between a soft hush and a prayer.

Chapter Nineteen

Sunday nite, June 4, 1944

Dear Viola,
I received two of your letters. One yesterday and the other to day. The one I got yesterday was written on the 16 of may and the second on the 29th. That one sure got here in a hurry.

I haven't been able to write for the past wk or so because of the problems we are having. We just got back from an over nite one. It was rather tough but we all lived through it. our biggest trouble is that it is so hot and we sweat so much and makes us weak.

We still go swimming but we seldom go on our own. And there isn't much fun in it unless we do. They try to teach us the G.I. way but aren't doing so well. I can swim a little but could of learned a lot sooner my own way. Half of the time they keep us on the beach instead of in the water and you can't learn that way.

Well, how is everything on the farm going by now? Is it still raining? I didn't think that dry spell would last very long. I sure hope it don't ruin the crops. That's what I hate about a wet year. You have to get in and hoe the weeds out. And I know what a job that is.

We aren't having as much rain as we have been having. It used to rain just about every day. I don't mind that as long as we are in camp. But sleeping in the woods with not much protection isn't so good.

So you have been fixing up the insides of the house. I didn't see anything wrong with it as it was. Of course that was quit a while ago. How is our house at home? Are they still working on it? I sure would like to see them when you are all threw. I probably won't recognize the place when I get home. That is if I don't get home in the next 3 or 4 years.

No, I didn't know that Walter is getting married. I haven't heard from Ted since I am here. who is he marrying the girl from Warren? I can't understand why the army hasn't gotten him. I sure expected him to be in by now.

I am glad to hear that Joey and Barbra passed in school. Joey sure is getting up there isn't he. I sure am proud of them two & I miss them very much.

So, Mother has a nice victory garden. Well she always does have every year. It doesn't seem to matter how much it rains she always has a nice garden.

I am glad to know that my trees are doing well. That is one crop that rain doesn't hurt very much.

It sure was nice of John S. to send Joey that bond. I wish I could have sent him one too. But I never seem to have the money or I forgot about it.

Well I must close for now. we are suppose to go to town tomorrow so I better go to bed. I am so darn tired I can't hardly stay awake.

Goodby & God bless you all.
Love, Claude

P.S. Have you heard from Johnny lately?

June 6, 1944: Operation Overlord, D Day Invasion

Commit to the Lord whatever you do and your plans will succeed. –Proverbs 16:3

Give us aid against the enemy, for the help of man is worthless. With God we will gain the victory and trample down our enemies. –Psalm 60:11-12

Tuesday, June 6, 1944; Fort, Jackson

Dear Viola,
It's been a long time since I've written to you but I just can't help it. we've been plenty busy lately taking ten mile hikes, field problems and all kinds of 2nd army and 9th corp. inspections. Everyone is running around here like mad. I don't even have time to breathe anymore.

I thought you'd be surprised to hear that I might get married. I figured if I stay in the U.S. much longer I might as well get married and get started. If I get married I can get an allotment taken out for Ceil and she can be working and that will help us get a better start when I get back. If I don't get married I'll never save any money and besides I'm getting pretty old too. Joe was right I should have got married long ago.

We went through the nite infiltration course last nite. I'm sore all over from it. I was pushing more dirt in front of me than a large scraper. I'd better tell you a little about it so you'll know what I'm talking about. Two machine guns are fixed and firing over our heads while we crawl from a trench toward the guns on our stomachs. Land mines explode in our faces while going through then too we have all kinds of barbed wire entanglements to go under. I sure could have used a pair of pliers last nite. I acquired plenty of scratches and rips in my clothes in the process.

How is everyone at home? Well I hope, I suppose you're all plenty busy now in the field and house.

So Joe is going fishing to Canada with Jim soon? It kinda made me home-sick when I heard that. Gee, I sure would like to be going with them. Oh well, maybe someday soon I'll be going with them.

The big fire works started to-day and that's all we can get on the radio now. I wonder where my boys in the 411th are now? I haven't heard from them for some time now.

Well Vi, I'll have to leave now. Give my love to all and write soon.

Goodnite. Love, Johnny

Wednesday, June 7, 1944; Somewhere in English

Dearest Viola & Family,

I received your letter to-day and one of my letters that I sent you. I did not put Ohio on it so it came back. I have some time to day to write because I am on Guard.

We are busy all the time. I sure wish this war will soon be over with. So we can come home.

I was glad to know that you all are feeling good & that the kids are doing good in school. So Babs in second grade & Joey is in fifth doing O.K. I see the kids are like me. get it?

I hear that John Smida's wife had a baby boy. I know how he feels about a boy. tell him to keep up the good work. How is he doing on the muck?

So Joey likes to fish well Joe sure likes it to. I sure see some good fish here but can't fish. Tell Joe to take you some place or he can't go fish ha ha. You don't have to tell me about him. I know him.

The weather is cool in English. I sure hope you are having good weather by this time so you have a good crop this year.

So mother got us a new bed & dresser for herself that's good. I sure hope I get home soon to see it. I think John will be home soon by his letter. Well it's time for me to go so I'll close for this time.

*May God Bless you all.
With all my love, Frank*

Friday, June 9, 1944; S.W. Pacific

*Dear Vi,
I was certainly happy to receive your letter dated May 25th and to know every thing is okay back there. Sure makes me happy to know you folks are so happy to hear from us boys. We feel the same hearing from you. We over here, do just like Joe does, when he come from work, asks "any mail today?" It's a pretty low feeling when they say, no. I don't know what we'd do without letters from home. It sure helps.
You say Claude is in Hawaii? That's quite a nice place. Course I'm quite away from there, but I heard it's a beautiful place. What do you think of the invasion of France? We down here, thought it great. The sooner it is over there the sooner it will be over here. I just wonder whether Frank is in it. I've been quite worried about it the last few days. If he is may God watch over him and bring him home safely. Glad to hear Johnny is still in the States, hope he stays there. Heard from Charles the other day. He's in New Guinea. Said it was quite wet and muddy over there, also hot. He said it looks like a good place to go fishing and will the first chance he has. Good luck to him. I've been busy lately besides doing my other work. I've been cutting hair. Course I make a little on the side.
Yes, I hope Johnny is still home when I come. We will probably whoop it up some. Hey! I dropped him a line yesterday. I gave him hell for not writing to me. it's been three months since he wrote last. I wrote him a few times in between that. Course he told Beth that he thought I was coming home soon and didn't want to write. But I told him if I wrote, his letters would get to me any way. I still don't know when I am coming home. It's one of*

those things that just come all at once and you go. Ha.

Sorry to hear that the weather has been so bad. I hope it's better now. I'm glad Joe plowed a piece of our muck. It will help him and also keep our muck in shape. How does Joey and Barbara like working on the muck? I don't blame them. I never really cared much when I was a kid. But I know they are willing to help. It was really swell of the children to drop me a line. I really can't express my feeling but I was really happy. I think they are wonderful. Don't forget to send me some of those pictures, of Joey and the folks.

I was really glad to hear that the two Joes are doing so good at fishing. I sure wish I could be there and go along. Man! When you mentioned about fried fish with crackers and crumbs, I was sure hungry. We'll have to make some that way the next time we go fishing. Okay?

Well honey, I'll close for this time and drop you a line again. Good luck and may God Bless you all. Say hello to all for me. Love and kisses, John

P.S. Tell Veronica Hello and that I rec'd your lovely letter.

Dear Joey,
Rec'd your swell letter and am very proud of you. First, for making your first Holy Communion and for writing me such a long letter. I suppose by this time you are quite a fisherman. That's swell! When I come home you and I can go fishing. I haven't got much time to write and I know you are busy too helping Mom & Dad. So I'll not take no more of your time, all I want to say is be a good boy and do what Mother & Dad tell you to do. And pray every day for your Uncles in services. Goodnite and good luck at your next fishing trip.

Love and kisses, your Uncle John

P.S. I'm proud of you for passing to the fifth grade. Keep it up Joey that's swell.

Dear Barbara,

Thanks for your lovely letter too. And I like you wrote in your letter. I love you too. And miss you and Joey very much. Do you and Joey go to shows much? When the picture "Lost Angel" come around tell Daddy to take you and Joey to see it. it's about a little girl like you. When I saw it, it reminded me of you, when I use to come over to your home. I bet by this time, you are quite a big girl. I'm also proud of you for passing into the second grade. Good work Barbara. Good night and be a good little girl. Pray every night and in that way, we will come home sooner. Your Uncles love you and Joey.

Love and kisses, Uncle John

Monday night, June 19, 1944

Dear Sister,

I received your letter today and was vey happy to hear from you. It sure was a nice long letter and I enjoyed it very much when I read it. I am sorry I made you worry about me just because I haven't been writing. I am not as busy as I have been so maybe I will be able to write more often.

I sure am glad to hear that the farm is doing well despite the wet weather you have been having. You say Dad has the nicest corn in the county. Well that is something to be proud of. Yes I don't know what dad would do if it wasn't for Joe and his two daughters to help him. I know you are glad to help him and I also know he is glad that you are.

Yes the invasion is on and doing pretty well. I always listen to the radio or read the news paper to find out how things are going on the fronts. It sure can't end too soon for me. It's too bad Frank had to be in on the invasion. But I am sure he can take care of himself. He was a man that always could no matter what came up.

  I still haven't heard from Johnny. I wrote to him quite some time ago. But I can understand why. They sure do keep us busy. The only time I get to write is at nite. And after a day's work one is pretty well tired out and want to get a little rest. Yes, I heard about Johnny wanting to get married on his next furlough. Eugene wrote and told me about it. I was very much surprised to her about it too. He told me he wasn't going to until the war was over with. I just wonder what made him change his mind. Maybe he expects to stay in the U.S.A. I had intentions of getting married on my last furlough, but after thinking it over I decided not to. I don't know what Catherine thinks about it, but I suppose she is angry and I don't blame her. I am now sorry I haven't a long time ago.

  So Joe is planning on planting some carrots. Well it takes a lot of work and time. Especially if the weather is damp and the weeds get a start. If he does plant the carrots he won't be able to help father as much. And he wouldn't like that very much. Of course it wouldn't mean much money but I am sure Dad is willing to pay what ever he ask for.

  I went to Holy Communion last Sunday. It's been the first time for quite a while, but I hope to do better in the near future. I go to church as often as possible.

  So you and the kids were on vacation. Well I am glad to hear that you were able to. I am sure you deserved it. I just can't wait until I am able to take a vacation too. Of course I intend to take more than five days.

  Well I must close for now. I want to write another letter before it gets to late.

  Goodby and God bless you all.
  All my love, Claude

Tuesday, June 20, 1944; Ft. Jackson

Dear Viola,

I don't know what's the matter with you people it seems I haven't heard from you in ages. I should talk for as often as I write. There really isn't anything hear for me to talk about. It's the same old thing day in and day out.

I thought I'd get home on a three day pass but it's all off now no more passes. I suppose you were kinda expecting me last week weren't you? I expected to get home then too but no such luck.

I might as well tell you now, that we're about ready to move out of here. I think we'll pull out of New York at least I hope so. Who knows I might get a chance to see Frank and my old buddies of the 411th.

Well how is everything on the home front? I suppose you're all busy as heck with the farm work.

We've been busy as heck here to lately. We've had about a thousand clothing checks already and will probably have a thousand more before we go.

Well Vi, I'll have to close for now. give my love to all and write soon.

Goodnite.

Love, Johnny

It was June 21st, Frank and his buddies of 793rd Field Artillery would sit huddled and anxious on the streets of Southhampton for two days. This waiting to cross the channel to Normandy seemed like an eternity, and for a brief moment, Frank almost would have preferred the discomfort of that pup tent he called home since landing in England and living virtually on top of the artillery ranges where they trained every day.

The training was grueling and redundant and Frank spent

countless hours firing the small 155mm howitzer ordinance used for training on the artillery range or in school learning about strategies, mines and aircraft identification. When he wasn't on the range, he was sent to one of six beachfronts for personnel landing training. Loading the howitzers on the landing craft began as an almost insurmountable task and at first it seemed as though few of the guns would ever make it both onto and off of one of the landing craft without damage and or injury to the men. However, the daily grind of those assignments were eventually met with the utmost efficiency that would be demonstrated once the 793rd landed in Normandy and fired their first rounds in battle.[19]

    The journey of the 793rd was very much like that of the 37th Buckeye Division. Both followed behind the initial confrontations all the while training, so that when they finally did see battle, they were like a well-oiled machine. This seeming overkill of preparation would prove indispensable as it reduced the number of casualties and conveyed a quiet, mounting attitude of success as the only outcome.

    On June 24th, the 793rd landed in Normandy where the scene of wreckage and carnage from the past two weeks could still be experienced through the nostrils of each of the men as they hit the beach, leaving the battalion in shock and sleepless that first night.

    The allies had been stockpiling armament, supplies and personnel in England for almost two years while planning the D Day Invasion, and from what Frank had witnessed, it looked like most of it was left on this one beach. Personnel carriers lay partially submerged in six to ten feet of water, many with a gaping hole in the side of its hull, all of them riddled with bullets from what was once the enemy's stronghold along the cliffs leading to the beach. There were still corpses washing ashore as well as occasional small plumes of black smoke coming from destroyed jeeps and other equipment left in twisted heaps on the beach.

---

[19] www.793rdfieldartillery.homestead.com

Frank couldn't fathom what the initial scene was like, from the countless rounds expended by the Germans to the seemingly endless wave of allied troops landing on a designated shoreline. Suddenly he thought of his buddies, the "All Americans", with the 82nd Airborne and wondered how they were faring behind enemy lines. Frank had to work through the rising lump in his throat and do his part to help lick those Germans once and for all.

The Lord will fight for you; you need only to be still.
–Exodus 14:14

Monday nite, June 26, 1944

Dear Viola,

I received your letters with the pictures today. The pictures are very nice. I think I will keep a few of them. I haven't made up my minds which ones yet, but maybe I will before I get through writing. Yes I can see the two stars in the window but it isn't very plain. The bush in white blossom is awful nice. I can remember it as plain as day. I wish I could have taken some pictures to send you. I had a few taken of myself in town but they didn't come out very good. If I had a camera I could have taken some nice ones.

So Joe decided to plant some carrots. Well I hope he makes good with them. I bet it will sure keep him busy especially if the weeds get a start of course you and the kids can help a little.

It sure is too bad about what happened to the wheat and clover. But that is the way it goes. You get a good crop and then something happens to it. I sure wish I was home to help dad with the haying. Maybe if he had some help the clover wouldn't be out there rotting.

Well there isn't much I can write about myself. I am getting along very well and I feel pretty good. We have been having beer parties once in a while. And boy am I drinking my share of it. of course it isn't as tastey as the beer we used to get in the States. But it is better than none at all.

I got a letter from Johnny last Sat. He sure suprised me with the long letter. It was six pages. He sure had a lot to say. I answered it Sun. but I didn't write a very long letter. It is so darn hard to find anything to write about.

Well I have decided to keep four of the pictures. I am going to keep the group picture, one with Joey, the one with the white bush and of course the one with Joey, Barbara and the trees. Joey does look like Mahatma Gandhi but I like it any way. Why didn't he take his glasses off when his picture was take? I want you to get Joe and Eugene together and have some pictures taken of them. The two sure would make a pair.

Well I must close for now. I will write as often as possible. And don't worry about me. I will take care of myself. Goodby and God Bless you all.

Love to all. Claude

I am sorry I couldn't write a better letter, but I hope you understand how difficult it is for me. Please say hello to Joe for me. I am sending the other pictures in this letter.

As Claude and the 305th Infantry secured their gear in preparation for their journey toward Guam, Frank and the 793rd Field Artillery had set up shop near the crossroads of St Lo – La Luzerne and were into day four of battering enemy lines whenever directed. The 105mm and 155mm Howitzers could support advancing infantry units anywhere from 3 to 8 miles away.[20]

---

[20] www.793rdfieldartillery.homestead.com

Chapter Twenty

Friday, June 30, 1944; Somewhere in France

Dearest Family,
I hope you all are feeling fine. I am just as good as you would want me to be, a little tired but that's all.
France is O.K. I have a bottle of wine it's O.K. sure wish I could send you some of it. Maybe some day I can send you some.
The weather has been raining all the time, but it's hot here.
How are the kids getting long? I sure wish I could see them. I don't have a picture of them. All I have is a picture with Mother.
Oh Yes how are the folks getting long? If you all don't hear from me all time, don't get mad it's because I'm so busy and tired.
Just see mother because I'll write her more.
Well honey may God Bless you all. With all my love, Frank

P.S. I hope John is home, I didn't hear from him now for some time.

Sunday, July 15, 1944; Corporal John Lulek change of address

The 793rd was on the move, after holding a position for nearly two weeks, now some days the advance was so aggressive that there was no time to fire the guns. That was just fine with

253

Frank because there developed a shortage of two critical items for he and his men, ammunition and dry socks! HQ directed the men to fire only five rounds per gun per day. The ammunition problem would be remedied. As for the socks, the men were on their own.[21]

Monday, July 16, 1944

Dearest Family,
How are you all getting long? I hope you all are feeling fine. I received your box. I sure was glad to get it, thanks for sending it.
As I'm writing this letter in my foxhole it's raining like hell. I sure hope we would have one week of good weather. I hope you are having good weather back home. How are the things on the muck? I hope you don't have the weather we are having. By the way why the hell don't John write to me? I did not hear from him since I came hear. I'm getting mad at him.
We don't have much time to write. When I do I'll write. When I get time I always write to mother first.
How are the kids getting long? Tell them I said hello. I sure would like to see them. Is Joe working in the mill?
Well I'll close for to night. May God Bless you all. Thanks again for the box.
With all my love, Frank

P.S. Tell Winnie M to send me some V mail soon.

---

[21] www.793rdfieldartillery.homestead.com

Sunday, July 29. 1944; Some where in France

Dearest Family,
It's been some time since I heard from you but I know you are busy at home. We sure are. If you get some time please write me.
France is a busy place. We sure are busy all the time, I hope this is over with soon, I would like to come home soon. How are the kids getting long? I hear from mother and she said everything is fine at home. I sure would like to hear from John L. Will you tell him to write to me? The weather is beautiful for the last week. It's been hot in two ways if you get what I mean. We sure are working hard, some of them back home should work like us. Well I'll be closing for to night.
Please write soon. May God Bless you all.
Your brother, Frank

Friday, August 3, 1944

Dearest Family,
Just a line to let you know that everything is fine. I sure was glad to know that everything was O.K. at home, & that Joe had a good time in Canada fishing. I sure wish I could been with him.
The weather has been O.K. it sure is hot. I like France, but not the war it's hell. I hope this place will be the last place I go to. The place I want to go is home & soon maybe some day soon I'll be home.
Well I'll close for this time may God Bless you all at home.

255

Take care of yourself and the family.
  All my love, Frank

Saturday, August 4, 1944; Some where in France

Dearest Family,
  I received your letter last night Honey boy was I glad when I got the letter from you in a week. I just write & give you hell for not writing. I take it all back.
  I didn't like to hear that John was in New York. Maybe I'll see him once here. don't worry he'll be O.K.
  The weather here is fine. I sure was glad to no that you are going to have some good carrots.
  I hope the kids are fine. I sure miss them so much. So the kids will be going to school soon. I know you will be glad. Then you can sleep all day? Ha ha. I sure wish I could sleep all day. Just once.
  I'll be closing for to night may God Bless you all.
  Love, Frank

Since we belong to the day, let us be self-controlled, putting on faith and love as a breastplate, and the hope of salvation as a helmet. For God did not appoint us to suffer wrath but to receive salvation through our Lord Jesus Christ. He died for us so that whether we are awake or asleep, we may live together with him. Therefore encourage one another and build each other up, just as in fact you are doing. -1 Thessalonians 5:8-11

Friday, August 17, 1944; V-mail

Dearest Family,
Just a line to let you know that I am O.K. & hope you are the same. Well the kids are going back to school soon. I know you will not like that much. ha ha. How is Joe working? I hope he is working O.K.

I just received a letter from John he is in England and had a good trip over. He don't like the English girls but he likes the beer. Wait till he gets the beer here he will not like it. it's about time he wrote to me. I hope he comes to France maybe I'll see him.

Well I'll close for this time because I have to write him to night. With all my love, Frank

Saturday, August 25, 1944

Dear Viola,
Well I'm somewhere in France now. I sure do get around don't I? We've been moving around so fast that I don't get much time to write. If mail keeps coming in like it has been the past few days I'll never answer half of it. I've been getting anywhere from five to fifteen letters a day. That's the way I like to see it. Celia's been writing about twice a day for the last month.

I wrote to Claude and Frank when I was in England. I got an answer from Frank but I haven't heard from Claude in two months. I imagine Claude was plenty busy if he was in on the Guam deal.

I might get a chance to see Frank while I'm here. Wouldn't that be swell? My old outfit is here too who knows I might run across them. I'm having a rough time trying to talk to these

French people. I wish I would have taken the course when I was in school. We usually do more motioning than talking and after a rough struggle we manage to figure each other out.

You asked me if there is anything that I needed, well there are two things to be exact. A lot of letters and cigars. Try to get me El Verso cigars they're real dark. Groves can get them for you just tell them they're for me.

Those pictures certainly came out swell. The kids sure are growing fast. I'll hardly know them when I get home.

Well Viola, I'll have to close for a while. I'll try to write in a couple days. So long. Love to all. Johnny

Relief washed over Claude's face as he and several of the men punched through the underbrush to a clearing North of the beachhead where defensive positions had been established since the 77th had landed on Guam. Thus far they had met greater resistance from the habitat than from the Japanese army and now that they had met up with the 3rd Marine Division, they had become a formidable force essentially connecting and securing both south and north beachheads on the island.[22]

Monday, September 11, 1944; Guam

Dear Viola,
Received your last letter today and was very glad to hear from you. I don't know what I would do without your letters. They sure do help my morale.

I am sorry I haven't been writing. I really wanted to write a long time ago. But I just couldn't find time to write. Every time I started a letter I was called away and couldn't finish it. it sure is bad you have to find out how I'm doing from Kalas's folks, but I

---

[22] www.history.army.mil www.Wikipedia.org

couldn't help it. he just had the breaks and was able to write.

I haven't written to Catherine for a long time. I don't know what she will think. Maybe I can explain why I haven't been writing. I'll try and write a few lines to her tomorrow.

I am glad to hear that the market on pickles has been fair. I only wish I could have been there to help you with them. Well maybe next year I will be home so I will be able to.

Sure was glad to hear that dad got his citizen papers. I thought he had given it up. I guess if it wasn't for you and the rest of them he would have.

So you had to buy a new battery for the car. Well you can't expect one to last forever. You know how hard it was for John and I to keep the tractor, car and truck going. We were always buying something for them. If it wasn't one thing it was another. You always thought it was easy to run a car didn't you?

I got a letter from Ceil quite a while ago. I haven't answered because I could never find the time. I don't know why she should think I am sore at her. If she knew the situation she would feel different. I'll try and write to her though. I have so many letters to write I don't know if I will ever catch up.

Well I suppose by now marketing is all over with. You should have made pretty good money. Did you ever sit down and figure out just how much you really did make? I am beginning to think there is good money in raising pickles. I was just thinking when I get home we would go a little deeper in the business. That is if the folks are willing to help us. Maybe we can talk John in to lending us a hand once in a while. But I suppose it will be asking too much from him ha ha.

Well I must close for now. I haven't much time to write just now. I will write more when I write the next time.

So long. Love and kisses, Claude

Please say hello to Joe and the children.

Frank had covered so much ground in the past two weeks that he swore the 793rd had crossed Belgium and was now in Holland as they received their orders to fire on the German town of Geilenkirchen. This was the first round to be fired at the Germans on their own soil![23]

Thursday, September 21, 1944; Some where

Dearest Family,
I received your letter & was so glad to hear from you. It was some time since I heard from you all. I received a letter from John L. to day. He is some place in France. I hope to see him soon one day. I seen his outfit B, Battery I didn't know he was in it.
The weather is beautiful it been raining some but not much. I hope this war is over soon so I can come home. I sure miss the farm. I hope we all come home soon. What a time we will have to gether. Well to day I got two packages from Winnie Matson.
Well I'll close for this time. I hope Joe is working & the kids are getting long with there school work. Tell them I miss them with all my love may God Bless you all.
Love, Frank

---

[23] www.793rdfieldartillery.homestead.com

News Clip About John Soukenik's Outfit

37th Holding Islands

Gen. Beightler Informs Friend of Pacific "Step" Positions

Certain islands "in the south Pacific considered the most important of all the "stepping stone" with the exception of Australia and Hawaii," are being held by the 37th Division, composed mostly of Ohioans, Major General Robert S. Beightler, the division's commander, wrote recently to an army friend, it was revealed yesterday.

Gen. Beightler gave the information in a letter to Major Harry H. Kerr, Camp Perry post executive officer, which was received last week. Exact whereabouts of the division is a military secret.

Sunday, A.M., September 24, 1944

Dear Viola,
Well, I finally got a chance to write. I probably wouldn't have, but since it is Sunday they are letting us have the day off. I started writing a few days ago, but it got so hot and I began to sweat so much I couldn't finish it. It isn't so bad today the sky is clouded over and there is a little breeze.
Yes, I came through the campaign with flying colors. Of course it wasn't as easy as it sounds. We had a tough battle for 21 days. We not only had to fight the Japs but also the mosquitoes

and flies.

The natives here are a nice bunch of people. At least the ones that I met were. They can understand and talk English. I mean most of them can. Some of the older people can't very well, but we manage to get along. I have had meals with them in a certain town here and they sure can cook. Well anyway it tasted good. After eating C and K rations for a month any cooked meal tasted good.

So, Johnny is in France. It sure didn't take him long to get there. I haven't heard from him in a long time. But I suppose he is busy with the Germans. It sure would be nice if he would meet Frank over there. I was hoping to meet John out here, but it looks like I won't. I haven't even written to him, I'll bet he will think I am a fine pal. I have thought of him a thousand times but never did I write. He should be coming home before long. Of course being an M.P. he may be over here for some time yet. I understand a lot of soldiers are to be discharged after the war in Europe is over. I am hoping I am one but no such luck.

Well I suppose by now dad has the silo filled and all of the corn cut. I sure wish I could have been home to help with it. I can remember when you and I cut corn. We had quite a time at first but after we caught on to how it worked things went swell. You know John left without showing me a thing about it. When I get home I'll have to learn all over again. But it won't be so hard this time. I sure do miss all of that work cutting corn, hauling soybeans and such things as that. It makes me lonesome to go back on the farm. Well, maybe it won't be too much longer that I will be.

How are Joey and Barbra doing in school? Barbra is in the second grade isn't she? Time is moving so fast I can't keep up with it. Well what ever grade they are in I bet they are doing all rite. I just can't picture Carol Jean going to school. She seems so young. She can't be over 5 years can she?

Tell mother not to worry I'll come back safe. I'll just have to after knowing I have a thousand dollars waiting when I get there. I sure will need it too. Gee, but I never expected her to do that for us. It sure makes me happy to have a mother like that. That will do any thing and give any thing we want. I miss her and all of you very much. and wish this would all end so I could be with all of you again.

Well, how is Joe doing at the shop? I suppose he is making a lot of money. After working there so long I don't suppose he will ever want to go back to the muck farm again. I think when I get back I'll go to my old job. I think I was doing pretty good there. That will be one place that will be kept going in good time and bad.

I'll have to close for now. it's getting so darn warm that my sweat is droping on the paper. I will write again as soon as possible. I hope to do more writing this evening when it gets a little cooler.

Goodby for now.
Love and kisses.
May God Bless you all. Claude

Say hello to Joe and the kids for me.

Saturday, September 30, 1944; Belgium V-mail

Dear Viola,
It seems I never get time to drop you a few lines. I'll try to do better in the future. I'm with the First Army that might give you some idea where I am. I got a v-mail from Claude last week. If it's not to late I'd like to have a fruit cake for Christmas and cigars of course. We've been getting plenty of rain here lately. The market stuff didn't last very long this year did it? How were the prices this year? I wish I was back to go there again, I kinda miss it. I suppose Mother is plenty busy canning and Father probably has his hands full too. Last year at this time I was helping him fill

silo. Well Viola I'll close for now, I'll write in a day or so.
      So long for now.
      Love, Johnny

                    Sunday P.M., October 1, 1944

     Dear Viola,
     I am just fine sister and hope you and the family are the same. No I haven't seen any more action, but have been rather busy and wasn't able to write very much. But from now on I hope to do more.
     I guess the Yanks are doing pretty good out here. they take everything that they attempt to. We have a radio here, but never get a chance to listen to it except at nites.
     So dad is having trouble getting fertilizer. Well that is the trouble with farming in these times. It is hard to get things needed for farming, but things will be changing as soon as the war in Europe is over with. I suppose dad has his silo filled and his field corn cut by now. well the next thing will be to husk the corn and dig the potatoes and the farm work will be almost through.
     It's too bad about Mrs. Frydrych dieing. I remember pretty well when she used to sing in the choir. I even remember when you used to sing too.
     So you made pretty good money at the market this year? Well I am darn glad to hear it. this is the time to make the money because after the war there will be a lot of changes made. But I hope it don't happen until I get some of that easy money.
     I hear Joey is learning to play Veronica's trumpet. Well he should be able to play as good as she did. He has a pretty good teacher to teach him. He is the same fellow that taught Ted Misiolek how to play the accordion. Ted said he really knew his stuff.
     It's a little better around here except for the ants. It sure

is hot out here and it rains every time you turn around. it's a darn good thing it does too or you couldn't stand it very long. I am sweating like a horse just sitting here writing. We have a post exchange so it makes matter a little better of course we can't get much but it's better than nothing. I go to the show every nite to pass the time away. We see some of the latest pictures.

Have you been hearing from Johnny lately? I heard from him once since he has been overseas. He must be seeing a lot of action or he would be writing. I guess I can't say much I only wrote once. But I don't usual write until I hear from him.

Well Viola, I must close for now. I would like to write another letter before it gets to late. It is just about chow time and it gets dark soon afterwards.

Goodby and don't worry about me. I will take care of myself.

May God Bless you all. Love, Claude

Excuse the poor writing.

Chapter Twenty One

This brief respite from the ever-changing elements was a great morale builder for John and his men as they woke from their first deep slumber in weeks to the feeling of hand-hewn oak floors just beneath their blankets. The 557th had confirmed their first two downed enemy aircraft and had been on the move through a bone chilling rain as of late. This brief R & R at the old farmhouse was much needed by both guests and hosts alike. It brought a fleeting moment of clarity as well as memories of what family life once was and all longed for, and they would fight to have once again.

Stay in that house, eating and drinking whatever they give you, for the worker deserves his wages. –Luke 10:7

Tuesday, October 3, 1944; Belgium

Dear Viola,
Received your letter and was very happy to hear from you. My morale is going up now, all I need is more letters. I'm trying to answer all my letters as soon as I get them. There'll probably be times when I won't be able to do it but I'll do my best.
We're still getting plenty of rain and it's getting colder every day. How is the weather at home now? I'll bet the trees are turning all beautiful colors. I miss the beautiful fall scenery. Most of the trees here are evergreen and the ones that aren't don't seem to be turning colors yet.

I'm with the First Army. You probably can get more information out of the paper than what I can tell you.

We're near a house where a widow and her four children live. We kinda moved in on her. I'm writing this letter in her house now. She's a swell old lady we call her (ma). She's been doing a lot of our washing for us. She seems happy to have us around. I got a loud speaker which I hooked up to the radio and ran it up to the house. We have good music on it most of the day also we get the latest news. When there isn't any thing on the radio Mom and us boys sing songs. She knows several American songs, she sings in French and we take our usual part. We all have a grand old time.

Tell mom not to worry about me and that I'll be home to collect that $1,000 before long. Don't worry about Claude either he'll probably beat me home.

I got myself three German blankets that I picked up in the field. We were supposed to be issued two more to keep warm. I'm going to pick up all I can find the more the merrier. One thing sure I'm not going to freeze this winter. I don't know how much snow they have here but I hope it don't get to deep.

I don't think I'll get a chance to see Frankie now. by the way have you been hearing from John lately? I'm sending some French and German currency to the kids as a souvenir. The French franc is worth two cents in our money and the German Mark is equal to ten cents in our stuff.

Joe ought to see some of the jack rabbits we have here they're as big as dogs. He'd have a picnic here hunting them, they run faster than lightning. Any time I get hungry I'll go out and shoot one.

I suppose by now the kids are well on their way to another year of school. How does Joey like Miss Christy for a teacher? I think he'll really like her he should and he'll learn something. Who does Barbara have for a teacher this year? I really miss the kids a lot.

I figured mom would make good on the market this year.

She shouldn't do it though she's working entirely too hard. Father also has been working to hard poor guy. I tried to tell them to sell out and take it easy but they won't listen to me.

Well Viola, I'll close for now, see you in a couple of days. Give my love to mom and dad.

So long for now. Love, Johnny

The 793rd was able to settle in to a daily routine with only occasional periods of firing to clear out the enemy's random blind attempts to pinpoint and counter their location. During this time, Frank and the 793rd Field Artillery Battalion would receive The Bronze Star for their part in the invasion of Normandy.[24]

Because of the Lord's great love we are not consumed, for his compassions never fail. They are new every morning; great is your faithfulness. –Lamentations 3:22-23

Friday, October 6, 1944; V-mail; Somewhere in Holland

Dearest Family,
I hope you are all feeling fine? I am doing O.K. so don't worry. It been some time since I have wrote to you because of being busy all the time & the weather has been raining & cold.

It's been two weeks since I heard from John L. I don't know where he is. He may be some place in Holland I don't know. It's so damn cold to-day that I just can't write.

So Viola, if you don't hear from me just see Mother because I'll be writing to her first, O.K. well honey I'll close for this time.

May God Bless you all. Till next time all my love, Frank

---

[24] www.793rdfieldartillery.homestead.com

Thursday, October 12, 1944; Guadalcanal

Dear Vi,

I finally got around to answer your sweet letters. I rec'd your last one a few days ago. It was dated Sept 26. Some how are mail hasn't been coming in any too good or maybe I'm losing my friends. Who knows Ha. Well may be it's better that the mail hasn't come too fast 'cause I been quite busy and find little time for writing. I try to write to Mother as often as I can and I know that way you all have a chance to read it any way. So if you don't receive any from me for awhile just read the one I send to Mother and that way you will know how I am. Right now Vi I'm a little home sick and wish I could come home but outside of that I'm feeling fine. As you probably know by now I'm the Co. Barber and doing okay. Wish I could've had the job the 24 months I've been over Seas but that's the way it goes. You can't have every thing.

Heard from Frank yesterday and he's okay but quite busy too. Said he was in three different countries all in one day that's going. Isn't it? he said he was some where in Netherlands. I know they are having a hard time of it but he still said it isn't bad. Wish this thing was over with so we could all come home again and live the life we love. I haven't heard from Johnny or Claude for some time. I lost Claude's address and Johnny haven't wrote to me since he went over Seas so I can't drop them a line. When you write again, give me their address. Glad to hear Claude is okay. I know they had a hard time too. Regardless of where you are in the war it's no fun.

You ask me in your letter if I saw Bob Hope. Yes, and also the Jack Benny Show. They're okay but I don't think it builds are moral any. I just soon hear them on the radio anyway they tried.

Yes the canal or sock as the boys call it down here is much larger than most people think it is. If you look at you map it looks awful small but it's a good three hundred miles around. That's the way most of them are course some are most larger and some are smaller. We have a farm here, quite big. That way we have vegetables all the time. Tomatoes and things like that don't do so good. It's just a little too hot, but we do get a few now and then.

Glad to hear your folks have their Silo filled and with the frost getting the other things like pickles and etc. It relieves you all of some work. I was surprised to hear how long your market season was. The farmer should've done pretty good this year. I hear E. Smida is making so much he doesn't know what to do with it. Well he can give us boys in the Army a little when we come home.

How's Joe doing? I suppose he's getting ready to do a little hunting. I was hoping on coming home for hunting season this year but it doesn't look so good. They're now giving furlough for 31 days or you can wait for rotation and that's just what I'm going to do. If you take a furlough you come right back to your outfit after your furlough and go another two years. If I had to do a nother two years in a place like this, I'll go nuts and I mean nuts. I now have 29 months over seas and I think I can stand a nother few more months if I have to. I hope it's no longer. Boy, my morale is low and I think every boy that has 24 months over seas is the same. Just think of those young boys that just came over, they've got two years more to go and may be more.

I don't know whether or not I sent you a letter thanking you for the swell pictures you send me of Joe, Babs and my folks. If not thanks, and they're swell. They all look the same as when I left. Course Joey and Babs look a lot bigger. Did you see the picture I send Mother of my self at my Barber shop. It's not so hot but it will give you a idea of what I look like.

Well I guess I've taken up enough of your time and will close with love to all. Hope to see you all real soon. If I don't see you all at Xmas time, here is wishing you a Merry Christmas and a Happy New Year. Good nite and God Bless you all. Love and kisses, John

P.S. Write as often as you can I love to hear from you.

Friday, October 13, 1944; V-mail; Somewhere in Germany

Dearest Family,
I hope this letter will find you feeling in a good way. I am O.K. just have a cold but nothing to worry about.
How is Joe working? I hope he works all the time, because when I get back I am not going to work the hell with the work.
I did not hear from John L. for some time maybe he is busy like me, but I think he have more time to write? Maybe not.
We been have some bad weather rain & cold. I sure hope this will be over by next year.
Well honey I'll close for this time and see if I can get some sleep. May God Bless you all.
With all my love, Frank

Monday, October 16, 1944; Luxemburg

Dear Viola,
We moved again that's why you didn't hear from me for a week. We are now in the little country of Luxemburg. I can't see any difference in any of the countries I've been in. it rains just as hard and often everywhere. I'm having a hell of a time trying (censored)
Oh well! I guess things are tough all over now.
It's two o'clock in the morning now and I have three more hours to go on the switchboard. I hate this midnight shift it seems you don't get any sleep at all. I have quite a time trying to keep my eyes open at this hour in the morning. The light on the board isn't very bright so don't expect too much of me then too I'm liable to fall asleep any minute. I wonder what it would feel like to sit down at a nice big desk and bright lights to write a letter???

I was surprised to hear that Mrs. Fredrych died. I imagine it was quite a shock to all the people in the neighborhood. She seemed so young yet.

Things are getting tough here. I mean the tobacco situation. I'm down to the point where I'm smoking home grown German stuff. Wow! Is it strong, it's enough to make my helmet raise up off my head. It seems everyone is out of cigarettes too. You hear so much about all the cigarettes going over seas-well I sure in hell would like to know where they are. Cigars are something you just dream about here. you see what the situation is so I'd certainly appreciate it if you'd keep the cigars coming. If you can't buy a whole box at once buy a few at a time it doesn't matter if you have a mixture, I'm not particular anymore anything will do so long as it's a cigar.

Oh yes. Thanks for the air mail stamps. You shouldn't have sent them though cause I got plenty of airmail envelopes now. I'm having a hard time trying to find writing paper as you can see by the letter.

I was surprised to hear that v-mail is so much slower than airmail. It's true too that you can't write very much on them. I don't like the stuff very much myself. I very seldom write v-mail anymore, unless I don't have paper or envelopes.

What are you trying to do make a (Harry James) out of Joey? I think he'll make out good if he works at it hard enough (the trumpet).

Have you been hearing from Claude and the other boys lately? I got a nice letter from Claude not long ago. It seems the other boys have lost my address. Frank owes me a letter for some time now.

I've been going to church and Holy Communion almost every Sunday.

Well Viola, I'm going to leave you for a while. Give my love to mom and Dad and keep the letters coming. So long for now.

Love, Johnny

This was taken in Planstadt Germany just before we hit the Elbe. The guy pointing the gun at me is Hans Hafer from Johnstown, Pa, my wire lineman!

Tuesday P.M., October 17, 1944

Dear Viola,
I got your letter today and since I have time I decided to answer it rite away. No telling what tomorrow might bring. I also received your birthday card to me. It sure was nice too. I wish I was home though. It would be a much nicer place to spend ones birthday. But there are many more like me so I will have to make the best of it. a birthday is just another day to an Army man. At least when he is so far from nowhere.

Yes, it is 2 yrs. That I am in the service and it'll probably be another before I get home. But when I do I will be one happy guy.

Yes, Johnny wrote to me some time ago. And I answered it too. I don't know maybe he never got it or I would have heard from him since. I guess I will write again as soon as I have time. John sure is getting around plenty. Well that is one way of seeing a lot of country. Of course it isn't my way of seeing it. I don't think he is having a hard time of it. I sure wish I was in his outfit. It is much easier than the Infantry. He never does much walking. And as far as the heat is I don't think it gets very hot. I know darn well it doesn't get as hot as it is here.

Yes, it is tough on the farmers. It's a wonder more of them don't quit and go in some other kind of business. But I guess that is a hard thing to do. If it wasn't for the patient farmer I don't know where we would be in the war.

Well, I must close for now. it is just about time for chow and I would hate to miss that. Of course I wouldn't miss much but one has to eat you know.

I will try and write more later.

Goodbye and God Bless you all. Say hello to Joe and the kids.

Love, Claude

Tuesday, October 17, 1944; Some Where in Germany

Dearest Family,

Just a line to let you know that I received your letter & was so glad to hear from you, I hope everything is O.K. at home. I am feeling fine so don't worry I'll get long. I hope so.

It been some time since I heard from John & Johnie, I guess Johnie's busy & John may be on his way home. I sure hope so for he's been over seas for a long time. It would be good for

Mother to have him for Xmas. I sure would like to see him.

How are the kids getting long? And Joe is he working every day? Tell the kids to be good.

...Next Day 10/18/44...

Just received a letter from John and he don't think he will be home for Xmas, and Charles Jackson wrote me a letter he said he received a letter from you the day he wrote me, and he is doing O.K.

Well good night may God Bless you all
All my love, Frank

Wednesday, October 25, 1944

Dear Sister,
Received your letter today and was very glad to hear from you. It really does me good to hear from home and know everything is going fine.

I am not doing much this afternoon. In fact we don't do much any day in the afternoons. And it's a darn good thing we don't either. It is so hot we can't hardly stand it a half day.

We have a Post Exchange now and are able to get a few things we need. I have been running back and forth with things. You see we can only buy only a certain amount at a time and besides we don't get a chance to look around so I go again. So now I think my buddy and I have all we need for a while.

Yes, I know it is a lot of trouble sending packages to us boys. And we appreciate it very much. It sure is nice to have such a good sister that will send us things that we want.

I haven't received any of the packages yet. But I will watch myself when I open up the cans. We have been getting beer in tin cans and I am getting pretty good at opening them up.

Yes we are living in tents. It would be pretty hard to fill one of them with packages though. Because there are two sides open. Maybe these tents aren't to good a place to live in but we manage alrite. About the only trouble we have is with the ants, rats and mosquitoes at nite and by day it's the heat. So it isn't so bad is it? I have no idea what length of time we are to be here. but it is as good as any of them I guess.

So, you had the carrots pulled and you only got 18 crates. Gee, that is a surprise. I thought you would get more then that. The woodchucks sure must of raised hell with them. Well that is one crop that never paid for itself.

Where did you and Veronica pick the nuts? At the Jackson's place I am sure. You didn't pick that many around home. At least I was never able to get that many.

Boy, I sure would like to see your mansion. A house would look darn good rite now. After living in tents for over six months.

Well my birthday is past, but I didn't have a very good time. It was too bad we didn't have beer that day or I would have. I will make up for it when I get out of here don't you think I will. I am going to make up for a lot of things.

I got a letter from Johnny a few days ago. And have already answered it. He told me about being in Belgium. The way he talk he is awful anxious to get things over with there. Aren't we all? He said he is darn glad to be over there instead of this side of the world.

Well I must close for now. Will write again. Please say hello to the folks, Joe and the kids. Goodbye and God Bless you all.

Love and kisses, Claude

Sunday, October 29, 1944; Some Where in Germany

Dearest family,

Just a line to let you know that everything is fine & hope you are the same. The army is more work every day. We are busy all the time. It has been to-day I hope it don't rain for 3 months. it's cold but I don't mind the cold if it don't rain.

How are the kids getting long? Hope the kids are doing good in school. How is Joe? Is he working in the mills. Tell him not to work too hard.

I didn't hear from John L. in a long time maybe he's too busy with the girls over here. I sure had a time when I was in Holland & France with the gals. Got all I want ha. ha. You know me.

Well I'll close. May God Bless you all. Love, Frank

Monday, October 30, 1944, Some where in Germany

Dearest Viola & Family,

I received your letter & was so glad to hear from you, the pictures are so good. I just love them, thanks for sending them to me. I was glad to hear that everything is O.K. I am O.K. just my back is not so good. It's the rain & cold weather we are having.

I just got a letter from John S. and he said he was busy. I wish he was on his way home but he didn't say nothing about coming home.

I went to Church & communion for Mother for her birthday in 2 days so, that's all I can give her. I got a letter from her the same day I got one from you.

We are just as busy as befor working all the time. To day is a beautiful day I sure wish we have more like this.

I am the same old man, I sure give the girls hell when I get time. All the gals like me & want to come back with me. I tell them yes, ha ha. getting all I want ha ha.

Oh yes, I was in the same Army John is but not no more, I have been in it since I came over seas. I didn't hear from him for some time, to busy I guess? With the gals.

Well, I'll close for to day. Maybe I'll get more time some day. May God Bless you all.

With all my love, Frank

Saturday, November 4, 1944; SomeWhere in Germany

Dearest Viola & Family,
I received your letter & was glad to hear from you. Thanks for the pictures of the kids. I sure love them. I have them in a prayer book. How is Joe? Getting long with his work? Tell him not to work to hard.

I sure hope your cookies get here soon. I sure miss your cookies & candy. We don't get much candy or cigarettes I the last two weeks. I hope we get more soon.

This war looks like we will be here for one more year. I hope to make it home by next Xmas. Maybe John will be home soon. I hope so he has been over seas for a long time. Well Viola, I don't weigh so much any more, about 175 working to hard I guess. With all the work and gals ha ha, no I don't have much time with the gals.

Did you hear from John L. lately? It's been some time since I heard from him. I was in the same Army but not at this time. My A.P.O. is 339 so when you write him tell him will you.

Birr, it's sure cold. We thought we'd have frost last night & it sure didn't disappoint us. There was ice on the water.

Well good night. May God Bless you all.
With all my love, Frank

Sunday, November 5, 1944; Somewhere in Holland

Dear Viola,
Received your letter some time ago but didn't have time to answer it right away. Your letters haven't been coming in so good lately either. I haven't received much mail in the past few weeks. I suppose I'll get a bunch of mail at once when I do get it. mail does much better coming from the Pacific than it does here. we'll probably get our Christmas packages about Easter time.
I located some of Frank's outfit the other day. I think I'll get a chance to see him one of these fine days. Won't that be swell if I do get to see him? A buddy of mine from the old outfit is located somewhere near me too. I'd like to see him too if I can get around to it. I met this fellow from New York just before we pulled out, I think I told you about it before.
The pictures you sent me of the kids turned out swell. I always wanted a picture like that of them, I put them in my wallet with the rest of the collection.
You were right I was near the town you mentioned. I'm away from there now. Tell mom not to worry about me cause I'm in a good spot and as safe as can be.
The other day was All Saints Day and I went to High Mass in one of the churches near by. They really have some beautiful churches on this continent. I went to church this morning too this church has a wonderful choir.
How is my dog getting long? I suppose the boys are all set to use him for hunting this year. Tell Joe I said he should take good care of him.
Well Vi, I'll have to close for this time being. Give my love to Mom and Dad. Write often.
Love, Johnny

Wednesday, November 8, 1944

Dearest Viola & Family,
I just received your letter & was so glad to hear from you and to know every one is fine. Guess that Johnie was here to see me but I wasn't here. I just seen him for two minutes but he is coming back to see me this week he looks good he is a Sgt. Did you know that? He's about 6 mi from me, I'll see him Sunday.
How is your family getting long? I hope every thing is O.K. Tell Joe to not work too hard. I hope John gets home soon. He sure been there a long time. Well, I'll close. As soon as I see Johnie I'll write more.
May God Bless you all. Take good care of the kids.
Your brother, Frank

Sunday, November 12, 1944

Gelukkige Kepstdagen En Een Voopspoedig Nieuwjaar
Frank

Greetings in Dutch. May God Bless you all.

Monday, November 13, 1944; Somewhere in Holland

Dear Viola,
Just a few words to let you know I'm O.K. and am feeling fine.
Don't worry about me being cold this winter I probably have more clothes than any two other soldiers. I now have six

blankets and a nice comforter. I wish you could see the comforter it's filled with feathers at least that is the way it feels. It has a satin cover. It gets so hot at night that I have to throw some of the covers off. I have to guard this comforter with my life cause there's too many guys that would like to have it. Don't ask me how I got it, cause it's a military secret. Ha! Ha! I usually do alright for myself don't I?

  I suppose you know by now that I saw Frankie. He really looks swell, just as fat as he always was. He hasn't changed a bit, still as crazy as usual. I got a pass the other day and we spent a few short hours to-gether. Most of our time was spent in a beer joint in a near by town. We had several beers and talked of old times and home. I probably could have seen him long ago if he'd write to me and let me know where he is. Now that I've found him maybe we can see each other once in a while, if we're not separated to much. I've been looking for him ever since we hit the beach. It's quite a job finding someone with so many soldiers here. he said he saw our outfit in France but didn't have time to look me up. If I had to wait for him I don't think we'd ever see each other.

  I'd like to see Barbara play the piano. If she's really interested in it she ought to make out alright. I got a letter from Claude last week he seems to be doing alright. He was telling me about having some good beer that almost killed him. I often wonder how a good bottle of beer would taste.

  I wrote John a long letter to-day and gave him the low down on things. I think he owes me a letter if I'm not mistaken. I was glad to hear he got a little break. Two and a half years on the islands is about enough to make any man go crazy. I thought he'd be coming home by this time, a good deal of his unit has been sent back to the states hasn't it?

  I hope the packages start coming in soon. You asked me if I needed writing paper, I did before but I ...(censored)......

  By the time you get this letter Joe will have had a few days of good hunting, let me know how he makes out. By the way how is my dog doing? Joe ought to have a good season with him this year.

I voted this year, I don't think you have to ask me how! Did Eugene's boys make out alright? Eugene's pretty good, the only time he writes is when he wants my vote.

We had our first snow last week, the weather is getting plenty rough plenty of rain. You probably know more about it than we do.

Well Viola, I'll have to close for now. Give my love to Mom and Dad. Keep the letters coming.

So long for now. Love to all. Johnny

Chapter Twenty Two

The 9th army stood at the gates of hell in conjunction with the rest of the allied armies. This was to be a knock down drag out affair with the ever-looming possibility of a fierce counterattack.

Frank stood soaked to the bone in almost four inches of mud with wet socks and boots that he figured he would never experience dry again in his lifetime as he was about to drop back into his foxhole. The only benefit the on-set of winter in these parts was that the ground was beginning to freeze and the thick, tacky surface would soon be transformed into a slick, rutted landscape. For over a month, towing the howitzers was like trying to coax a stubborn mule into its stall. Now the problem would be keeping the wheels from seizing up from the freezing rain and mud. The axles often loosened themselves as they hit the now bone-jarring frozen trail.

Be strong and let us fight bravely for our people and the cities of our God. The Lord will do what is good in his sight. -2 Samuel 10:12

Wednesday, November 15, 1944; IN GERMANY

Dearest Viola & Family,
Just a line to let you know that everything is O.K. with me & hope you are the same, & how is Joe and kids getting long? John L. and I had some time again. We met some Czech boy. Can Johnie drink the beer & liquor & So can i. I had about 12 beers &

some liquor, the liquor's hard to get.

The weather is so bad it rains or snows. I sure hope this war is over soon. I wrote to Claude & John to-day, Johnie said he was going to write to John but he's so busy working. It's so hard to write when it's raining all the time and you are working in it.

Well I'll sign off for this time. May God Bless you all. Take care of the family.

With all my love for you. Frank

Sunday, November 19, 1944; Holland

Dear Viola,

Do you recognize this paper? You should, it's the stuff you sent me. I think this is the first time I wrote to you with this type of paper. This paper came in handy cause we do have a hard time getting paper. We get all the v-mail forms we want but I don't like it you can't write very much on it. I know the censors would like us to write v-mail it's much easier on them. I don't think I have written over five v-mails since I've been here.

I got my first package last week it was from Helen. I didn't expect it cause she never said anything about it. it was a swell package but I was rather disappointed in it-<u>no cigars</u>. I suppose the packages will be coming in quite regular now—I hope.

Has Joe been doing any hunting yet and how is he making out? He should have a good season if he can get shells. I wish I could be there just to get one good day in would make me happy. After this is all over I'm going to take a six month vacation in Canada and do nothing but hunt and fish.

I haven't seen Frank since the last time I wrote to you. We wanted to have some pictures taken the last time but the studio was closed. I expect to see him again in the near future, maybe we'll make out better this time. I'll bet his mother was happy when she heard we met wasn't she?

I wrote to Claude and John last week. You know I get Claude's letters quicker than I do from home.

I went to High Mass again this morning. I haven't gone to communion for several weeks, I just haven't had the opportunity. I wish you could see the church it's beautiful and they have a wonderful choir too. I'll have to close for now. give my love to Mom and Dad. So long.

Love to all, Johnny

Wednesday, November 22, 1944; a letter from Viola to Claude was returned to sender and remains sealed today. Letter was returned approximately one and a half months after it was mailed.

Wednesday morning, November 29, 1944; letter returned to sender and later opened

Dear Claude,

How are you? Here's hoping that you are doing fine. Haven't heard from you for some time. I bet you aren't getting any mail right now. You'll probably get all the letters at once. You must be in a battle again. Gee! I'm so sorry, I thought you'd get to stay there for a long time.

We have been getting mail from Johnny pretty regularly now. I received mail from him and Frank yesterday. They say they both wrote to you. I don't suppose you know that the two boys met on the Western Front? I guess they were a couple of happy lads as long as it lasted. They drank beer together. Each one wrote and told me how well the other looked. Of course they lost some weight.

We are watching the papers every day. Yet we can't find

out what the 77th is doing. Every day we hurry to the mail box and no mail from you. Irma & I usually meet out there and when we don't we holler over and ask "any letter from Claude yet?" the answer is always <u>no.</u> I sure hope it will be yes to-day or some time soon. Mother is so disappointed and worried. It seems if it isn't you it's Johnny but one of you are always in some mischief.

The B29 Bombers have bases on the Mariannas, Saipan, Tinian & Guam. We know that they are flying from there to bomb Tokyo. But that doesn't seem to be the reason you aren't writing.

Thanksgiving is past. We really had a lot of snow that day. I suppose on Christmas we won't have any.

Johnny has received Helen's package already, have you gotten any yet? He said it was a good package but looked for a cigar and there weren't any. It's too bad because his tongue is hanging out for a smoke. I suppose by now he has the cigars we sent.

Well so-long Claude dear. May God Bless you.
Love & Kisses, Sister Viola & Family

Thursday, November 30, 1944; Guadalcanal; V-mail

Dear Vi,
Just a line or two to let you know how I am and that I rec'd your swell Xmas packages. Sure was swell of you. I also rec'd one from Mother the same day. Heard from Frank today and he said he saw Johnny and boy were they happy to see each other. He said they would get together again, any way we hope so. I am still cutting hair and it keeps me quite busy. I find little time for writing, so if you don't hear from me too often, don't be angry with me for not writing. I think of you all often and wish I could be home with you all soon. I'm really home sick and now that hunting season is here. How is Joe doing? Is he getting any thing? I'm glad the children are doing so good in their school work. I'm

proud of them. May God Bless you all.
   Love and kisses, John

Sunday after noon, December 3, 1944; Guadalcanal

   Dearest Vi and Family,
   Just got through writing to Mother and Frank, and have a little time left so I thought I would drop you a few lines and let you know I am okay and that I received your swell Xmas package. And God Bless You and Family for thinking of me at Xmas time. I think you're swell! I got a letter from Frank the other day I guess I told you in my v-mail letter that he met Johnny and was so happy to see him. Wasn't it swell of them to meet over there. It just seems that I don't have a chance to see any of my folks over here. when I was M.P. I used to check the ships as they came in to see if any of my friends were on them, but no luck. I'm really glad they don't have to come on this hell hole any way. There's nothing here any way. No towns nothing like that least some of these other places have towns where you can go to, Fiji Island wasn't so bad, I had a little fun over there.
   I don't know if I told you in my last letter that I received your last letter dated November 16th. Sure enjoyed it too. Wish you could write more often, but I know it's hard when you have to write to all of us and still do your other work. I was glad to hear the children were doing so well in their school work. I'll bet you're proud of Barbara in that school play. I hope I could make it to see her in that (Waltzing Doll). I know it will be anxious.
   I think I will be home some time this spring, anyway I hope so. This damn pen I'm using is no damn good, so if my writing isn't so hot, just overlook it. Ha. How's Joe doing with those boxes of shells? Is he getting any thing with them? I wish I could've gotten home for hunting season, sure miss it. Remember how Joe, Johnny and I used to go hunting. Boy those were the

good old days. I will never forget the time Joe and I took Veronica hunting. Boy she was game! Tell her I said hello. I'll bet she'll miss Rudy and you can't blame her. I know he'll miss her too. I'm glad I haven't got any girl waiting for me. I wouldn't want any to. When I come back I'll have plenty of time to get one. Ha. I hope. Since I been over seas, I've seen plenty of friends lost their girl friends. One of my best friends lost his girl friend just a few months ago. She got married to one of his best friends too! Now he's coming home and you can bet he's quite disappointed.

  You ask me if I heard from Johnny or Claude. No, I haven't heard from Johnny since he went Over Seas and Claude never did write. Course I know they're busy and as long as I hear from you that they're okay. That's all that matter. Frank said that Johnny told him, he was going to write to me. so I'm waiting. You sure were right when you said that maybe Johnny & Frank would meet over there since they had the same A.P.O number.

  I heard from Charles a few days ago and he's doing okay. Sure is a little home sick. I could tell by his letter, I really feel sorry for him, he's so young. He always mentions you folks in his letters and all good you all were to him. He's having quite a time with Natives. He said he takes their pictures and how they live. I got a kick out of his letter telling me all about it.

  I sure was glad to hear you were going to Cleveland to see Ceil's baby girl. She sure has a nice name, Patricia Ann, beautiful. Isn't it?

  Well Vi, I got to close and do some work that has to be done. So be careful and may I thank you again for your Xmas package. It was swell, and they're really good too! Have some ready for me when I come home, you know Like I used to when I came over to cut hair, and please don't listen to those stories on the radio so Joe can get some sleep. Ha. Ha.

  So long and Merry Xmas and a Happy New Year to all.
Love and kisses, John

  P.S. I'll write again soon. You do the same.

For this reason, make every effort to add to your faith goodness; and to goodness, knowledge; and to knowledge, self-control, and to self control, perseverance; and to perseverance, godliness; and to godliness, brotherly kindness; and to brotherly kindness, love. For if you possess these qualities in increasing measure, they will keep you from being ineffective and unproductive in your knowledge of our Lord Jesus Christ. -2 Peter 1:5-8

Chapter Twenty Three

Monday, December 4, 1944; Leyte

*My Dear Sister,
I received three of your letter yesterday. All at the same time. And I was very happy to hear from you. I haven't been able to write very often lately because we were on the move so much. Your letters all came within a month's time. That isn't so bad, but not so good either. I guess the stamp don't mean very much. They all go about the same time. Yes, Viola I got your stamps that you sent but forgot to mention it in my letters.
So Johnny is in Luxembourg. Well he sure is getting around. You say he is a Sgt. Now? I knew he would make it. That is where they are made. On the battle front and not in the states.
I don't know anything about Guam, but I suppose there still are Japs. It is hard to get rid of them all. They usually are prowling around looking for food. What ever you read or hear about the happenings at Guam are true.
You say you saw Catherine's cedar chest. I guess she thinks a lot of it. She's been wanting one for a long time. She has been telling me about it. I guess she wanted a large one so she could put more in it.
I sure am glad that the folks getting there work done. They deserve a rest. I imagine it's been a hard year for them taking care of all the work by them self.
I am glad to hear the children are doing better in school.
I haven't been going to church very often lately, but I do when I get a chance. As you know I am in the Philippines and we*

don't have things set up yet. Yes, it sure would be nice if both of us could come home by next June. But I don't think it will happen. There is so much to be done yet. But when we do get home you can bet there will be weddings. I hope we can have a double wedding. And I personally will see to it that you enjoy yourself. Of course you probably start working like you always do. I can remember yours and Helen's weddings.

I haven't received the cigars that Veronica sent. In fact I haven't gotten any of the packages that was sent to me. I only hope I get them for Xmas.

Yes I got the Combat Infantry badge but I sure did earn it and so did every body else. I got it just after the battle of Guam, but I forgot to tell you about it. Art Halas received the same honor as I did.

I don't think it will last much longer over there. They seem to have the Germans cornered. It might happen most any day now and it won't be any too soon to suit me. The quicker it ends over there the sooner it will end over here.

So Dad had his straw bailed. Well, that is good. It is always good to bail it to save space. If he can't sell it he can always keep it. There may be times he won't have any.

Yes, election is over with and I am glad it turned out the way it did. I don't blame Eugene for being happy because it meant a lot to him. Yes, I voted and for the very man that won too. I am glad that Mother and Dad were able to vote.

You say Joe is working afternoons. Well that isn't a bad shift, but it isn't as good as days are. Tell Joe I will keep writing as often as I can.

We haven't had any entertainment since Guam, but I guess we can get along without it for a while. We had a paradise there but it was to good to last.

I have lots of buddies but Kalas is one of the best. I get along with them all but that is because I have to.

Well, Viola I must close for now. Please excuse ink on the paper. It's raining and my tent leaks. I will write again as soon as

possible. Say hello to the children and Joe.
Lots of love and Kisses and God bless you all. Brother Claude

The initial push since landing on Leyte went fairly uncontested other than the few encounters from Kamikaze pilots while being transported to the island. This allowed Claude and the rest of the 305th to move from the western shore of the island and drive north toward the Ormoc Valley. Meanwhile, the Japanese Army had caught wind of the U.S. plan and sent reinforcements in an attempt to hold the valley.[25]

It had been raining since Claude set foot on Leyte and it was not worth it for him to even try to remember the last time he felt something not completely rain soaked and steaming from the humidity beneath the jungle canopy. The world as Claude knew it felt like a wet rag that had been wrung out and left in the heat of summer only to be rained upon once again. "The sooner we sweep this island the better", he said to himself as he mopped his face with his forearm.

He finished his K-rations, broke down his tent and secured his pack for the morning hike. He was told there was a small ridge line to cross before descending toward the valley floor and a rendezvous with the 304th and 306th infantry. The travel was painstakingly slow, not simply because of the formidable swamps and terrain but more so because the Japanese had held this island for some time and it was all too easy to step from the copious undergrowth into a clearing and right on top of a machine gun nest.

It was eerily quiet this particular morning. Claude could scarcely hear his footsteps aside from the occasional squishing of his boots on the muddy and moss-covered ground. The buzzing and droning of mosquitoes and other biting insects had long since been consumed by the simple desire to be able to stand erect and see more than a few yards ahead of oneself. It sometimes felt as if the jungle was growing at such a rate that if you didn't keep

---

[25] www.Wikipedia.org   www.history.army.mil

moving, you might find yourself a part of it as it slowly crept around you and eventually swallowed you one layer at a time.

Claude had once again assumed the right flank of the point because he had grown accustomed to both the responsibility and vantage point from that position, and he was a creature of habit comforted by routine. Claude's many years of hunting rabbit in the thick brier patches back home had greatly improved his peripheral vision making him extremely astute to the slightest of movements. His eyes had adjusted to the intermittent rays of sunlight that managed to fight their way through the three layers of canopies seemingly to achieve their goal of reaching the forest floor.

It was the end of the typhoon season and much of the vegetation was once again transforming itself from a rain and wind battered mess to a lush and blooming array of colors. From the ferns and orchids to the palms and Philippine mahogany[26], the jungle floor had a way of muffling any distant sounds and leaving a person feeling as if he was held isolated from the rest of the world and wrapped in his own cocoon.

Claude was able to make out a small natural clearing less than fifty meters ahead of him and slightly to his right. He moved with caution and slowly crouched sweeping an opening in the ferns in front of him with his left hand. His eyes darted quickly to his right as he saw movement about ten meters above the ground in the next canopy. It was just several flying lemur moving from a tree. He had heard about them, but this was his first encounter actually seeing this creature that looked something like a cross between a squirrel and a bat. Claude watched for several minutes and then slowly rose from his crouched position. He thought it odd to see the lemur this time of morning for although many portions of the canopy were so thick that it always appeared as night, the lemur was a nocturnal creature.

He made his way through the next small stretch of jungle

---

[26] www.Wikipedia.org

and approached the following woods line that opened to his left and appeared somewhat level. Claude figured he and the men had reached the plateau of the ridge and would soon be making their descent toward the valley floor. He cautiously stepped out with his left foot followed almost a minute later by his right foot. Claude had honed the art of stalking, hunting fox squirrels in the hardwoods back home during many early fall seasons. Back then his patience often paid dividends with his daily limit in his game pouch.

    As he stepped into the clearing, Claude scanned the next bit of cover that stood before him, the closest ranging approximately two hundred and fifty meters in any direction. He moved toward a small wash every step guarded, as he looked to his left and saw his point man along with Kalas and several of his other buddies just having emerged into the clearing. The rain had not let up but the wash that he moved into was no longer a raging river formed by the torrential downpours of the past two months but rather a trickling stream leaving what now looked like one long foxhole.

    As Claude slowly rose from the wash, he suddenly felt his knees buckle and his body being thrown back into the opposite bank. The silence was abruptly followed by the sound of a single gunshot. Claude scampered back up the bank in front of him and unloaded his clip in the direction of the sniper. What ensued next was a several minute barrage of small arms fire and mortars coming from both edges of the clearing.

    Claude replaced his third expended clip as he tried to reposition himself for a clearer shot. As he moved, his hand almost instinctively touched his midsection where his shirt had become warm and blood-soaked. Claude's adrenaline was quickly replaced by shock as he looked down and saw where the bullet had cut through his shirt and entered his stomach. The bloodstain was spreading in a peculiar circular pattern around the entry wound like some sort of virus consuming the original color of his shirt! He shot wildly through his fourth clip as a hot searing pain began to rise up from his belly and into his throat. He lowered himself back into the protection of the wash and eventually rolled onto his back as he began to call for a medic. The world around him began to slacken as each minute seemed like an eternity. The initial firefight had transformed itself from a frantic melee of discharged hot shell casings flying from rifles to dirt and tree limbs spitting fragments from near misses of return gunfire and mortar rounds to a slowed almost out-of-body experience.

Claude felt it was much like a baseball player being in the zone and tracking that perfect fastball as it crossed home plate. Eighty plus miles per hour seemed impossible to catch up with until he guessed at that one pitch being released from the pitchers finger tips and realized that this was his pitch, his body poised for the ball's approach, his weight shifting like a pendulum, hands high, bat off the shoulder, the knob of the bat being driven toward the ball as it was about to cross the front edge of the plate only for the barrel of the bat to suddenly appear and come around in time to meet the ball over the front third of home plate. It was almost as if the batter could reach out with his hand and adjust the ball to his liking prior to hitting it. And then the world was back to its seemingly normal pace.

Claude's third attempt to speak was met by a stammering and some fluid in his lungs. He mustered the strength to cry out once more for a medic only to be met with gunfire followed by a grenade as it exploded twenty meters in front of the wash. His mind was awakened briefly by the explosion and suddenly it began to race frantically from his days working on the muck for Mr. Rutenik to the church hall dances to Sunday gatherings with family that started with church, migrated to his mother or Vi's kitchen and finished with a smoke and light conversation or horseplay. The farm, he so wished he was back home again.

His eyes flittered slightly and began to fog as he saw the movement of an arching grenade enter the wash nearby… it seemed almost suspended in time. Strange the thoughts that entered one's head…Claude thought of Catherine and just holding her, the excitement she expressed in her letter regarding the new cedar hope chest, he thought of Mom and Dad and how proud they would be to see him returning home in his dress uniform and oh boy, the wedding they would have. It would be one swell time at the wedding, and the kids, boy would it be nice to see Joey and Barbara again when he got home, and his sister Vi; don't you worry Viola everything is going to be O.K... He was coming home.

For none of us lives to himself alone and none of us dies to himself alone. If we live, we live to the Lord; and if we die, we die to the Lord. So, whether we live or die, we belong to the Lord. - Romans 7:8

Tuesday, December 5, 1944; Lockwood, Ohio

Dear Claude,
Still haven't heard from you. But hope and pray that you are safe wherever you are. I even dreamed about you the other nite.
Yesterday I was 31. Gee! I'm really getting old. I'll have to start going back don't you think so?
Here's hoping that we hear from you before Christmas or mother will go bugs. I hope that you have been getting our mail.
Last week we had a few days of terrifically cold weather. To-day it's warm and looks like rain. Our neighbor that bought Ruby's place wrecked his car last Friday on the way to work. It was terribly slippery. Sunday, Charles Roscoe wrecked his car in Greene on the way home from Church. He lost control of his car. His mother was bruised. I don't know just how seriously.
Have you received any of your packages yet? Last week I sent a small box with a few smokes and candy.
There isn't much to write about. The children have good report cards.

Dad has two cows that came in in the past week. Maybe he will be shipping more milk soon. Their test is (4.0) which is better than they used to get.

Joe caught about 20 rabbits so far and 2 pheasants. He sold several rabbits and gave a few to his folks and to mom. Dicky (the hound) just loves to go hunting and he also loves to ride. Any time a car is open or the truck door he jumps in before you know it.
I made myself a birthday cake. Chocolate and chocolate icing. The kids sure like it. I took a piece over home and Veronica thought it was pretty cute that I had to bake my own cake. But, that's the only way I get one, ha! ha!
Eugene stopped in here for dinner to-day. He had a great big trailer truck with slag and taking it up north.
I really will end here and write a few more short letters. I figure that a card doesn't mean much if there isn't a letter accompanying it.
Love & Kisses, Sister Viola and Family

May God Bless You.

p.s. I shouldn't write on both sides on this thin paper, but I don't want the letter to weigh too much.

Tuesday, December 5, 1944

Dear Viola,
Just a few lines to let you know that I'm feeling fine and in the best of health.
I haven't received a letter from you in so long that I hardly know what to write. I usually try to answer your questions when you write other than that there isn't much here to write about. We do the same thing every day.
I want to thank you for the swell box of cigars. I'm pretty

well fixed on cigars for a while.

How is everyone at home? I suppose everyone is doing their Christmas shopping already. I won't be doing much shopping this year. I wish I could get to a big town for a while I'd like to get Mother something nice as a souvenir. Maybe before it's all over with I'll get my chance.

Has Joe had a chance to do much hunting yet? He should have a good year with my dog-if he can get the shells.

I went to communion again last Sunday. I go every chance we get.

Well Viola, I'll have to close for now, write as often as you can. Give my love to Mom and Dad. I wish you all a "Very Merry Christmas" and a "Happy New Year."

So long for now.

Love to All. Johnny

Thursday, December 7, 1944; v-mail from Private Claude Lulek to Helen (Lulek) Drabek (envelope and postmark only)

Saturday, December 9, 1944; Some Where in Germany and it's not raining

Dearest Viola & Family,

Just a line to let you know that everything is OK & hope you are the same. I sure hope the kids are getting long O.K. in school? Tell them I miss them all the time & think of them every day.

The weather has been bad it rains or snows every day but to day is a beautiful day. I sure wish we would have more like to day, then the war would be done soon. Tell mother you heard from me so she don't worry because I don't know if I can write to her to day.

Oh yes, I heard from Johnie L. to day he's some place close to me but I just can't see him, maybe some day I'll see him again.

So the calf doesn't want to get caught? I'll be home soon ha ha. how are all my gals back home? I sure do get mail from 4 or 5 of them, and most of them think I love them ha ha. Helen writes every day.

Well I can tell you I am in the 9th Army & XIX Corp. I have been in the 1st Army for a long time but we are in this Army.

I'll sign off for this time. May God Bless you all.

Love to all. Frank

p.s. How is Joe working & is he feeling O.K.? Tell him not to work to hard, how is hunting this year?

So long

The Lord is my light and my salvation-whom shall I fear? The Lord is the stronghold of my life-of whom shall I be afraid? - Psalm 27:1

Saturday, December 9, 1944; Christmas card from Frank Soukenik with sketch and description of the Meuse River

XIX CORP. U.S. ARMY CROSSING THE MEUSE RIVER AT MAASTRICHT, HOLLAND

The Meuse River was the last obstacle between us and Germany. Maastricht is the oldest town in Holland. It, like the Trier, was an outpost of the Roman Empire. On the site of a Roman wooden bridge "pons Mosae", the foundations of the present "Massbrug" were laid in 1280, it was restored in 1683, altered in 1932, destroyed by the Dutch Army on may 10, 1940 to slow up the German advance; repaired in 1942; blown up by the

Germans on September 13, 1944; and repaired as shown by XIX Corps on 30 September 1944.
   With all my love, Frank

Monday, December 11, 1944; Czech Christmas card to Claude from Joseph and Anna Soukenik, Jr.

Infant of Prague, so small yet a king.

God , the Creator, the Word, His splendor He's hiding, although angels sing

And reverently worship their Lord.

May this dear Prince of Peace be given the sway

And rule as the King of your heart.

The blessings and peace of the Savior's Birth Day.

Be with you and never depart.

Thursday, December 14, 1944; letter from Viola to Claude returned still sealed

Friday, December 15, 1944

Dearest Vi,
   Here's wishing you and family a Merry Christmas and a Happy New Year. I wish I could be with you all this Christmas time, but the way it looks I'll not make it. May be I'll be with you

all for Easter. Any way I hope so. This will be my 3rd Christmas over seas. Sure seems like a long time. Heard from Mother today.

Sure was happy to hear that every thing is okay. Got a letter from Johnny. He saw Frank and they had a wonderful time. Too bad I couldn't have met Claude over here or Charles, but that's the way it goes. I haven't heard from Claude or Charles in some time, but I suppose they're quite busy and I know how that is, it's pretty hard to write if you can't say any thing about the place.

Well, I suppose Joe is bringing in the game from the woods, or is he just shooting at them Ha. wish I was home to show him how it is done.

How's the weather out there? I suppose it's pretty cold. Mother wrote that it was snowing so hard that she couldn't see Jackson's place. Sure will be glad to see that snow again.

How are the children doing are they still doing great in school? Tell them I'll look over their report cards when I come home. It better be good Ha. Well, I'll have to close and say good night.

God Bless You All.
Love & Kisses. John

Chapter Twenty four

Battle of the Bulge December 16, 1944-January 25, 1945

Saturday, December 16, 1944; Some Where in Germany

Dearest Family,
Just received your letter & was so glad to hear from you and was glad to no you all are feeling fine. I am O.K. so don't worry. Some time my back is not so good. It's been some time since I seen Johnie, but last week I got a letter from him. He's still in the same Army, the 9th, I was in the 1st but not no more.

I wrote to John & Johnie this week. It sure was good to see in the paper that the 37th Division is coming home. About time. I sure would like to see him home & maybe some day I'll be home, <u>maybe</u>.

The weather is cold for the last two days. I sure hope this weather be like this for one or two.. censored...

I was glad to hear that the kids are doing well in school. I sure hope the kids have a good Xmas maybe some day I'll do something for the kids.

I received a letter from mother and it make me so happy to hear from her, I think she's so good. When I get back I'll take care of my folks. If Mother and Dad would only no how much I miss them, I miss you all but Mother & Dad are first.

Well dear I'll close for this time. Oh yes, is Joe working hard? I hope he don't have to, how is the hunting this year? Tell me in your next letter.

May God Bless You All.
With all my love, always, Frank

Wednesday, December 20, 1944; A letter from Viola to Claude was mailed and eventually returned remaining sealed

Wednesday, December 27, 1944; Lockwood, Ohio

Dear Claude,

Christmas is over and now we can relax a little. Everything was fine except gloomy when we thought of you boys so far away. One thing we could be thankful for was that we did hear from you and Johnny the week before Christmas. Although just before we received Johnny's letter the Germans were counter attacking the Allies especially the First Army. I hope we hear from both of you this week. We don't know just where each of you are. I had the folks and the Drabeks over for Christmas Eve <u>Dinner.</u> Then the children opened the gifts. Of course none of us were too thrilled over the packages but the children were happy. This year presents don't mean much to us. The best present to us would be if the war ended very soon.

Laura Glowe and her family got stuck in front of our place Christmas Eve. She came in for help and we had quite a reunion. She seemed so happy to see us and was glad that they got stuck. We all kissed and laughed and almost cried with Joy. Joe laughed at us as she came in and none of us could hardly recognize her because she is stouter and has changed a little.

All of us went over to see Catherine's gifts on Christmas Day. She received many pretty gifts.

Joey & Babs received quite a lot of money so I put it into a bank account for each. Now they each have $20 in book and I bought them each a bond. Barbara got a cradle for her dolls and other gifts. Joey got games and other gifts. He also got a puzzle which we have spent hours on and have only a small portion put to-gether. Mother gave us an all wool blanket.

We are really having a hard winter. Since that snow 2 weeks before Christmas we haven't seen any ground. It keeps snowing more and more. We don't mind it but the roads are terrible to travel to work & Church. Because that's the only place we go. Oh yes, I got Joe a bill fold for Christmas. Now he needs money to put in it. he usually has any where from $.10 to a quarter to his name. so the bill fold won't get much wear ha! ha! and when he has any change I borrow it from him for stamps or something for the children for school.

The children are on vacation now. the Christmas play went over big last week. I was told Babs looked like a doll. Her pink full dress, pink ribbon, blonde curls, black slippers and white stockings. She was a waltzing doll and danced around alone and then a boy wound her up and she danced some more. Junior was an Eskimo.

Joe caught two rabbits on Christmas without any shells. There's so much snow the rabbits can't get away.

The Drabeks are supposed to come out to day for a short vacation. Eugene intends to do a little hunting.

Well so long Claude dear and be careful. May God Bless You.

With Love & Kisses, Sister Vi and Family

p.s. Joe sends his love. you should see him when there is any kind of news on the radio. We all have to be quiet and turn on the radio louder. The way things look they are going to take older men soon again.

Monday, January 7, 1945; Lockwood, Ohio

Dear Claude,
Just wanted to let you know that everything is quite all right on the home front! But we would like to know how it is over there. Are you well and doing fine? Here's hoping because we haven't heard from you for about 3 weeks now. it seems like 3 months. all we live for from day to day is for a letter from overseas. That's one thing that perks us up. But it's so bad lately. No letters from anyone. Frank doesn't even have time to write to us anymore. But he does write home often. He wrote that Johnny was up to see him again. Isn't that wonderful? We haven't heard from Johnny since the time we heard from you. That is he wrote on the 5th and you wrote on the 4th of December. He is right in the thick of it on the Western Front. The germans are counter attacking for the second time in 3 or 4 weeks. I hope the boys can give it to the Germans good and proper pretty soon.
How are you doing and what and where? You boys over there are really taking over the Philippines fast, which is good news. Hope you are safe and be careful.
There isn't much to write about. It is Sunday nite and I just put the youngsters to bed after reading them a bedtime story. I'm listening to the radio and trying to write. Joe is working and will be home by midnite. The roads aren't what they used to be. We have had continuous snow now for about 4 weeks. Every week the wind blows and the roads are drifted and no one can get out for a day ot two finally the scrapers get out and clear the roads. Then the next week the same thing over. The children have missed two weeks of school this winter because they can't get out. Then they had their Christmas vacation so when they go back to school I won't know how to act, I have had them home so long. Joey made an ice house in our ditch. He pulled chunks of snow that looked more like ice (from what they have been scraping off the roads) and made a tunnel to crawl into the house and the mail man asked

me if that was Joe's house. I said yes, little Joe's house.

Last week Joe and Veronica boarded at Helen's. Joe stayed 2 nites. I doubt if Helen makes much on such boarders do you?

We made a thousand dollars at Christmas collection this year. Pretty good no hey?

Well so-long Claude dear and watch your step. May God Bless You.

Love & Kisses, From Sister Viola & Family

p.s. Write just a few lines when possible. You don't have to say more than that you are OK and we will be happy to hear that. I know you can't feel very much like writing when it's so hot.

To you O Lord, I lift up my soul, in you I trust, O my God. Do not let me be put to shame, nor let my enemies triumph over me. No one whose hope is in you will ever be put to shame…Show me the way O Lord, teach me your paths; guide me in your truth and teach me, for you are God my Savior, and my hope is in you all day long. –Psalm 25:1-3, 4-5

Monday, January 7, 1945

Dear Viola,

Just a few lines to let you know I'm feeling fine and in the best of health-here's hoping this letter finds you all the same.

I'm sorry if I caused you folks to worry from the absence of my letters. We've been moving around so much and it's so darn cold that I just hate to write.

I received your box of hand kerchiefs the other day-thanks a lot. I know I have several more packages on the way but heaven only knows when they'll get here. I hope the box containing clothes gets here soon-the hoods especially would come in handy.

I saw Frankie again a few days before Christmas. We had quite a time to-gether.

I guess you know all about the first army being pushed back into Belgium. We're somewhere In Belgium helping check on the situation. it won't be long that we'll have the "Jerries" chased back to the <u>fatherland</u>. It's a new year now and we've got to finish the job this year. Remember when I told you it would be over in 1945-mark my word. I have several bets as to which month it will be.

Joe seems to be doing alright with my dog-I'd like to be there with him. The season is all over with now, boy how the time does fly. It's hard to believe that we're starting a new year.

I wrote to Claude some time ago but never got an answer as yet- I suppose he's to busy to write at the present time.

Well Viola I'll have to close for now. Give my love to Mom and Dad.

So long for a while.
Love to all. Johnny

Tuesday, January 8, 1945; Some Where in Germany

Dearest Viola & Family,

It's been some time since I have wrote to you but dam we have been busy, and it's been cold we have about 6 inches of snow or more. We work night and day some time. I didn't see Johnie since week before Xmas. We are about 30 miles from one another. To-day I seen Helen B.'s old man. He's in the same Amy as me.

I didn't receive your box. Maybe the Germans got it but it may come this month. I sure hope so. It about time I hear from you again. I love to hear from you. I don't have the time to write much, but I'll think of you all at home it so cold to write some time.

We had a home but this time we are in the woods and we are in tents or foxholes.

So, I'll sign off may God Bless you all. Till next time. With all my love, Frank

Saturday, January 12, 1945; Lockwood, Ohio

Dearest Claude,

We hope to find you well and safe. Haven't heard from you for so long.

John Soukenik came home this week January 9th. He left Guadalcanal December 16, 1944. He looks fine and feels fine. He is certainly one happy soldier. Boy you don't know how good it is to see one of our loved ones return from combat. Our hearts ache for you who are left back there to fight for some time yet. May God be good to us and keep you boys safe and end this war soon. John told us many of his experiences and we listen with our mouths open. It is so interesting and it brings us closer to the battle and you. We know and understand what it is like over there. He brought home a <u>cheesy hat</u> that the Japanese Navy wears. Also a small flag with the rising sun. he showed us a picture a friends took of a dead Jap and one of their Chevrolet trucks. This picture is so much plainer than the ones that are printed in the newspapers. It looks so real.

Yesterday was Joe's day off also to-day. He goes out to-nite midnite. So Joe, John and Tom Smida went hunting yesterday. John got 2 rabbits and I guess Joe caught one. They let John get the first cracks at the bunnies. Boy were they tuckered out when nite came. We had supper at Soukenik's and after supper the boys sat in the living room listening to the news and they dozed off. We finally awakened them and played cards. We had a nice evening and someone was always calling for John. The Smidas are very good to him. He uses Steve's car when he wishes. I guess they all want to take him out some evening.

Well the children have finally gone to school all this

week. This is Friday morning. It is raining on all that snow we have. I hope it doesn't freeze to-nite.

Joe went over to help the folks to butcher their first <u>hog</u> this winter. It was too bad weather before Christmas and Mother doesn't have any one to feed anymore. Veronica is so fussy and doesn't eat much and stays by Helen's a lot. Of course there is dad to feed but they can't use much meat.

It took John 16 days to cross the Pacific then they went to <u>Angel Island</u> off San Francisco and were issued winter clothing and sent home to an Indianan camp and from there the boys went there way. In 21 days John has to report to Miami Florida for reassignment.

We haven't heard from Johnny since we heard from you either. Frankie wrote to his mother December 29th that was very good it came in about 10 days. He also claims he saw Johnny again. So long dear brother and write. Love and kisses and God Bless You. Sister Viola & Family

Wednesday, January 16, 1945

Dear Viola,
Yes, this is your bad brother again the one who hates to write. I made a new year's resolution that I'll try to write more often. When you and Helen get a letter from me tell Mom. So she won't worry cause I can't write to everyone as often as I'd like to. You'll hear from me quite often from now on even if I don't get a chance to say anymore than hello. How is that?

I see Joe did alright with my dog this year or I should say last year. Tell him I said he shouldn't get to familiar with Dickie. Ha! Ha! One of these fine days <u>soon</u> I'll be home and of course the dog goes with me. I'll be home for next hunting season you can bet your life on that.

Tell Mom I got the package with the hoods and socks.

The hood sure feels good on these cold frosty mornings.

I hear you've been having plenty of snow lately-we got our share of it too. I wish I had my skates here I'd have a little fun. With all that snow you're having Eugene must be working night and day!

Well viola, I'll have to close for now. give my love to Mom and Dad and write often. So long for a while.

Love to all. Johnny

Friday, January 18, 1945; V-mail

Dearest Family,

Just a few lines to let you know everything is fine & hope you all are the same. I received your box last night the cookies & candy & sardines and all things was O.K. thanks a lot for send me the thing you did.

I didn't see Johnie for some time we are about 20 miles for one another that's what I think. Maybe some day I'll see him. I seen Joe Sewich, Helen B's old man. He's looking good. Last two days I got 48 letters, but just can't write to all. I write to Mother the most because she's first. I'll write to you all as much as I can Mother will tell you when she hears from me.

Say hello to the kids for me.

With all my love & may God Bless you all.

Always. Frank

Saturday, January 19, 1945; Lockwood, Ohio (still sealed)

Wednesday, January 30, 1945

Dearest family,
Just a few lines to let you know everything os O.K. and that I received your letter. I was so glad to hear from you. To day I received a letter from John he is not in Germany, he's in Belgium but is OK so don't worry we are all busy.
The last time I seen him was just before Xmas. Maybe we will see each other again soon.
How are the family getting long? Hope the kids are O.K. I received 50 some letters this week most of the letters are December and 3 boxes and 2 from Mother. She is so good to me.
The war looks O.K. to me. maybe it will be over this year. I sure would like to get home & be with the family.
Well dear I'll sign off because it's so hard to write when you work out in the cold some time we work all day and <u>night.</u>
With all my love & may God Bless you all.
Your brother, Frank

Chapter Twenty Five

And we rejoice in the hope of the glory of God. Not only so, but we also rejoice in our sufferings, because we know that suffering produces perseverance; perseverance, character; and character, hope. And hope does not disappoint us, because God has poured out his love into our hearts by the Holy Spirit, whom he has given us. Romans 5:4-5

Thursday, January 31, 1945

Dear Viola,
I just received some old mail, about five weeks old. In a way I hate to get old mail but it's better than not getting any at all. I suppose you get my mail the same way?
We're on a few days rest now-It's almost like a furlough to me. we've got a room in a pretty nice house and the people are swell. I've got a special chair just like the one by the floor lamp at home. I spend my evenings smoking a good cigar and listening to hot jive on the radio. The woman of the house or (Mom as we call her) fixes us midnight snacks every nite. Wow! What a life, I would stay here for the duration. I'm afraid this soft life is spoiling me. it'll be hard to go back to the field. oh yes, there's a set of twins here too-not bad numbers either. Ha! Ha!
I'd have loved to see the kids in the Christmas play. I can remember when I used to be in it, of course that was a long time ago but I still remember it.
I haven't seen Frank since the time before Christmas.

Maybe we'll be going back up his way again.

Have you been hearing from Claude lately? I sure wish he'd get time to write me.

Well Viola I'll have to close for now. Give my love to Mom and Dad and write often. Love to all. Johnny

Thursday, February 7, 1945; Miami, Florida

Dear Vi and Family,
Just arrived in Miami Beach, Fla. and am staying in the New Yorker Hotel. What a place! I'm having a wonderful time, but it will only be for ten days. I don't know where I am going to be sent to, but I hope it's near home. Have you heard from Johnny yet?

I hope so. say hello to all.
Love & Kisses. John

Saturday, February 10, 1945

Dear Viola,
So John finally got home-it's about time! It's a funny thing I was thinking about it the day I got your letter. I also received a letter from John that day it was seven weeks old. You didn't seem to say much about him-how does he look? Do you think he's changed much? I sure wish I could be there to see him, we'd probably take off on some of our specials.

To-morrow is Sunday I hope I get a chance to go to Church-I haven't been in Church for two weeks now so you'd better pray hard for me. I was all set to go to Church last Sunday but something came up the last minute which prevented me from doing so. one nice thing about the Army you never know what you're going to do the next minute.

I'm getting rather tired of this life everything is so uncertain. Another thing if anyone mentions moving to me after this war I'll shoot them.

You were asking about Ceil-there's nothing wrong. She's got a new job now with the secret service and I guess it keeps her plenty busy then to she's been working at the printing shop nights. The weather hasn't been to pleasant for driving either has it? She'll probably drop around as soon as the weather breaks if she hasn't been there already.

I'll have to close now Viola. Give my love to Mom and Dad. Write soon and often. So long for now. Love to all. Johnny

Monday, February 12, 1945; with the 9th Army in Germany

Dearest Family,

Just a few lines to let you know everything is O.K. with me & hope you are the same. It's been so long since I heard from you., but I hope to hear from you soon!

It's been a long time since I seen John because he is about 30 miles from me with the 1st Army. He wrote to me last week or 2 weeks ago. Getting long O.K. but he said it was cold, but wrote he will be O.K.

How did John look? I sure would like to see him. I know he was the same old John. I sure miss him it's been ages since I seen him. I received 15 letters last night and all the letters was Jan. the mail in good time is 10 to 12 days. I sure hope to day mail called. I heard from you and home. I miss Mother and Dad so much & you all.

How are the kids? No school since you have so much snow? We had more snow last night. It's been raining all week. I sure hope this war is over soon.

Well dear I'll close for this time. Say hello to all for me & tell Joe not to work to hard.

With all my love may God Bless you all.
Frank

Monday, February 19, 1945; Syracuse, NY

Dear Vi and Family,
I'm now in Syracuse N.Y. and doing M.P. duty in the city. I don't know whether I will like it or not, but after I am here for a while, I'll know better. The people around here seem very like and so far been swell to me. I'll write more about that in my letter some time this week. Have you heard from Johnny yet? I hope so. I just wrote to mother and asked for Johnny's address. So when you write please send it to me. I can't seem to find it and would like to write to him.
    Say hello to all.
    Love, John

Wednesday, February 21, 1945

Dear Viola,
I feel like a million dollars now. I just had my second shower this week. Showers are a great treat to us especially when there's plenty of warm water. I'm usually the last man out. I just love to stand there and soak. We usually have to take a (hobo) bath in our helmets. When I get home I'm going to get in the bath tub with plenty of hot water and soak for about a week to make up for all I've missed over here.
    I wish you wouldn't write v-mail anymore it takes longer to get here then you don't have much when you do get it. I can't understand why it takes my mail so long to get home. It makes me

so darn mad, I don't get a chance to write very often then when I do it takes a month or more to get there. If we should ever get in the position we were in before and I don't get a chance to write much I'll write a few lines just to say hello so the folks won't worry so much. Your mail isn't coming in here very well either. I won't get any for some time then I'll get a whole stack at once.

I'm sending Mother a fifty dollar money order as soon as I can get it. I want several masses said for Claude. It kinda made me feel good to hear of all the people that attended the Memorial Service you had for Claude. A friend of mine is getting the Cleveland Press they're kinda old when they get here but I enjoy reading them anyhow.

Well Sis, I'll close for now. Give my love to Mom and Dad. Don't worry about me I'll be back soon.

So long and write often.

Love to all. Johnny

Though he slay me, yet I will hope in him. –Job 13:15

Why are you downcast, O my soul? Why so disturbed within me? Put your hope in God, for I will yet praise him, my Savior and my God. –Psalm 42:5

Chapter Twenty Six

It was early morning, February 23rd, and the 793rd commenced with its next objective. They were to lay cover fire for the 29th and 30th Divisions who had just crossed the Roer River. Frank was in awe of the number of rounds fired by he and the boys over the next three days. They would expend nearly 3,900 rounds, all the while Frank prayed for Johnny knowing that he was somewhere near this melee. The night sky was sometimes so full of artillery and arms fire from both sides that it had the eerie appearance of a dull grey morning.[27]

Johnny knew that he had to get that communication wire down and operational. The Roer River crossing had already turned in to a free-for-all and the Germans fought as if every battle might be their last for the front was now embedded on German soil. Johnny gathered his men, spoke of a plan and then stopped to say a prayer before heading into the thick of it…

Monday, March 5, 1945

Dear Vi,
I finally got around to answering your most welcomed letter and it was swell to hear from you again. I am sorry I didn't have time to answer right away, but I will do the best I can. I been quite busy working. We don't get much time off. I am doing M.P. duty here in the N.Y.C. railroad station and by the time I get

---

[27] www.793rdfieldartillery.homestead.com

through there I am ready for bed. Ha. I am quite away in back in my writing. I have so many letters to answer. I wrote Johnny a long letter the other day. I know he will enjoy it. It's been some time since I heard from him. I'm glad you heard from him any way. It takes so long for letters to get there and back, seems like years. Right. I think this War will be over with soon and we can all be back together again. I hope so. All this War does, is bring sorrow and pain to us all. All we can do is pray to God to end all wars and bring our boys back. I know how sad it is for you and your folks, to lose the one you love. It's hard to take. I feel sad about it too. That's why I left without seeing you all. When I went back from my furlough. I just couldn't come back any more. I hope you understand. I am going to try and come home some week end but when, I don't know. I hope it is soon.

The weather here was sure nice today. The sun was out shining and it was just like a spring day. I thought of the times, when I was home and how I would like to go fishing. I hope Johnny and Frank come home this summer. We'll all go out fishing together.

How are the children? I bet they like this warm weather. Is Joe working every day yet? I suppose he is. I bet he can't wait till it warms up so he can go fishing too. They say there is some good fishing here too. I'll have to try it this summer.

I heard that Rudy was home. I don't suppose Veronica could enjoy it much any way. To bad. She was planning on it so. When you see her, say I said hello and I will write her a letter as soon as I have time. Say hello to your Mother and Dad too.

I will write again when I have time and you do the same. I love to hear from you. So long and God Bless you all.

Love & Kisses. John

Sunday, March 11, 1945; Germany

Dear Viola,

I got another hood from Helen to-day. I don't know why she sent it. I never asked her for it. We're having darn nice weather now for this time of the year. Funny thing I thought I'd have a lot of use for the hoods but I only wore it once. It was pretty cold when we were in Belgium but we didn't stay there very long.

I wish you wouldn't write v-mail anymore a lot of them don't photograph very well and are hard to read then too you can't write very much on them. Air mail gets here just as fast if not faster (none of it's to speedy). I haven't heard from John yet I suppose he's too busy to do any writing. The last letter I got from him before he came home took seven weeks. I hear from Frank quite often now. I was quite surprised to hear that Jim and Ann Cerny got married. I didn't think Jim would ever get Ann.

We have quite a time in the evenings frying potatoes and pancakes. The kitchen gives us the butter if there is any left over. I'm getting to be an expert at flipping hotcakes. You'd probably die laughing if you could have seen me when I first started cooking. Ha! Ha!

Vi I'm sending you girls some money I want you to buy Mother something for Easter. The reason I'm sending it to you girls is that I'm afraid if I send it to Mother she'll put it on my bank account and I don't want that. I want to be sure you spend all of it on her. The first money order which is in this letter is for $75 and the one to follow will be for $38. You ought to be able to buy something pretty nice for that.

I've been reading about the terrific floods in Southern Ohio. I expected that to happen when all that snow started to melt it seems to be the worst flood in history. I'll have to close for now. Give my love to Mom, Dad and the kids. I'll write more in a day

or so. So long.
   Love to all. Johnny

   This picture was taken at noon on the Super highway coming down to Bavaria. I was pouring gas in the truck at the time the rest of the boys are getting their K rations and coffee.

Thursday, March 22, 1945; Easter Card

Dear Vi,
Happy Easter to you and family. Wish I could be with you this Easter Sunday. I'll try. How's everything with you and family? Fine I hope. Have you been hearing from Johnny lately? I heard from Frank a few weeks ago? I wrote to Johnny and Frank the other day and am waiting to her from them. The weather here has been nice. Today it's raining and snowing together. Real spring weather. How's Joey and Babs? Still enjoying school I suppose? Say hello to your folks and I'll drop a letter soon. Love, John

Both Frank and Johnny remained on the move, Frank and the 793rd offering cover fire for the 9th Army that had crossed the Rhine and Johnny and the 557th laying communication line and keeping what remained of the German Air Force at bay.[28]

Tuesday, March 27, 1945; Somewhere on the Rhine

Dear Sis-
I see you people are getting big time now buying a new De Soto. How much did you get for your old car?
I got a nice long letter from John last week. He sure has a good set up now-if anyone deserves it he does, he put plenty of time in hell for it. he ought to get home quite often there-maybe every weekend if he works it right. Frank hasn't written to me for some time again-he gets those spells quite often. I have no idea of where he is now that we've been moving so fast. Who knows I might run across him again one of these fine days.

---

[28] www.antiaircraft.org www.793rdfieldartilery.homestead.com

We're having beautiful weather the kind of weather that makes you want to go places and do things. I'm almost tempted to go down to the Rhine and do a little fishing.

I still hate to wash clothes as much as ever. One nice thing now is the Germans furnished us with an electric wash machine- that helps a lot. We practically ruin the machine by putting to many clothes in at a time. The rolls on the ringer look like the termites were working on it after we get done. We run stuff through the ringer that anybody that knows anything about a washer wouldn't try! Buttons fly in every direction! It looks like an artillery barrage. Can't you just picture a bunch of men doing that? Ha! Ha! More fun!

Well Viola, I'll have to close for now. give my love to Mom and Dad. I want to wish you all a Happy Easter.

Love to all. Johnny

Saturday, March 31, 1945; With the 9th Army

Dearest Family,

Just a few lines. It's been a long time since I wrote you. This letter will not be much because we are busy. I sure hope it ends soon. It sure look goods to me. I hope I don't have to C.B.1 just pray to God so I don't have to go. I been in action 9 months. I have 4 campaign stars and I have seen a lot since I been here.

I have a letter from John last week he's the same place close he about 30 mi. from me. I hope to see him soon. How are the family getting long? Tell Joe not to work too hard. I hope he don't have to go to the Army. Well I'll close for this time hope to hear from you soon.

Take good care of yourself & the family. Wishing you a Happy Easter.

With all my love. Frank

Saturday, April 21, 1945; With the 9th Army

Dearest Family,

Just a few lines to let you know I am O.K. and hope you are the same. It's been a long time since I wrote to you but dear, it's been a long time since I heard from you.

The weather is beautiful. I hope you are having the same weather at home. I sure would like to be home on the farm.

I didn't see Johnie for some time he didn't write to me for some time he is busy to. We been so damn busy last 3 weeks. I didn't write to no one but mother.

I received some pictures from Jo Brkayk and you look O.K. and the family look good. How is Joe getting long working 7 days a week? Tell him not to work to hard. I know him.

Well dear I'll sign off. May God Bless you & family.

With all my love. Frank The pens no good so if you can't read it to bad ha ha

323

Saturday, April 28, 1945; Germany

Dear Sis-
I received your package yesterday- I was afraid it was lost. The R.G. Duns were like gold to me, it's the first I've seen of any since I left the states. I got about ten boxes of German cigars but they're not very good. Every time Frank writes he teases me about having a good supply of cigars on hand and that if I'll drop over he'll give me <u>one</u>.

Frank hasn't been writing very often the last letter I got from him was written in March. I'll send him the pictures of the kids the next time I write. The pictures really turned out swell. I'd like to keep them but I have more than I can carry now. The one picture of Barbara really shows the depth of snow, it's a wonder you were able to get out this winter.

What's the jive about being married?!! Don't worry <u>(when I do)</u> get married you'll know about it.

I washed all my clothes last week and I can still feel it <u>(my poor back)</u>. We weren't so lucky this time no electricity and no wash machine. We washed in teams it's a lot easier that way. Now I know why women want a wash machine before they buy anything else. We had several pictures taken during a project I hope they come out alright it'll be a sight to see.

Well Vi I'll have to close for now. Keep your chin up and don't worry about me.

Goodnite. Love to all, Johnny

Both Frank and Johnny met up with the Russians not two weeks prior to VE Day, May 9th.

With God we will gain the victory, and he will trample down our enemies. –Psalm 60:12

Death has been swallowed up in victory. -1 Corinthians 15:54; Isaiah 25:8

Where O death is your victory? Where O death is your sting? -Hosea 13:14

Chapter Twenty Seven

Saturday, May 12, 1945; Germany

Dear Viola,
I've been waiting to take a bath for three days now and I see someone beat me to it again to-nite. The house we're living in has a pretty nice bath tub but we don't have hot running as yet-give us time.
It seems hard to believe that it's all over with here somehow or other it doesn't seem to phase me. I suppose if I were at home it would be a lot different. I could feel that it was the real thing. we got a little ration of whiskey for our V.E. day celebration but it wasn't enough to even get feeling good. There's so darn many men over here that I think it was nice of them to give us what they did. I'll make up for all this lost time when I hit the states believe me. Most of the people at home practically went mad when they got the news, most of them have good reason to celebrate.
I forgot to tell Veronica that I got the box of cigars and the package that Mother sent. The package come through pretty fast now from four to five weeks isn't bad. I think I told you in one of my previous letters that I got your swell box-I'm telling you I'm getting so absent minded that I don't know whether I'm coming or going anymore.
We're going to be occupational troops for a while then I don't know what after that.??!
I suppose Veronica is on her way to Florida by now-I hope she has a nice trip. I'll bet when she gets back she'll say never again-I travelled that route too many times and I know what the

transportation problem is.

How is the weather at home now? it's beautiful here-the kind of weather that makes you want to go places like fishing and joy riding in the country. I suppose Joe has all his fishing equipment ready to go?!

Well Sis I've got to go now. give my love to Mom and Dad and write often. So long. Love to all, Johnny

Sunday, May 20, 1945; Germany

Hi Sis-

I guess Veronica is having a good time way down south. She dropped me a card from Washington and I got a letter from Florida yesterday. I can see her now-big time-splashing her dough on everything-I don't blame her she might as well enjoy herself while she has the opportunity. She's made pretty good money for a kid and besides money don't mean a damn thing now days-so I say enjoy it while you can.

I got the papers yesterday and you can bet your bottom dollar that I'll do my best to get out. I only have 52 points and 85 is supposed to be the minimum in consideration for a discharge but I think I have the best reason in the world for a discharge and I'll fight it with everything I got.

You shouldn't feel the way you do about Claude I know it's hard to take but we just have to. We won't see him anymore on earth but I know he's with the good care of God. You should want to carry on all the more you have the two sweetest children in the world and a one swell guy for a husband.

When I heard the tragic news I didn't care to live either but then I settled down and told myself I just had to come through for Mom and Dad's sake. We were making preparations for the Roer River crossing when I got the news-this was one of my most dangerous missions and it sort of made me afraid for I knew if anything happened to me Mom and Dad couldn't bear it. I prayed harder than ever and went to mass and communion the Sunday before and everything came out OK.

The crossing was one of the greatest things I ever witnessed in all my days of war experience. The Battle of the Bulge was rough but nothing compared to this. We were right on the river bank with our guns and on the 23rd of February at 0300 (am) hours all hell let loose the sky was lit up like daylight. Shells were flying both directions my jeep had all kinds of holes in it from mortar shrapnel the more shells that came in the harder I prayed and the Good Lord saw me through. I think I'm very fortunate for as many close calls as I had.

Just to give you a faint idea of what took place there listen to this-we had seventy six battalions of artillery consisting of twelve guns per battalion firing in our corp. area besides a great many machine guns and small artillery pieces. After seeing all that I often wondered how anything could live through this hell of fire. All these guns were firing at one time for three hours straight a consistent barrage.

I had charge of all communications in our battalion which was a pretty rough job. I had orders to put in the wire in such a manner that it wouldn't fail no matter how heavy the enemy fire was that in itself was a project. The hard part was to keep the wire in under such in tense mortar fire but once more Lulek comes through and keeps the news system working through the whole show.

One nice thing about being a Sgt. You go ahead and your men follow if they have enough (guts). My job keeps me up front where things are plenty hot all the time. I only took two boys from my section, up front with me that nite, the rest stayed back. When they left that evening they all shook hands with me and bid me the best of luck and I know they all prayed for me too-most of my section is Catholic. When I returned from the front the next day after my mission was accomplished they all seemed relieved-confidentially so was I.

In addition to keeping the wire in I was hauling ammunition with a jeep. I didn't have to do that but the jeep driver was hit with a piece of shrapnel from an 88 at Gielenhicken and was a little shaky so I took it. it's all over and I'm still alive without a scratch so that's all that counts. I'll tell you of some of my other experiences in another letter. I could go on and on but I don't have the time.

I'll tell you a little about our trip across. We left from Ft. Slocum, N.Y. We pulled out of Brooklyn Navy Yard on the 23rd of July on the Queen Mary an enormous ship. We were unescorted most of the way. Incidentally, the Queen Mary is the second largest ship in the world. Elizabeth is the largest by a few feet. We had a nice trip. It took us 5 days and 8 hours to make it.

We docked at Clyde, Scotland (beautiful country). There were 18,000 of us on the ship 400 of that number were nurses. Couple days before while on pass in N.Y. we met five nurses in a night club had a nice time there with them. The funny part of it was they told us to meet them on such and such a boat and I'll be damned if they didn't get on the (Mary) with us that made our trip a little more enjoyable. I think we were pretty lucky. The small ships in convoy take about 14 days to cross.

I sent Dad a German rifle and a saber. I hope it gets there. Have Joe try to put the rifle to-gether if he can and tell him not to lose any of the parts. I also have a nice little ash tray a souvenir of Paris that I'll send one of these days soon.

I'd better go now there's a dozen guys hollering for hair cuts and I also have a wire line to fix. Give my love to Mom, Dad and the kids. May God Bless you all and keep you well. So long for now.

Love to all. Johnny

But encourage one another daily, as long as it is called Today, so that none of you may be hardened by sin's deceitfulness. We have come to share in Christ if we hold firmly till the end the confidence we had at first. As has just been said: "Today, if you hear his voice, do not harden your hearts as you did in the rebellion." -Hebrews 3:13-15 and Psalm 95:7,8

Thursday, May 24, 1945; Germany

Hi Sis-

I got all the papers and they're on their way. It all has to go through channels so it will take a little time. I'm doing all I can to make it work.

As for being on my way to the Pacific I don't know about that. I don't think Japan will last over three months maybe six at the most. If we go at all it will take at least three months to get there.

I see the first army is on it's way via the U.S. already. As far as I know I only have 62 points not enough to amount to much.

Things are being changed so often that it might go up.

We're having some pretty bad weather here too quite similar to what you're having at home. During April we had beautiful weather now it's cold and practically every day.

I'm glad to hear that John gets home quite often. He must have a pretty soft life if he's putting on all that weight of course I guess beer helps the situation along a bit.

How are Mother and Dad these days busy as ever I suppose!? Gee! I wish like hell I was home now so I could help them. When I see the farmers doing work in the fields it makes me homesick as heck. You know they use cows to work in the fields it seems funny to see the crude methods used here, it makes you wonder how they ever get anything done. I've often seen a cow or ox and a horse working to-gether.

We're moving back all the time. We occupy a place for a little while then move on. Most of the guys are cleaning up their equipment and drilling putting on a show for the German people. I'm kept plenty busy-I'm laying more wire now then I did when we were in combat the only difference is the shells aren't flying over head. I usually lay about 10 to 15 miles of wire in a position and we move just about once a week or ten days so you can see how much it takes (there's usually nothing left). One of my men has had a pass to Paris and all the rest have had a pass to some town way back where you can fraternize. Being a chief of a section isn't all grapes although it does have its advantages at times. If any of my men do anything wrong I get hell for it of course I pass it on to them and add a little more. I'm signed out with thousands of dollars worth of signal equipment if anything is missing or lost I'll have to pay for it if I can't get out of it any other way. This army is a lot of dull jive no matter how you look at it.

It looks like Veronica's really enjoying herself I can't say I blame her I'd do the same if I had the opportunity. I'm still thinking of going to Canada on a vacation if I ever get out of this army. I've got to use both sides of the paper now cause this is the last tablet I've got. I sure hope you can read this scratching-I'm going like a horse on fire so I don't know if I'll be able to read it myself.

I got to go now Vi. I'll write soon again. Give my love to Mom, Dad and the kids.

So long for now. Love, Johnny

Wisdom's instruction is to fear the Lord, and humility comes before honor. –Proverbs 15:33

Tuesday, June 5, 1945; Germany

Dear Sis-

I received that box of cigars the other day. I wish you would thank Celia and her husband for them for me. if I had their address I write to them myself. It sure was swell of them to do that. It surprised the heck out of me when I saw who they were from.

Our chow is terrible now. They cut us down twenty percent since the war ended. We weren't getting to much before so I think you can imagine how much we get now. I'll be a walking shadow in no time. I'd send for some packages but I have a funny feeling that I might be on my way home in not to distant future, I hope! The worst part of it is we can't steal chickens or potatoes like we did when the war was on. I don't know what I'm going to do but I'll figure a way out pretty soon.

Did Dad ever get the German rifle and saber I sent him? I sent a German uniform home last week- a hat, coat. It also had a steel helmet and a nice little ash tray a souvenir of Paris in it.

Well I'd better go now Vi-you probably won't hear from me for a week or so cause we're moving down to Bavaria. Give my love to all.

So long. Love, Johnny

Enjoy the enclosed commendation letter:

HEADQUARTERS
557TH AAA Auto Wpus Bn (Mbl)

30 May 1945

SUBJECT: Commendation.

TO : All Officers and Men of the "557th".

Since activation back in '43 we have all been justly proud of the "557th". By hard work you established yourselves as one of the outstanding AA outfits to come out of a training camp.

Since coming overseas your record has been one to justify all early hopes. You have operated successfully with three divisions and two armies, under both American and British leadership. At times the going has been "tough" but you never complained. In the extreme cold of the Ardennes "Bulge" in one of the bitterest campaigns of this war you convinced all that you were top grade fighting men. At the crossing of the Roer it was due in a large measure to your splendid support of the infantry that casualties were light. In the crossings of the Rhine and Weser and the rapid advance through Germany to the Elbe you were always ready for action, inflicting heavy losses in men and equipment on the Krauts. When the Luftwaffe finally came out you were ready for them. The result—23 planes, shot down in a two week period—testifies to your professional ability. The drivers have all done an outstanding job, not only in moving this organization, but on innumerable occasions helping to move other units. You have been subjected to heavy artillery and small arms fire, to strafing attempts and to the dangers of enemy mine fields under black out conditions, but you have met and overcome all obstacles.

It is a privilege to have been your commander. It is with a sense of great pride that I review your accomplishments. I know that whatever you do and where ever you go you will continue to do the same outstanding job you have done in the past. I salute the officers and men of the "557th".

Victor L. Groff
VICTOR L. GROFF
Lieutenant Colonel, CAC
Commanding

B.S.- In ten months of combat he paid us one visit. Yes men you've done a great job- now he's brave and raking in the glory. He finally came out of his hide out now that it's safe. He talks about the bitter cold and the shelling we got in the Andennes but he didn't care to come out and see how the men were living nor did he care how much or what kind of food his men got. Now he's got courage enough to send us a commendation on our wonderful work in the past. I'd like to punch him right in the nose-for a commanding officer he isn't worth a damn all he worries about is his own hide.

Friday, June 15, 1945; Germany

Dear Sis-
I haven't had any mail for ten days now- I know you people are writing but our moving around so much has things messed up a little. My morale is getting low so I hope some letters get here to-nite.
I never did send the pictures of the kids to Frank the hell with him he never answers my letters anyway. Besides those pictures are darn nice so I think I'll keep them-I love to look at them once in a while so I won't forget what they look like. I can't get over how big the kids have grown since I left. It seems that they were first babies when I left home and now they're a grown

up young lady and man. I noticed in particular the one picture where you're standing with them that Joey is almost as big as you are.

You're not going to like this but I might as well tell you-my papers went to Div. Hq. and bounced back. We're going to try a new angle so I got the clerk typing up a new letter it should be ready any day now we've been delayed on account of moving so much. The darn trouble with this army everything has to go through channels. Here's the line up it goes from our headquarters to Division from there to corps then to army and finally to the adjutant General in Washington D.C. and back to me. I think you can see now why it takes so long.

Now that it's all over I can tell you of a little incident that happened to us while coming ashore in France. They unloaded our trucks on a big barge from the liberty ship - we started for shore and one of our motors went dead so we plugged along with one motor for a while when another liberty ship bumps into us knocking the other motor off into the water. This is when we began to sweat; it was dark and we had no way to contact shore for help, on top of that the water was rough and we were heading out to sea fast! Fortunately for us another barge happened our way and pushed us in. that being our first experience of that kind had us worried a little, now we'd think nothing of it after what we've been through.

This patch I'm sending you is the patch we wear it's the Lincoln Div. patch of the 84th Railsplitter Div. we've been with this Div. since last Nov.

Well Vi, I've got to go now. I'll see you later. Give my love to Mom, Dad and the kids. So long for now.

Love Johnny

Tuesday, June 19, 1945; follow up letter

HEADQUARTERS

557TH AAA Auto Wpns Bn. (Mbl)

U.S. Army

APO 339

19 June 1945

GENERAL ORDER)

NUMBER 21)

I. Under the provisions of Par 3 a (2), AR 600-68 and Sec I, Cir 32, Headquarters European Theater of Operations, dated 20 March 1944, the following named EM are awarded the good conduct Medal for exemplary behaviour, efficiency and fidelity.

Grade	NAME	BTRY
S/Sgt	Alvin R. Montgomery	A
Sgt	Leslie Frith	A
Sgt	John T. Lulek	B
Sgt	Frederick H. Saul, Jr.	A
Sgt	Earl M. Smith	A
Sgt.	Thomas O. Watson	A
Tec 4	William F Thomas	A
Cpl	Daniel Buchan	A
Cpl	Henry J. Chrostowski	A
Cpl	Harvey K. Kratzer	B
Tec 5	Michael H. Dick	A
Tec 5	Roman J. Dorsch	B
Tec 5	Calvin F. Ingram	A
Tec 5	Lawson V. Feinour	B
Tec 5	Stephen W. Tomaskovich	B
Pfc	Albert Catino	B
Pfc	Richard L. Crump	A
Pfc	Roy S. Moyer	A
Pfc	Wilby J. Nall	A
Pfc	Claude M. Roth	B

Pfc	Charles E. Sawtell, Jr.	B
Pfc	Granville G. Schaffer	A
Pfc	Edward J. Sparrow	A
Pfc	Clarence J. Wilson, Jr.	A
Pfc	Frank J. Wilson, Jr.	A

By order of Lieutenant Colonel GROFF:

DAVID R. PRICE
1st Lt., CAC
Adjutant

OFFICIAL: David R. Price
DAVID R. PRICE
1st Lt., CAC
Adjutant

Wednesday, June 20, 1945; Germany

Dear Sis,

I received your v-mail to-day-I don't like v-mail but I was darn glad to get this one it's the first letter I've gotten in about ten days. I read in our army paper that they held up our mail from 15 to 30 days before we go to the states- I wonder if there is anything to that??!! That's a long time to go without mail-it just isn't good for ones morale that's all.

We're living in an old hotel; it's not as nice as some of the houses we've lived in but I can't complain my section and I have a pretty nice room. I'm sleeping on a bed too so Frank doesn't have anything on me. Of course these beds aren't at all like ours at home;-I don't think they know what innerspring mattresses are over here. they're far from being soft but it's a lot better than sleeping in a fox hole or on the ground. I have one of two twin beds my radio operator has the other and the rest of my men have folding canvas cots which aren't bad either.

I hope your watermelon and muskmelon crop turns out

alright-who knows I might be home in time to help you dispose of them. I hope! I really think we will be coming to the states one of these days-It might take longer then I think cause it takes quite a while before they can move all these troops.

I saw one article in our army paper telling of a large shipment of bananas to the troops in the E.T.O. (European Theater Operations)- 6,000 tons to be exact, also 2,000 tons of tomatoes they're to come from the Canary Islands. Oh, happy day I'm crazy about both so I should do alright. We've been getting oranges quite often they come from Spain.

I was kind surprised to hear the kids got a pony-it's a good thing for them as long as they don't get hurt. If he's as old as you say he is they shouldn't have any trouble. When I heard what you paid for him my hair stood up-I thought you could buy a pretty good one for fifty dollars. Horse steak must be pretty high at that rate. Ha! ha!

I'd love to go fishing with Joe and John again-I'll never forget the swell times we had-didn't get many fish but had a swell time! We've been doing a little fishing here too but the darn fish don't want to bite on worms. We use other methods much more effective (hand grenades) that really does the trick! We find a nice spot where we think there should be some fish and drop half dozen grenades then send one man in after the fish-some fun!

You had a nice turn out at the Alumni Banquet, of course that's a small number to feed compared to what I have to sweat out three times a day and then I don't get all the good food you mentioned. We feed from 160 to 170 men at every meal in our battery. It will be nice to get home and sit down to a good meal and not have to wait in line for an hour. I can dream can't I!!

I did get the hand made cigars some time ago and I want to thank you for them. You folks certainly have been taking good care of me and making sure my supply of cigars don't run out. I really appreciate it-you know I'm lost without a cigar. I'm known as "Big John with the cigar" to all my buddies. No, things haven't changed a bit I'm still recognized as the man with a rope.

I thought I told you that I sent the gun and Saber-maybe you never got the letter. I sent another box some time ago maybe you've got it already it contained a air corps Capt. cap and coat a helmet and an ash tray souvenir of Paris. I've got a few other things I want to send one of these days.

I'm going on a pass to Paris the 22nd so you probably won't hear from me for about ten days. I'll try to drop you a few lines from there if I have time. Ha! ha! I'm going to try to get you all a souvenir of Paree if the prices aren't to high and I heard they are.

If I'd have known you can't get that white material I would have wrapped a whole roll with the gun.

Well Vi, I have to go now cause I've got a lot of work to do- got to look sharp when I go to "Gay Paree" Ha! ha! Give my love to Mom, Dad and the kids.

So long for a while. Love, Johnny

Thursday, July 5, 1945; V-mail

Dearest Family,
I just received your letter. It's been a long time since I heard from you but I know you are busy working. I was glad to hear that John was home and that Joe was still working. As for me I am still the same. Well the 9th Army is coming home but not me maybe I'll get home some time. Now we are in the 7th Army. Every time some army goes home we are put in a new army!

Well I'll close for this time. I haven't seen Johnie for a long time if you write him tell him to write me.

Love, Frank

Sunday, July 22, 1945; Deauville, France

Dear Viola,

We're still traveling around like a bunch of Gypsies-I think we covered more of this country than any other unit in the E.T.O. Moving around so much is one reason why you don't hear from me very often and when I do get a little time off I like to spend it on the beach. Deauville is one of the greatest summer resorts in Europe- so I'm told-I can't see it myself although the beach is pretty nice. I'm trying to get a sun tan on my time off-you know we can't work with our shirts off.

We're guarding P.O.W.s while they clear mine fields and clean up the beach. We're also hauling or putting 9th Army Hq. stuff on the boat at Le Havre they're supposed to leave for the states in a day or so . I thought we'd go back with them for sure but maybe it's better we don't. the longer we stay here the less chance of us going to the Pacific. We'll probably work around the port for a while and then I don't know what we'll do.

This isn't a bad job only the hours are so long and they're not regular. I don't mind the day shift but the midnight one kills me it's hard to sleep in the day time. Boat after boat is pulling out of this port that goes on every day.

I got the package of shoe polish and stuff thanks a million. I also got a nice package from Irene the same day.

I wish my papers would hurry back so I'd know what to do. I bought several things in Paris that I'd like to send home but I'm holding them for a while just in case we do go home. At second thought I think I'll pack them and get it off my hands so I won't have so much to carry if I do go home soon.

I sent a certificate of mine home the other day take good care of it I want to frame it. It means a lot to me and there's a long hard story behind it.

I'm sending you a few pictures I had taken in Paris and a few that were taken on the beach here in Deauville. How do you like my girl friend? We messed up on a few pictures as you can plainly see there are no heads on any of us-we were all feeling pretty good that morning. I guess that accounts for the bad job. I really had a swell time in Paris though.

I hope you can read this writing cause I can't-I'm getting worse every day. Ha! ha! I try to go to fast!

You know I only got 5 letters in the last five weeks. Pretty rough isn't it?

I'll have to go now kid. Give my love to Mom and Dad and the Kids.

May God Bless you all. So long.
Love, Johnny

Stand firm. Let nothing move you. Always give yourselves fully to the work of the Lord, because you know that your labor in the Lord is not in vain. -1 Corinthians 15:58

Chapter 28

Sunday, August 5, 1945; Le Havre

Dear Sis-
I'm sorry if I worried you people by not writing but I don't have much time to write the way we move around. the trip to Paris kinda messed things up a bit too-I didn't get back to the outfit for almost two weeks. When we got back from Paris the outfit moved to Northern Germany so that was the great delay.
We're in Camp Phillip Morris just out of Le Havre waiting for shipments to England. We're scheduled to pull out day after to-morrow the 7th. I thought I'd better drop you a line cause I don't know when I'll get a chance to write again-at least you'll know what the score is and won't worry.
I don't think I'll be home for a while we're scheduled to stay in England from 30 to 60 days and return to Antwerp. I don't count on that too much cause orders change faster then the weather in the army. I'll tell you one thing don't expect me home till I walk in the door. I'd rather stay here a little longer there's less chance of going to the Pacific. I'd much rather stay here longer and come home for good when I do. I went through one war and that's enough for me.
I'll have to leave you for a while see you in England.
So long and may God bless you all.
Love to all, Johnny

Tuesday, August 14, 1945; Postcard from Monte Carlo

Dearest family,

Just a few lines to let you know everything is O.K. and I'll be on my way back to work this week. I sure had a good time.

I'll write more when I get back.

With all my love, Frank

Tuesday, August 28, 1945, Eye England

Dear Viola,

I kinda figured you'd stop writing when you heard the 9th Army was coming home. I thought we'd go home with them too but no such luck-maybe it's better we didn't cause I think a lot of them will go to Japan as occupational troops. I think I can stand this place a little longer.

We had some pretty nice times on the beaches of Deauville and Frauville. I kinda wish I was back in France-it's so cold here you can't even go swimming.

I'm glad you got the certificate of merit. I can't understand why you haven't received any of the packages yet I sent some of them first class mail they should go as fast as letters.

You certainly are doing alright on the market this year! I was surprised to hear it. I didn't think you'd be going to market this year. I wish I were there to go-it would seem good to get back in the groove again.

I went to London two days after V.J. day and the people were still celebrating! I can imagine that all the people back home went wild now with gas off the rationing list. Conditions should improve fast now that it's all over many of the critical items should be back on the market. I see Clark is up to his old tricks again-what the neighborhood needs is another thrashing machine.

I'd better go now got a lot to do to-day.

Write as often as you can-see you later.
Love to all, Johnny

P.S. Now A.P.O. 592

Friday, September 8, 1945; Eye, England

Dear Sis-

I'm on the switchboard to-nite from 5:30 to 7:30 in the morning so I thought I'd try to write you a few lines between calls. If it keeps as busy as it has been I won't do very well. I have 120 lines on a double board also a teletype and broadcasting system to operate. We really should have two men here all the time but there's a shortage of good help.

Veronica never did tell me how the thrashing came out. I suppose Dad will be filling silo soon won't he? Did he get all his soy beans in yet?

I was very happy to hear that John got his discharge. It makes me homesick when you tell me about the boys doing a lot of fishing. I might be able to join them before the year is over. Oh happy day!!

I'm sending you a bunch of foreign currency-I wanted to send it long ago but always forgot about it so I'll get rid of it now. One of the bills is Russian I got it when we crossed the Elbe in a kayak.

I guess I'll have to go-the air corps that's left on this base is leaving to-morrow and they're all calling up their girls. I'm glad they're going I won't be so busy after they leave-I hope!

I'll see you later. So long and may God Bless you all.
Love to all, Johnny

Thursday, September 14, 1945; Eye, England

Dear Viola,

I should be home by spring at least, cause all the troops are to be shipped out of England by that time. I quit trying to figure things out anymore-they got this point system so messed up that I don't know whether I'm coming or going.

A bunch of men left our outfit to-day and more are going to-morrow. One minute they say all men with 60 points and less will stay with the battalion. Now the story going around is that men with 45 points and less will stay so I don't know what to think. We sent men out with less than 60 points and turn right around and get new ones in that have 6 to 60 it just don't add up.

I sure would like to see John in his new suit-I'll bet he looks sharp. Tell him to drop me a line some time. Just because he's a civilian and I'm still in the damn army he don't have to act so stuck up.

Where in the heck is Frank anyway? He hasn't written to me in six months. he should have enough points to get home I think.

I'm sending you some more pictures. You're probably getting disgusted with so many but we got to do something to pass the time away.

The pickles are holding out fairly well this year aren't they?

I guess the kids are well on their way to another year of school by now-they'll be so grown up when I get home that I won't know them. It won't be long now that it will be two years since I was home last and I served three long years already.

I've got to go now Vi. See you later.
May God Bless you all. So long.
Love to all. Johnny

P.S. I got 62 points and 8 coming from V-E Day to V-J Day if that means anything!!!

Tuesday, September 26, 1945; Eye, England

Dear Sis-
Your letter the 16th is the first I received in about two weeks. I figured you were to busy to write now with canning in progress and all that stuff.
Speaking of tomatoes I could really go for some now-my favorite fruit. We don't get them in army rations very often and when we do they're real small. I trade the British kids around camp candy for tomatoes.
Don't send any packages cause I kinda think I'll be home by Christmas. I hope!
I sure would like to go fishing with the boys! Maybe I'll be home in time for hunting. It's been a long time since I hunted or fished. We did do a little fishing In Germany with grenades. Some fun-We'd fill our pockets with hand grenades and head for some small streams every evening until we ran out of grenades. One nite we came back with a string of about thirty all pretty good sized too!
In the last bunch of pictures I sent home I think there's one of me on my super racer. Most of the pictures aren't very clear cause the boys developed them in camp and the stuff they had to work with wasn't very good.
Where is Frank any how? I haven't heard anything about him in six months.
I've got to go now. See you later. Write often and may God bless you all.
Love to all, Johnny

Tuesday, October 10, 1945; Lockwood, Ohio

Dear Johnny,

I'm going to try and write to you this morning. Veronica is here and I can't even think straight. She started out to work at Smidas but the big rain yesterday made it impossible for them to even get into the field. It is still raining here. I hear you have plenty of rain over there too. So all your friends are leaving you? Well it's time they do something with you!!

I have been doing some sewing this week. Made Carol a housecoat and to-day I want to make Babs'. Last week I cleaned houses. It sure feels good when it's clean. Saturday and Sunday we spent in Cleveland at the Romanchiks. We went to theater while there. Of course we had to go to Brookside Park on Sunday with the children. They have a train there for the children to ride on. It's pretty nice. Also ponies. Imagine Babs wanted to pay to ride the ponies when ours is just loafing around in the woods. He is getting stubborn lately. Takes Junior under trees and he gets all scratched up.

John went to Canada for another week. He had about 2 days rest in between. Frank went to Cleveland yesterday. He said that you are <u>fat</u> as ever.

Johnny, you had better be home for some hunting. Shirley just went back yesterday. Love and Kisses, May God Bless You. Vi & Family

Monday, October 17, 1945; Lockwood, Ohio

Dear Johnny,
Gee! I hope you are on your way home soon. But according to the papers 70 point men will be home by Nov. 30 so

you are in that class I guess. Before they said 60 point men will come home in Nov. I guess they change more often than the wind does.

It seems ages since we heard from you. Are you still operating the switch board? I bet your buddies do miss you! I know we do. You have a way with people. It's too bad you couldn't all come home on the same ship, and at the same time.

Well Johnny we are having a few nice days, believe it or not, but the sun has been shining now for 3 days. It must be the long awaited Indian Summer.

The folks are husking the corn next to the road in front of Glowes' places. You know halloween <u>is coming</u> and you just can't trust the corn next to the road. My own son might try to do some halloweening! He's quite a man now.

Yesterday I went to the school house and helped the cooks. They are serving hot lunches. Then in the afternoon I took Mother to Middlefield with pumpkins. She sold about 60 (different size) for $10.00. then in the evening I went to P.T.A. Boy I really had a busy day. So to day I must get after my ironing.

Joe is finally working in the woods finishing up some of the wood he started last fall at this time. You know all last winter there was so much snow we couldn't get into the woods & this fall again too much rain until now.

Last Sunday we had mass for Claude. His birthday is to-day or to-morrow I never can get it straight. 30 years old he would have been.

Love & Kisses, Sister Viola & Family

P.S. Babs & Joey send you their love and will certainly be happy when you come home.

December 1945

It was mid morning and the once gloomy black and purple skies that often accompanied an early winter storm off Lake Erie, began to give way to vibrant aqua blue hues as the sun punched holes through the seemingly impenetrable cloud cover. John had hitched a ride the last stretch toward home for he so wanted to surprise Vi and the rest of the family. It wasn't very difficult for a soldier to hitch hike just about anywhere. People were eager to help as they held on to that feeling of celebration and relief as they drew ever closer to a return of normalcy, family and routine. He was at State Routes 45 and 87, the crossroads that made up tiny North Bloomfield. This little crossroads had played a part during the civil war with the "underground railroad" and the transportation of slaves north, often as far north as Canada.

Only a couple miles from home now, John sat up almost pressing against the windshield trying to catch the very first glimpse of Joe and Vi's place. Viola's house was on the northeast corner of their intersection. You typically saw the front right-hand corner of the house, once a resting place for weary passengers travelling by stagecoach during the late 1800's. As the car made a left hand turn John could see the half-oval drive already scraped clean of the most recent snow, the garage and picket fence facing opposite of the back entry to the house and Joe burning rubbish out by the burn barrel which stood between the cage for the dog and where he planted his garden each spring.

It was almost surreal the way Joe looked up at the approaching vehicle still some 100 yards away to make eye contact with John through a grin so big you could have hung ten cigars from his lower lip! At the same instant, Vi was looking out the kitchen window only able to see her husband Joe, putting down the garbage can and walking toward the vehicle smiling and then laughing to himself.

Could it be? Over three years in the Army, and God had

brought John back home, back home safe to us! Viola grabbed her coat and ran down the three small steps between the kitchen and the landing and right out the door. The twenty or so squares of cement that made up their walkway seemed like they didn't even exist as she arrived at the vehicle just as John stepped out…

…God's work-which is by faith. The goal of this command is love, which comes from a pure heart and a good conscience and a sincere faith.   -1 Timothy 1:5

Clothe yourselves with compassion, kindness, humility, gentleness and patience. Bear with each other and forgive whatever grievances you may have against one another. Let the peace of Christ rule in your hearts… whatever you do, whether in word or deed, do it all in the name of the Lord Jesus, giving thanks to God the Father through him. –Colossians 3:12-13, 15, 17

www.ingramcontent.com/pod-product-compliance
Lightning Source LLC
Chambersburg PA
CBHW022049160426
43198CB00008B/167